Working-Class Lesbian Life

York Studies on Women and Men

General Editors: Haleh Afshar and Mary Maynard

Haleh Afshar
ISLAM AND FEMINISMS
An Iranian Case-Study

WOMEN AND EMPOWERMENT
Illustrations from the Third World (*editor*)

WOMEN IN THE MIDDLE EAST
Perceptions, Realities and Struggles for Liberation (*editor*)

Haleh Afshar and Stephanie Barrientos (*editors*)
WOMEN, GLOBALIZATION AND FRAGMENTATION IN THE
DEVELOPING WORLD

Haleh Afshar and Carolyne Dennis (*editors*)
WOMEN AND ADJUSTMENT POLICIES IN THE THIRD WORLD

Myfanwy Franks
WOMEN AND REVIVALISM IN THE WEST
Choosing Fundamentalism in a Liberal Democracy

Judy Giles
WOMEN, IDENTITY AND PRIVATE LIFE IN BRITAIN, 1900–50

Mary Maynard and Joanna de Groot (*editors*)
WOMEN'S STUDIES IN THE 1990s
Doing Things Differently?

Haideh Moghissi
POPULISM AND FEMINISM IN IRAN
Women's Struggle in a Male-Defined Revolutionary Movement

Shirin M. Rai (*editor*)
INTERNATIONAL PERSPECTIVES ON GENDER AND DEMOCRATIZATION

Carmel Roulston and Celia Davies (*editors*)
GENDER, DEMOCRACY AND INCLUSION IN NORTHERN IRELAND

Yvette Taylor
WORKING-CLASS LESBIAN LIFE
Classed Outsiders

York Studies on Women and Men
Series Standing Order ISBN 0–333–71512–8
(*outside North America only*)

You can receive future titles in this series as they are published by placing a standing order.
Please contact your bookseller or, in case of difficulty, write to us at the address below with
your name and address, the title of the series and the ISBN quoted above.

Customer Services Department, Macmillan Distribution Ltd, Houndmills, Basingstoke,
Hampshire RG21 6XS, England

Working-Class Lesbian Life

Classed Outsiders

Yvette Taylor
University of Newcastle

First published in 2007 by
PALGRAVE MACMILLAN
Houndmills, Basingstoke, Hampshire RG21 6XS and
175 Fifth Avenue, New York, N.Y. 10010
Companies and representatives throughout the world.

PALGRAVE MACMILLAN is the global academic imprint of the Palgrave Macmillan division of St. Martin's Press, LLC and of Palgrave Macmillan Ltd. Macmillan® is a registered trademark in the United States, United Kingdom and other countries. Palgrave is a registered trademark in the European Union and other countries.

ISBN-13: 978–0–230–00871–7 hardback
ISBN-10: 0–230–00871–2 hardback

This book is printed on paper suitable for recycling and made from fully managed and sustained forest sources. Logging, pulping and manufacturing processes are expected to conform to the environmental regulations of the country of origin.

A catalogue record for this book is available from the British Library.

Library of Congress Cataloging-in-Publication Data
Taylor, Yvette, 1978–
    Working class lesbian life : classed outsiders / Yvette Taylor.
        p. cm.
    Includes bibliographical references and index.
    ISBN-13: 978–0–230–00871–7 (cloth)
    ISBN-10: 0–230–00871–2 (cloth)
        1. Working class lesbians—Great Britain—Social conditions. I. Title.
HQ75.6.G7T29 2007
306.76′63086230941—dc22   2007060080

10 9 8 7 6 5 4 3 2 1
16 15 14 13 12 11 10 09 08 07

Printed and bound in Great Britain by
Antony Rowe Ltd, Chippenham and Eastbourne

For my granny, Agnes McKelvie

Contents

Acknowledgements

Enormous thanks to the women who took part in this research, who spent time with me and who told so many interesting, funny and sad stories. Thanks to friends and colleagues in the School of Geography, Politics and Sociology at Newcastle University for their input, enthusiasm and support over the last couple of years. Thanks to Stevi Jackson and all staff and students at the Centre for Women's Studies, University of York, for past and ongoing support and encouragement. Still, thanks Alice.

Permission has been obtained to reproduce:

• Taylor, Y. (2004) 'Negotiation and Navigation: an exploration of the spaces/places of working-class lesbians'. *Sociological Research Online*, 9(1): 1–24.

• Taylor, Y. (2005) 'What Now? Working-class lesbians' post-school transitions' *Youth and Policy* 87: 29–43.

• Taylor, Y. (2007) '"If your face doesn't fit . . .": the misrecognition of working-class lesbians in scene space' *Leisure Studies* 27: 161–178.

• Taylor, Y. (2007) 'Brushed behind the bike shed: class and sexuality in school' *BJSE* 28(3).

1
Reviewing the Literature: An Introduction

Here I seek to set out the ways that class and sexuality have, or have not, been discussed, suggesting a tendency to deny, abstract, separate, to 'complicate', these two categories so that instead of emphasising their relevance, interconnections and urgency, they become detached and disconnected, far removed from inequalities faced by actual people. The actual people I am concerned with are working-class lesbians – I'm not just 'putting them back in', filling a 'gap in the literature' but asking why they weren't included in the first place? While this may seem a weighty accusation, I believe it is substantiated by the absences and silences about working-class lesbian lives. I am indebted to previous, and current, academic debate on both class and sexuality – this book has been written from a critique of the in/adequacy of such approaches and it is with respect, which occasionally turns into scepticism, that I make such an intervention. Academic debate often involves 'abstract' 'theorising' and to engage with this can involve reifying such abstraction. This first chapter provides an overview of academic theories that I deploy and critique in my analysis but this chapter may be passed over; the further six chapters present and deliberately centre the empirical data which lies at the heart of this research.

The production of knowledges remains a classed practice – rarely are working-class voices heard or legitimated, and sometimes the louder they shout the less they are heard. In trying to establish this book (and myself) as academically rigorous I too am investing in classed processes, with unease as well as confidence (Taylor, 2005a). Rather than trying to reconcile the dilemma of the production of knowledge, theirs and mine, I will attempt to offer further contributions and challenges to place working-class lesbians' experiences at the centre of my analysis, rather than my own dis/satisfaction. But what of those 'other' academic voices – what do they say, why do their views differ from mine? Re-reading the headlines, articles and debates I will look for the missing and the missed out, forging out a new space to think about the interconnection between class and sexuality and create an enduring and respectful, if not an exclusive or final, account.

I start this chapter by exploring class definitions, meanings and erasures, that is, 'Class in a new/cold climate'. The 'newness' refers to the ways that class is seen to belong to the ever distant past, while in a 'new' climate class is replaced by flux, fluidity and freedom from class constraints (Bauman, 1990; Beck, 2000b; Giddens, 1992). The coldness references the feeling of being left out of this, of taking away that which explains and informs. This applies not just to the economy but also to identity formation and continuation; the need to 'identify yourself' may not be a need at all if you are marked as 'one of those', and classified accordingly. When 'what you see is what you get' questions have to be asked about the continual production of class tables – the contrast between method-ological precision and substantive issues of material inequality. I then go on to explore the gendering of class in 'a certain class of women': those who criticise class models by arguing that the class position of women is ignored, rarely consider the class position of lesbians.

As I move on to Hennessy's (2000) attention to the 'political economy of sex', the interconnections between class and sexuality are re-established. This is rather unique given its usual separation. Nevertheless, Hennessy's material 'interconnections' are remote from the lives of actual working-class people, who rarely appear in her account. There is a danger of abstracting class from actual everyday lives when talking about class 'out there': poverty does exist in wealthy capitalist countries and an analysis of class in such places serves as a reminder that everyone is implicated in class, everyone has a class position (Mahony and Zmroczek, 1997). I then look at Dunne's (1997) empirical study on 'lesbian lifestyles' and argue that her account ignores the experience of working-class lesbians; her sample and subsequent conclusions contain a middle-class bias.

Movements and 'mobilities' are structured through class and I turn to Bourdieu's model of classed 'habitus' and class capitals to provide a sense of the ways that class still affects access into positions, travelling through space. Having the 'right' cultural, economic and social capitals (which, when legitimated turn into 'symbolic capital', a resource which the working-classes 'lack') produces opportunities and advantages across various social spheres. I suggest that these capitals influence 'economic achievement', more so than lesbian credentials (Dunne, 1997). Capitalising on the self, 'performing' at work, can be difficult when the performance is not that good, is self-deceptive and not economically rewarding, as I explore in 'fixed smiles, emotional labour', where both class and sexuality are interrelated, connecting and dis-connecting theories of performativity and materiality.

The inter-relationship generates controversy amongst feminists and here I locate the demise of class within as well as outwith feminist circles. In topical work on sexuality much of the agenda has been set by queer theory (Butler, 1990; Fuss, 1991) and most claim that this 'cultural turn' has deflected attention away from material inequalities, as more performative aspects of identity construction are prioritised (Barrett, 1992; Jackson, 2001). Queer theory is seen to unhinge sexuality from the social structures that organise it as sexuality is the primary and often isolated site of analysis (Hennessy, 2000). 'Queer' or 'materialist', where are the working-class lesbians? Bourdieu's (1984) social theory offers many potential connections with contemporary feminist theory and Butler (1990, 1997) has detailed the relations between performativity and Bourdieu's framework of social positioning in social space.

Spatial aspects of classed and sexualised movements, opportunities and dis/comforts also need to be explored: 'Opening the map'. Profitable or marketable identities legitimately, though precariously, occupy public space, which raises particular problems for working-class lesbians, who may not be able to 'buy into' existing queer scene space – available on the market, for a price (Jeffreys, 1994; Hennessy, 2000; Chasin, 2000). Looking is equated with being – someone or no-one, hence I move on to look at the ways class and sexuality are 'written on the body'. Such a focus draws upon varying theories of identity in space, particularly the ways that certain bodies, appearances and identities are rendered unentitled to occupy space because of lack of capital, bodily or otherwise, to legitimately access that space and to receive interpersonal affirmations within it (Bourdieu, 1984; Skeggs, 1999, 2001).

Scene space is also contrasted with working-class space, as there is a need to look at everyday spaces. Such a contrast provides a focus on the often stigmatised places which working-class people inhabit (Howarth, 2002) in comparison to 'trendy' and fashionable scene space. Stigma and outsider status produces dis/identification, classification and boundary regulation between classed 'others' (Savage et al., 2001; Skeggs, 2001; Southerton, 2000). I look at the creation of classed and sexual boundaries working to create exclusion and feelings of not/belonging, combining attention to spatialised identity with the negotiated and embodied meanings and understandings of individuals in space.

In the final section of this chapter (Black sheep of the family) I look at the ways in which lesbian relationships are currently being discussed as exemplary sites of transformed intimacy (Giddens, 1992; Weeks et al., 2001). I suggest that emphases on 'equal, accountable' intimacy (Dunne, 1997), achieved in sexual relationships and through 'families of friends' (Weston, 1997) ignore the structuring of friendships, the class encounters within these and the continued structural inequalities within intimate relationships. I argue for the persistence of inequalities across class, rather than situating, for example, sexism and homophobia within the working-class. Class constitutes a significant gap in recent studies of family, friendship and sexual relationships where notions of the 'good' and the 'bad' family often still contain unspoken classed assumptions. I aim to look at the ways class and sexuality has been researched, in relation to meanings, effects, outcomes, participation and dis/advantage and have necessarily, and hopefully productively, drawn upon an array of theories in order to conceptualise interlinked working-class lesbian identities.

Class in a new/cold climate

There has been somewhat of a resurgence of interest in class across disciplines, for example, in feminist theory, geography and sociology (Charlesworth, 2000; Crompton et al., 2000; Ehrenreich, 2001; Nayak, 2003a; Skeggs, 2004; Zweig, 2000). In the United States, there have been several rich, ethnographic accounts of the continued effect of social class, as it intersects with other social positions, all of which challenge the popular myth of North America as a 'classless' society (Bettie, 2003; Kefalas, 2003; Lareau, 2003; Reese, 2005; Zweig, 2000). Yet defining class becomes difficult in a climate of supposed 'classlessness', where class inequalities are thought of as increasingly 'complex' or non-existent. Rather than there being a demise of class division, I argue that such pronouncements are in fact classed. Rather than 'moving away' from class, in an 'upward', 'unstable' and 'uncertain' manner I am remaining with it, due to its fixity and its ability to fix – to deny opportunities in a 'new' global market place (Hennessey, 2000).

Changes in the organisation of production and consumption, it is said, make it difficult to describe and analyse social class; occupations that have traditionally defined class have broken down, being replaced with service and information industries (Beck, 2000a,b; Castells, 2000; Urry, 2000a,b). Castells (2000) speaks of the 'power of flows' taking precedence over the 'flows of power' whereby capital flows are spread throughout interconnected networks, creating a fast growing electronic economy in which money is increasingly abstract and invisible; there is no such thing as a global capitalist class as the behaviour of capitalists depends on submission to global networks, which is less secure than claims to the ownership of production.

In contrast, I believe that such flows work to sustain class structures, rather than undermine them. The 'unpredictability' of the flows of globalisation is often thought of in terms of increased flexibility or, indeed, re-named as improved 'choices' for workers; workers have the 'opportunity' to change their careers. But the security of traditional working-class jobs flows away. 'Choice' is therefore a multifaceted concept, some choosers accrue more benefits than others and the 'choice' may be whether to accept working in a certain framework, or to suffer poverty. While changing socio-economic structures lead some to question the relevance of social class, or at least to rethink previous conceptualisations, less is said about what class continues to do – not just what it is, or could be. For example, Bradley and Hebson (1999) argue that while the class dynamic remains a powerful force, that dynamic is itself complex and fluid. This may be an accurate description of the new global economy, but attention needs to be given to the ways class inequalities are lived in and why they are still relevant.

Class still insists upon its presence. There are many proponents of this argument (Bettie, 2003; Devine, 1992; Skeggs, 1997) who contend that even in the midst of economic changes, persistent occupational divisions of wealth and poverty prevail. These may be occurring within a different historical moment, with specific social and cultural conditions but they are still here. Even in the 'postmodern' global age, class continues to be a reliable predictor of life chances affecting, for example, health, education and housing. Changes in class structure should not be mistaken for the eradication of class; every generation has suspected that class has been in decline, only for its persistence to be discovered later on, triggering another round of academic debate (Roberts, 2001). The need to re-think class, yet again, can prove to be very frustrating and it is from and against such a sentiment that my research occurred. Yet frustration alone cannot explain the insistence, among the women I interviewed, of the relevance of class in their lives.

Examining psycho-social aspects of class and gender and, in particular, the discomfort in transition, via education, felt by both middle-class and working-class girls, into a 'new', de-industrialised, feminised labour market, Walkerdine et al. argue that as the boundaries of social class are 'opened up' self-definition becomes a painful and confusing process where 'it is no longer possible to know who or what or where we are meant to be' (2001:10). While I agree that class identification can indeed be painful I am not convinced by the 'opening up' of class boundaries, or indeed of class identification. This work, like that which emphasises 'global' changes and flux, fails to address continued everyday identifications as working-class, even in 'unstable' places.

Identify yourself

Identity has become one of the unifying frameworks of academic debate, with concerns especially generated about 'transformations' in identity (Jenkins, 1996). But who decides who and what is 'transforming' and who is 'staying put'? Are we all really included in this transformative, reflexive process, where the 'choice' is not only about where to work but also what to be? While proponents of global flows dismiss the relevance of class at an economic level, such 'transformations' spill over onto identity concerns and similar key phrases mark out the supposed shift from class to ... what? In an all moving, uncertain, shifting climate society, the economy and the individual cannot, it would seem, be adequately described (Beck, 1992; Lash and Urry, 1987, 1994). Against such conceptualisations I situate my work within those debates which do concede the continued relevance of class, as a factor informing economic and social experience (Devine, 1992; Marshall et al., 1988). I also see the importance of enquiring into class identification, rather than denouncing its relevance without empirical evidence.

Although social identity has attracted considerable attention, there has been little recent research on the salience of class identities. Based on a UK study Savage et al. (2001) show that whilst class identities are 'ambivalent', they are also structured and coherent in their own terms, asserting that 'the ambivalence of class identities does therefore not entail breaking from class analysis itself.' Yet they claim that people identify with gender or locale with greater ease, with much less ambivalence, than class. Class is still deployed by interviewees as an external benchmark, as a peripheral marker used in the 'telling of stories' but not as an absolute, clear or definite part of such identity 'stories'. This research is part of a broader project on 'social networks, social capital and lifestyle'[1] through which they provide an account of contemporary class identity processes. Due to the 'threat' of attaching class to identity, respondents were concerned to establish their own 'ordinariness'. Ideas of class are seen to pollute references to 'ordinariness' and so this strategy is read as a 'defensive device to avoid the politics of being labelled in class terms', while 'ordinariness' both undermines and invokes class location, since a comparison with the 'non-ordinary' is utilised (Savage et al., 2001: 875). There are classed reasons why people may wish to avoid social fixing, at different times either 'playing up' or 'playing down' their position. Invoking 'ordinariness' may be difficult if you are marked as 'other' and cannot afford to play reflexively with ideas of class. Savage et al. (2001) provide interesting insights into the dynamics of class dis-identification, yet disappointingly, and in contrast to Skeggs (1997), do not relate material inequalities to identity formation.

Many researchers have outlined the difficulties surrounding issues of class identification, suggesting that to accept a working-class identity is increasingly to accept a 'spoilt identity' (Reay, 1996) a 'white trash' status, synonymous with degradation and shame (Bettie, 2003; Brown, 1997; Sandell, 1997). Working-class people are depicted more and more as 'dis-identifying' from their working-classness, reluctant to become known through the markers of class (Lawler, 1999; Reay, 1998; Skeggs, 1997). In fact Skeggs (1997) claims that for the working-class women in her study, identity was constituted upon disassociation and avoidance of the possibility of being labelled working-class. Her respondents were eager to prove their 'respectability', against the 'unrespectable' and the stigmatised; far from 'reflexively' playing with class, the women she spoke to were deeply afraid of being 'one of those' and rather than seeking 'ordinariness' an extra-ordinary effort was required to disclaim classed associations and prove themselves as 'worthy' and 'decent'.

McRobbie (2000), Brown (1997) and Bettie (2003) consider class resistance and challenges to traditional notions of femininity in the use of material goods. In *Women Without Class* Bettie's (2003) ethnography, conducted in a high school in California's Central Valley, examines how White and Mexican-American girls construct their identities within the school as members of various subcultural groups: 'Smokers' ('white trash'), 'Cholas and Cholos' ('hard core' Mexican-American students from hard-living families), Las Chicas (other Mexican-American students who had 'outgrown' the cholas/os grouping), Skaters (the mass of white students, self-identifying as 'alternative'), 'hicks' (mostly white students from hard-living and settled families) and, finally, 'Preps' (primarily white students from middle-class backgrounds). Bettie (2003) is concerned with the lived intersection between class, gender, ethnicity and sexuality and the ways these are perfomatively constituted and resisted. Similarly, writing about a group of white teenagers from poor and working-class families in rural Maine, Brown (1997) reveals how respondents resist masculine control and that, far from rejecting one's class positioning, class provided a source of group identity, solidarity and even resistance, challenging Skeggs's (1997) notion of dis-identification. Rather than investing in their femininity (like Skeggs's respondents) the working-class girls in Brown's research also provide a challenge to the constraints and understandings of traditional femininity, a signifier which is both classed and sexualised. Working-class women may not be able to positively invest in a (masculine) working-class identity, to claim a 'Real Geordie'[2] (Nayak, 2003a, 2003b), 'white trash' status (Wray and Newitz, 1997), but the increasing theorisation of class solely in terms of dis-identification can be interrogated to include a stronger sense of when working-class and middle-class women do and do not identify themselves as classed.

I draw upon Skeggs's work to highlight the negotiation of positive and negative meanings of working-classness but I suggest that for working-class lesbians, identity is not solely based on 'dis-identification': being working-class is hard to 'avoid' when it is so 'obvious'. In everyday situations identity is categorised and called into question, yet the continued classed aspects of this are under-investigated. Identity is constructed in interactions and institutionally, continually informing understandings of who we are and who other people are: 'the categorisations of others is a process upon which to draw the construction of our own identities' (Jenkins, 1996: 87). Our identifications also require validations from others. It is not enough to assert an identity, as we cannot see ourselves without also seeing how others see us; interpretations, readings and understandings are negotiated in social encounters. The presence of class reveals itself in everyday judgements and interpersonal interactions – informing not only the type of person we declare ourselves to be but also what we are seen to be and the structuring of this identity.

Symbolic interactionism focuses on the subjective aspects of social life, on actors actively negotiating, creating and responding to their social worlds: society is thus organised in the patterned interaction amongst individuals. The emphasis on the social construction of society and people's negotiated realities and identities therein causes attention to be focused on the meanings these have for individual 'actors' and the 'roles' created, or 'scripted', and responded to through language, gestures and actions (Gagnon and Simon, 1973; Goffman, 1968, 196; Mead, 1927). These negotiated reflections, expressions and rememberances are particularly important for marginalised groups in that they highlight agency, subjectivity and interpretation as the everyday meaning-making events are highlighted and challenged: it allows for voices and stories that would not otherwise be heard and seeks to elevate and validate these stories as a matter of urgency. By engaging with recent studies that explore identity in interaction I aim to highlight the material, subjective and interpersonal constructions of class and sexual identity across time and place.

As far back as in 1969 Goffman noted the importance of 'the presentation of self' during interaction and the significance of impression management strategies in the construction of social identity, recognising that identity could be 'spoiled' and devalued. The matter of identity claims, resistances and counter-claims is relevant to the study of working-class identity. For the women I interviewed, identifications as working-class were mediated by such processes, as they wrestled with the positive and negative meanings and experiences contained within the term, responding to and 'reconciling' this with an 'outsider's' view of them. I am convinced that class processes can be in play, even without 'accurate' affirmed definitions, but this is yet another contested terrain.

What you see is what you get? Defining class

There have been many attempts to define class, to say exactly what it is, raising much debate and controversy – followed by a long silence. There is little point in rehearsing such debates, especially as my purpose is not primarily to say what class is but rather what it does, achieved through a focus on working-class lesbians' experiences of class and the meanings which they themselves attribute to it.

There may be no agreed definition of class, but people are invariably classed on the basis of their occupations. The Registrar General's Classification,[3] which does not measure class in a theoretically sophisticated way, has been replaced by various other class categorisations. The main classes identified in the Goldthrope Scheme are the service class and a working-class. There are also intermediate classes: lower-level white collar workers and a petite bourgeois, comprising self-employed non-professionals and proprietors of small businesses. To these the 1998 classification added a bottom stratum, in effect an 'underclass'. The notion that people are somehow 'under' class, rather than part of it, is a contentious one. Nevertheless, the concept of 'underclass', with its connotations of stigma, regularly appears in political rhetoric and policy (Bradley and Hebson, 1999; Byrne, 2005; Ehrenreich, 2001; Zweig, 2000). What happened to 'classlessness' here? Re-definitions are not eradications and renaming is not resolving. The pervasiveness or importance of class inequality cannot be ascertained from categorisation and classification alone, but allocation to such positions, including 'underclass', gives an indication of the ways in which class is still, officially persistent.

Members of the 'underclass' are blamed for their own circumstances, unwilling to take advantage of educational and occupational 'opportunities' (Murray, 1990, 1994), marking an individualisation of class processes in neo-liberal times (Hey, 2003; Reese, 2005; Skeggs, 2004; Walkerdine, 2003; Wray and Newitz, 1997). A more accurate account is that of MacDonald and Marsh (2000), who suggest that while cyclical transitions can transform labour market marginality into what appears to be almost permanent socio-economic exclusion, there is not a class of people beneath the lowest class of the gainfully employed. Rather, there is a restructuring of the lower levels of the labour market typified by cyclical movements around peripheral work and unemployment (Webster et al., 2004). Many women I interviewed were unemployed but I view this as a result of their class position, rather than as a result of their being 'under' class. To categorise is not an easy or innocent process, but class schemes are easy to find, much debated and, I would argue, still inadequate; they cannot, nor do they attempt to, describe the experience of occupying these categories. The employment aggregate approach has little to say about how class is played out in everyday life, with the crucial question concerning how many classes there are, rather than what class does.

Although Crompton (2000) argues for a genuinely pluralistic approach to class analysis in order to capture its complexity, measuring and revealing 'who gets what', more qualitative approaches seek to understand how people perceive, experience and respond to their circumstances.[4] This is important given Reay's claim that the experience of working-class lives are documented in empirical analysis from a distance: 'the structural location of working-class groups is analysed in theory. Exploitation, urgency, struggle and necessity are lost in a sea of statistics or theoretical abstractions' (1998: 309). It is important to investigate both 'objective' and 'subjective' aspects of class. Working-class experience is different from middle-class experience because of economic inequality – but an exploration of how this is lived in requires moving beyond class categorisations alone.

A certain class of woman

Hennessy and Ingraham (1997) highlight the movement of capital into new forms of work, expanding the service sector, education and middle-management and the ways in which middle-class women can benefit from and capitalise upon these changes. Like others, I remain sceptical about these changes and question their benefits (Chasin, 2000;

Hennessy, 2000). The 'female future' may in fact be highly polarised, producing sharp divisions amongst women (Walby, 1997; Walkerdine et al., 2001). Furthermore, divisions exist between women who have educational credentials and skills and those who leave school with few qualifications and enter a labour market characterised by poorly paid part-time work. For many working-class women there is a greater likelihood of being employed in 'pink-collar ghettos', doing poorly paid part-time, insecure work. Thus, economic change has to be considered in relation to the feminisation of poverty (Gluckman and Reed, 1997).

In arguing for an analysis of the gendered constitution of the class structure, Crompton's (2000) analysis of household and family structures remains middle-class, which is acknowledged, and heterosexual, which is unacknowledged. Most labour market theory either ignores sexuality or considers it unimportant for the gendered operations of the labour market (Adkins, 1995, 2000). My work emerges from these gaps, making use of the focus on gendered employment inequalities, but suggesting necessary extensions, given the inattention to the experience of working-class lesbians. Women's disadvantaged labour position has been largely ignored throughout class analysis,[5] and lesbians have been further ignored, or presumed to be too 'confusing' for comment: Valentine (1993a), for example, argues that the class position of many lesbians is 'complex', 'fluid' and 'multiple' (Penelope, 1994; Raffo, 1997; Valentine et al., 2003). Although there has been attention to the linkages between sexuality and class or more accurately, between capitalism and sexuality, these occur without reference to classed individuals – putting class in but leaving working-class lesbians out.

There is some relevant work, including that produced by other self-identified working-class lesbians such as Munt (2000) and Allison (1988, 1992), cross-cutting literary, cultural and sociological disciplinary boundaries. Writing within a US context, Allison seeks to give the 'white trash' a voice, speaking against the misrepresentations of working-class women, lesbians and poor people, in general, as trashy, distasteful, excessive and wrong (see also Skeggs, 2004). 'White trash' life is characterised by Allison as harsh, brutal and often violent, mixed together by an all-pervading sense of hopelessness and despair and thus the romanticised myth of the noble hard worker is resoundingly questioned. However, while the working-class has been both vilified and romanticised, arguably it is the former positioning which currently dominates (Skeggs, 2004). Discourses of class, of taste and distaste, of propriety and respect, excess and waste are profoundly linked to discourses of sexuality.

Davis and Kennedy's (1993) ethnography charts the life experiences of working-class lesbians in the United States from the 1930s to the 1960s in Buffalo and New York, speaking of particular places and times when working-class lesbians had more recognisable cultures, communities and scenes. Also based in the United States, *Queerly Classed* (Raffo, 1997) charts the intersections between class and sexuality, based on the personal reflections of a number of academics and activists; this book challenges the concept of 'classlessness' within North America, revealing it to be one of the most pervasive lies (Gluckman and Reed, 1997). The dual consideration of class and sexuality highlights that to be on the outside on both counts is quite a significant burden to bear, the intersection amounting to an outlaw status as sexuality both compliments and negates class status. In naming the effect and impact of class across a range of sites, from education, employment and leisure to activism, attitude and esteem (Kadi, 1997; Willow, 1997), the collection seeks to put class and queer together, as two interlocking, inseparable spheres shaping everyday experiences, forcing a 'coming out' on two fronts (Becker, 1997; Brownworth, 1997; Witherow, 1997). The real, emotive, painful and happy experiences within this book surpass the theories that explain, numerate and account for class in an 'objective' manner, yet what is absent is empirical data, beyond the author's own individual, yet shared, experiences: clearly some of the authors have moved away from, although ever mindful of their classed 'pasts' (see also Penelope, 1994). Working-class lesbians have always existed while they have rarely achieved recognition or visibility (Faderman, 1991; Feinberg, 1993; Nestle, 1987). There is a need to chart the experiences of working-class lesbians who remain in this interlocked 'outlaw' space, both subjectively and materially.

Gluckman and Reed (1997) tackle the myth of the 'pink pound', of gays and lesbians as an economically advantaged, hedonistic, opulent and 'in your face' minority capable of acting up in and re-claiming a range of cultural spaces. Importantly, Gluckman and Reeds's analysis serves as a reminder that lesbians exist in every income bracket, challenging both gay and mainstream media. In a UK lesbian lifestyle magazine ('Lesbians: Loaded and Loving It', *DIVA*, February, 2005), lesbians were declared to be the 'new gay men', equally capable of matching gay men's income and spending power. This was followed by mainstream press attention which failed to question such middle-classification of lesbians and instead pointed out the historical lineage of lesbians' middle, even upper-class, capitals, re-endorsing the mythical 'pink pound' passage to full societal inclusion (Badgett, 2001; Gluckman and Reed, 1997).

Buying in to the in crowd

Consumption is one variable of social exclusion measures representing, for Crompton and Scott (2000), a collapsing of class and consumption. Indeed consumption, as a 'lifestyle generator', is seen to provide the focus for identity that once came from paid employment (Pakulski and Waters, 1996). In identifying consumption as a way of differentiating social groups, Bauman (1998) claims that the poor can be viewed as 'flawed consumers' in that they are failing in one of the most crucial duties of citizens in a consumer society. Similarly, Pahl (2000) discusses 'financial citizenship' as a way of differentiating social groups, arguing that new forms of money have a divisive impact on patterns of consumption, creating the credit rich and the credit poor, where a wallet full of plastic may be much more impressive than a purse full of real pounds and pence. Notions of 'flawed consumers' excluded from 'financial citizenship' point to class without pointing it out, while the intersection between class and sexuality makes apparent enduring forms of exclusion.

Roseneil (2000) charts the cultural valorising of the queer in popular culture, fashion, magazines and television. This is taken as evidence of the 'aspirational status of queer', rather than as the class-exclusive 'aestheticization of everyday life' (Fraser, 1999; Hennessy, 2000). Queer theory has been associated with the pursuit of a queer lifestyle, constructed through a 'postmodern consumer ethic'. To the lament of many materialist feminists, theories of lesbian identity are increasingly preoccupied with the queer subject of desire, rather than with material needs and constraints, representing a separation between gender and sexuality (Hennessy, 2000; Jeffreys, 1994, 2003). The queer emphasis on identities as 'performative significations' largely ignores the material factors at play in self-fashioning (Hennessy, 2000). As I have commented elsewhere, queer opportunities may be accessible and obtainable to middle-class urban dwellers, but lesbians living on the breadline may well have few opportunities for engaging in subversive parodic practices (Taylor, 2005a). Queerness may in fact only be accessible to those materially poised to occupy the position, in contrast to those excluded from both heterosexual privilege and the circles of the fashionably queer – or 'lesbian chic' (Hennessy, 2000).

Hennessy (2000) pays attention to the global nature of the structures of patriarchy and capitalism as sustaining a 'political economy of sex'. She rearticulates the materiality of sexual identity formations, transformations and commodifications, situating these in the global structures of late capitalism. Drawing upon a vast range of empirical, international evidence and varying materialist perspectives, she contests the relevance of queer theory and associated ideas of identity performativity. Furthermore, in 'Classing Queer' Fraser (1999) argues that queer's stance on visibility and recognition further marks a connection between identity and aesthetics, whereby queer becomes a brand name, an identity project assuming the form of aesthetic, consumer-based lifestyles (Featherstone, 1991; Hennessy, 1995). Yet Binnie (2004) challenges the 'myth of the pink economy' arguing that it compounds the idea of a 'special', even privileged, group who can more than afford their 'rights'. Class-based exclusions – and inclusions – are noted in terms of consumption and activism and proliferating 'McPink' lifestyle options. As such, Binnie further classes the politics of visibility and ensuing classed invisibilities, raised by Fraser (1999), while claiming that a queer framework need not be devoid of economic components; the focus on the 'cultural' is also, already, a crucial focus on the economic (Butler, 1997; Fraser, 1997; Jackson, 2001).

Moving on?

Bourdieu's (1984) social theory offers many potential connections with contemporary feminist theory and Butler (1990, 1997) has detailed the relations between performativity and Bourdieu's framework of social positioning in social space. Lovell (2000) compares Bourdieu's account of the social construction of the human subject through space, with Butler's (1990) account of subjectivity as performance; while claiming that Butler pays insufficient attention to the social conditions of 'performative subversions' she also argues that Bourdieu's concept of 'habitus' produces an over-deterministic view of subjectivity, being tied to the classed practices in which they were forged: Bourdieu is criticised for having an 'oversocialised' concept of the individual 'who is destined to be a mere bearer of social positions' (Lovell, 2000:17). Notably, Bourdieu's theory is framed mostly in terms of issues of class, having little to say about gender or sexuality (Adkins and Skeggs, 2004).

Yet the issues that Bourdieu (1984) raises are too valuable to lose sight of, as they provide understandings of the constraints on individual mobility and performance. Lack of symbolic capital affects access into legitimised social space and positioning, which is useful in thinking about how movements through spaces are constituted, facilitated or impeded. It also points to the entrenched, emotional 'value' of spaces, relevant to how social space is viewed and negotiated (Reay, 2000; Skeggs, 1997). It is still important to recognise the (classed) tension in negotiating social spaces, rather than the 'subversion' of the values which it holds (Fraser, 1999).

Bourdieu (1984) makes use of 'habitus' as a three-dimensional space, defined by the volume of human capital, composition of capital and change over time. Habitus can best be described as a 'feeling for the game' in which the embodied self always bears the marks of the starting point (Johnson and Lawler, 2005); it is generative of distinctive social practices or dispositions, which result from social conditioning related to one's position in social space. Class attaches itself to classed individuals and in so doing becomes apparent in the everyday interactions, which social actors in social space engage in. Bourdieu's model of classed capital and classed 'habitus' provides a sense of the ways class still affects access into positions, travelling through time and space.

Speaking of trajectories and fields enables an understanding of how bodies have access to different amounts of capitals. For Bourdieu, the relationship between the deployment of various capitals, within sets of social conditions, or fields, produce classed practices. Bourdieu's capitals include 'economic capital', 'cultural capital' and 'social capital', encompassing objective and subjective elements, which are convertible into usable resources and power, becoming transformed, reproduced and capitalised upon.[6] Capitals are classed: distribution of capital runs from those who are best provided with both economic and cultural capital to those who are deprived in both respects. This model of embodied capitals, where resources are attached to classed individuals, challenges straightforward notions of 'upward mobility'. Gradations of social status inform and prescribe movement through space while mobility with its 'rises' and 'falls' produces a one-dimensional view of social space, ignoring conversions and reproduction strategies (Bourdieu, 1984). Additionally, notions of mobility further pathologise those working-class deviants who do not 'escape' (Lawler, 1999).[7] However, Bourdieu's theory of classed capitals and classed 'habitus' is framed solely in terms of class, having little to say about gender or sexuality (Adkins and Skeggs, 2004).

Individuals do not move about randomly, or easily, in social space because they are subject to forces which structure that space, whether they are classed, gendered or sexualised or, more likely, an intersection of all three. Objective limitations and a 'sense of one's place' leads to exclusion from resources and places, and this structuring sentiment and material actuality cannot easily be discarded. Yet Dunne (1997) suggests an ability to 'capitalise' on lesbian credentials – 'escaping' heterosexuality and economic disadvantage, moving away and moving on. In exploring the social and economic influences for lesbians across the household and the workplace, Dunne concludes that there is an inter-relationship between lesbian lifestyles and financial independence: lesbianism then becomes an 'economic achievement'. But is clear that Dunne has a relatively privileged sample. Her research is based on a life history of continuity and change in the lives of 60 non-heterosexual British women aged 17–59. Only 25 per cent of Dunne's sample were from 'manual' backgrounds (using the Goldthrope Scheme) whereas 30 per cent were from intermediate background and 45 per cent from service backgrounds. It is little wonder that she does not speak of poverty, exclusion and disadvantage.[8] In fact, Dunne does admit that the district where her respondents lived had a particularly well-qualified population, but she denies the importance of this in her overall conclusions. However, educational provision is bound up with geographical location and is classed (Bettie, 2003; Devine, 2004; Lareau, 2003). Yet Dunne states that for those who questioned the giveness of heterosexuality during their schooling, the experience of being 'different' was consequential, supporting the 'mobilization of facilities which could facilitate the construction of a different life' (Dunne, 1997: 89).

If this 'mobilization' is classed, which it is, can only middle-class women then become lesbians? It is claimed that education may offer a context within which women can make a positive identification with lesbianism, which fails to acknowledge that the passage of a working-class student through the education system may be both problematic and painful, constituting an attempted erasure, rather than affirmation, of identity. Ultimately, Dunne (1997) ignores the reality of working-class lesbian existence and the relevance of class in structuring educational, and employment, outcomes.

The entrenched nature of classed habitus, informing 'economic achievements' or otherwise, alerts us to the structuring of opportunities, a factor which Dunne analyses in relation to sexuality and gender – but not class. Becoming a lesbian does not necessarily alter a working-class habitus, instead 'achievement' can be seen as constructed through, related to and informed by the intersection between class and sexuality.

There is potential and actual disjuncture between working-class habitus and that authorised in institutional space, such as school systems. The classed, gendered, and sexualised aspects of schooling have been investigated by many authors – but these do not combine in such a way as to cast light upon the interconnecting inequalities faced by working-class lesbians, or the outcomes of these (Bejamin et al, 2003; Epstein, 1994; Mac an Ghaill, 1994; Skeggs, 1997; Willis, 1977; Youdell, 2005).

The school curriculum itself is profoundly gendered, classed and heterosexist (Thomson and Scott, 1991), which is uncomfortable at best and devastating at worst, often the case for young women 'coming-out' in a hostile environment (Cockburn, 1987). Vulnerability is compounded by classed expectations and lack of legitimated channels of challenge (Reay and Ball, 1997). During the 1970s Marxist theorists developed theoretical frameworks suggesting that schools reproduced the social relations of wider society. In critiquing those theories, Willis (1977) presented a more complex picture, arguing that working-class students in actually resisting the schooling process, reproduce themselves inside social class relations. Transgressions such as 'havin' a laff' and 'dossing' represented strategies to deal with the vicissitudes of a schooling system that alienated them (Mac an Ghaill, 1994; Willis, 1977). Nevertheless, the 'gang of lads' model is insufficient in explaining the classed production of femininity and the resistances against this (Renold, 2000; Skeggs, 1997). Young women's contestation of state schooling is severely circumscribed by schools' institutional power, which enables them to act as key gatekeepers to future economic and social destinies (Bettie, 2003; Skeggs, 1997). 'Havin' a laff' can be difficult when occupying and experiencing combined inequalities and it is difficult to get the 'last laugh' when you are the one being laughed at.

The intersection of class, gender and sexuality combines to produce a heavy disadvantage within and beyond the schooling system, impacting upon post-school transitions and entry into – or exclusion from – the workplace. Lesbians are still subject to institutionalised heterosexuality despite the Employment Equality (Sexual Orientation) Regulations 2003[9] and workplaces can be experienced as deeply homophobic (John and Patrick, 1999). Given that there is an inter-relationship between employment and sexuality (Adkins, 2000; Dunne, 1997) working-class lesbians' experience should also be investigated: the interaction between 'coming out' about a devalued sexual identity and a stigmatised class position is captured in this book.

Fixed smiles, emotional labour

Drawing upon the work of Goffman (1969) and the tradition of symbolic interactionism, Hochschild (1983) documents how service sector workers' emotions and bodily displays are regulated and manipulated via institutional, occupational structures in order to extract profit (Leidner, 1993). Such routinisation calls into question taken-for-granted norms about social interaction and deeply felt beliefs about authenticity, individuality and personal integrity. Notions of 'surface acting' can be applied to working-class lesbians' workplace experiences where mis/readings and self-deception (i.e., not 'coming-out') had to be managed. Sexuality, class and gender are consequential to the ways in which the women's workplace 'performances' were mis/read – and indeed to the ways in which they themselves displayed and read these signifiers.

I also highlight the economic consequence of these: to be read as a lesbian often does not bestow economic advantages, with or without the smile. There are dual processes of mis/recognitions,[10] where to be recognised as worthy, entitled and 'in place' – a process occurring via the classed readings of 'in/appropriate' bodies and appearances – is dependent upon symbolic systems of knowledge evaluations (Skeggs, 1999). The consequences of these and the effects of being misrecognised, that is being undervalued in interpersonal interactions, classified as unworthy and unentitled to legitimately occupy public space are re-occurring themes apparent as working-class lesbians negotiate, accept and enact their classed and sexual identities in multiple spheres.

Various authors have given attention to the 'aestheticisation' or 'culturalisation' of economic life, whereby aesthetic components, such as appearance and bodily dispositions, are given economic value (Bourdieu, 1984; Hoschild, 1983): 'an increasing proportion of jobs in contemporary Britain involve the marketing of personal attributes, including sexuality, as part of the product ... selling oneself – one's body, sexuality and gender performance is part of the job' (McDowell, 1997: 76). An ample body of work has developed on the performativity of production (Holliday, 1999, 2001; Holliday and Thompson, 2001). Adkins (2000) suggests that the commodification of sexuality at work, especially lesbian sexuality, is highly prevalent. As well as constituting an opportunity for self-invention and empowerment, many stress that commodification involves an appropriation of lesbian identities, as well as their 'labour, leisure and purchasing power' (Griggers quoted in Adkins, 2000: 205).

Instead Adkins (2000) examines whether the commodification aesthetic can be seen as making, or constituting sexual subjects at work. This involves an investigation of the ways in which desires, sexualities, bodies and identities are figured through commodification aesthetics. A warning is issued against the simple conflation of aesthetics and identity, but Adkins (2000) looks at the example of hairstyles to show how particular aesthetics ('lesbian hair') may constitute 'the lesbian' at work. Stylised workplace 'performances' become potential workplace resources, linking cultural and economic capitals as each works to enhance the other.

In claiming that the aestheticisation of work allows for mobility and flexibility, the connection between performativity and materiality, a qualifier is given with regard to those workers with 'different ascribed identities' who are unable to enact multiple performances. It is unclear who these workers are but Adkins notes that such 'others' are 'unable to be mobile in regard to performances of sexuality and gender' (2000: 209). This is related to the process of fixing particular workers in specific genders and sexualities. But 'othering' also occurs through class processes, as Skeggs (2001) has shown in relation to leisure spaces. Those with limited economic and cultural capital are unable to be flexible and mobile as their identities and bodies, physical and embodied capital, are 'fixed' (Fraser, 1999; Skeggs, 1997, 1999, 2001). This has not been theorised in terms of both class and sexuality, or in relation to working-class lesbians who occupy both positions and whose 'performances' may be doubly out of place.

Holliday (1999) uses video diaries to explore the performance of sexual identities in work, domestic and social space, using this information to reveal performative 'comfort' and 'discomfort', which she links to theories of performativity and reflexivity (Butler, 1990; Giddens, 1992): the comfort of identity, expressed through clothes, becomes an external expression of what one feels on the inside, a 'wish to close the gap between performance (acting) and ontology (being), a desire to be self-present to both oneself and others' (Holliday, 1999: 481). Nevertheless, identities are subject to regulations and constraints, mediated by other bodies and by the appropriateness of dress codes for particular spaces; not everyone is able to power dress. There is a structuring of un/comfortable work and leisure 'performances', forcing attention toward the material aspects of identity construction. The performativity of identity is clearly demonstrated in the appearance and embodiment of sexuality (Adkins, 2000; Holliday, 1999): it can be extended by classing workplace aesthetics, giving attention to the ways that bodies and identities are rendered un/entitled to occupy workspace through in/adequate 'performances'. To be recognised as something is often also to be in receipt of material resources (Fraser, 1999; Skeggs, 1999, 2001); systems of evaluation are deployed and these have real effects on material movements through space – and for individual movers (Bourdieu, 1984). There are material, embodied and subjective consequences of occupying intersecting working-class and lesbian positions and identities.

Reinstating class in the analysis of sexuality, rather than abstracting class from sexuality, serves to address the subjective meaning of class location and sexual identity. Sexual and class identity, although social constructs, may be invested with emotional meanings, as part of our sense of self. This entails consideration of the ways that sexual and gendered identities intersect with class affiliations and localities, affecting spatialised perceptions (Corteen, 2002; John and Patrick, 1999; Namaste, 1996). Social environments powerfully shape subjective feelings and access to material resources and spaces, rather than just being the space where sexual identity can be displayed: the inadequacy of theorising identity as *only* performativity becomes apparent.

Opening the map – introducing space

Thomas (2004) notes that the primary concern with space and sexuality has revolved around urban homosexual identity (Brown, 2000) and dissident sexual citizenship (Bell, et al. 2001), expanded by recent explorations of, for example, sex tourism (Binnie, 2004) and suburban (Brekhaus, 2003) and rural sexualities (Binnie and Valentine, 1999). I believe it is important to put class back in to the study of space (Thrift and Johnson, 1993) and to the meanings that locations have to those within them – where we are and how we get there, as well as what we can do (or cannot do) when we are there (Bondi, 1998; Nayak, 2003a,b; Reay, 2000; Reay and Lucey, 2000). Class not only exists, it creates and divides territories; privileged enclaves or 'sink' estates, while lesbian and gay space must surely be more than scene space – the purpose then becomes finding out how these spaces are variously occupied and moved through.

Bell (1991) and Binnie (2004) note that the most visible and studied gay geography is that of white middle-class men; working-class lesbians are excluded from research agendas and little is known about the respective influence of class, gender and sexuality upon space and the meanings of such territories for those who occupy marginal and stigmatised spaces and identities.[11] By incorporating a concern for place and space, the ways in which class and sexuality are experienced by working-class lesbians moving through particular environments will serve to highlight the interconnections, setting an evocative background for the location of inequalities.

Space is constituted through social relations and material processes, it reflects the way life is organised, the way it is perceived and understood, and the ways groups react to it. Scene space may be seen as a space where lesbians and gays can be legitimately visible, as opposed to the felt, perceived and actual illegitimacy in occupying heterosexual space. However, there are divisions within this, where entitlements are bought and access denied, or at least made difficult, to those on the 'geographical fringes'. Attention has been given to the ways that such space is gendered. Many women cannot afford to 'buy into' such spaces (Bell and Valentine, 1995) – but who are these 'many women' in class terms? Lesbian space may meet a desire for identification, providing emotional and practical support for women 'coming-out'; thus I ask if the 'coming-out' process is differentially negotiated in terms of class and where, then, are the spaces in which working-class lesbians construct and negotiate their classed and sexual identities? (Valentine et al., 2003).

Shelf space and sexual geography

Subjects are rendered il/legitimately visible in city space; sexual identities can become categorised and commodified, trapped within commercial spaces. Although scene spaces can be seen to offer a range of possibilities – from going out to 'coming out', such possibilities may not be open to certain groups. Some groups, it seems, have more power to enter negotiation of 'possibilities' than others. This is demonstrated by Warner (1993) who looks at the pivotal role of the market in the construction of queer sexualities and notes its exclusionary tendencies: 'In the lesbian and gay movement … the institutions of culture-building have been market-mediated – bars, discos, newspapers, magazines, phone lines, resorts, urban commercial districts … the structural environment has meant that the institutions of queer culture have been dominated by those with capital: typically, middle-class white men' (1993: xvi–xvii). These spaces are exclusionary and attention directed towards them may perpetuate this by focusing on the more visible and open spatial expressions of sexual identity, rather than the hidden places (Bell and Valentine, 1995; Binnie and Valentine, 1999).

If many groups are excluded from the scene then it cannot be conceptualised as being representative of lesbian and gay lives; it may not purport to be, but claims and entitlements are inevitably made upon this space. Scene spaces need to be re-thought and re-located within a gender and class framework. In attempting such a re-conceptualisation, Binnie (2000) argues that 'queer cosmopolitanism' is based on knowingness and sophistication, with the distinction between cosmopolitanism and provincialism being articulated through discourses of 'sophistication'. Consequently, working-class and 'provincial' sexualities are marked as being unsophisticated and 'less developed' (Binnie, 2000). Similarly, Weston (1995) reveals the connection between 'coming-out', developing a gay identity, and becoming a 'sophisticated' city dweller. This requires access, both culturally and economically, to these spaces and positions.

While Knopp (1995) notes that those who feel distanced from the scene are quick to castigate it for being exploitative, it is necessary to criticise the way in which this space is structured and maintained – pro-capitalist discourses and practices facilitate many structures of oppression and someone's 'leisure' space may be another's work space (Skeggs, 1999; Hennessy, 2000). For there to be individuals who assert their status and tastes in consumption patterns (which is how class in contemporary market theory is increasingly being discussed) there have to be economic processes whereby surplus labour (classed workers) is 'performed, appropriated, distributed and received' (Gagnier 2000: 43), suggesting the necessity in combining materiality, performativity and spatiality.

Examining current conflicts over sexualised urban space, Binnie (2000) argues that as cities compete for mobile capital in the global market they strive to present themselves as safe, business friendly, controlled environments, which results in the most visible aspects of public sex being forced out by corporate interests.[12] He compares this process with the management of particular classed spaces, with working-class people being displaced through market driven gentrification. The spatial layout of cities clearly shows class divisions: industrial work areas are separated from residential areas, council estates from middle-class suburbia (Binnie, 2000; Brekhaus, 2003; Davidoff and Hall, 1992).[13] Both the sex industry and the manufacturing industry are seen as polluting and unsightly, which warrants their containment. In other words, more powerful agents in the economy force these sexualised and classed spaces out of 'respectable' areas.[14] Binnie (1995, 2004) argues for the reincorporation of the material into debates on sexuality and space, claiming that sexuality should not be subsumed under the more 'neutral' category of the cultural politics of consumption. I would endorse Binnie's assertion while still asking what 'material' is to be included in such materialist approaches?

Clear visibility/queer viability

Culturally, there can be resistance to the heteronormativity of space through creating lesbian and gay space and enacting a 'queer social visibility' (Binnie, 2000; Butler, 1990). For example, Pride marches 'queer' space and uncover the norms that space holds. Some celebrate this as 'reclaiming space', a subversive social practice contesting the production of space as straight. But it is necessary to ask what kind of space is being claimed and for whom/what. Do such demonstrations really constitute a challenge, or can they co-exist within, and even be assimilated by capitalism, re-producing classed space? 'Queer visibility' does not really constitute a radical challenge when it co-exists quite happily within these structures (Chasin, 2000; Hennessy, 2000). This may be a slightly cynical view but if the concern is with exclusion, then it matters that material inequalities are forgotten when highlighting cultural visibility alone. Nevertheless, Lovell (2000) still feels that 'less serious' spaces, of carnival and masquerade, are worthy of attention because it is there that cultural constructions become visible as such and therefore open to challenge.

In comparing Bourdieu's (1984) account of the social construction of the human subject through space, with Butler's (1990) account of subjectivity as performance, Lovell (2000) detects both over-determinism and abstraction. Materialist feminisms criticise queer theory as overly concerned with the academic, the textual and the cultural – rather than with 'real' life, and the ensuing *material* reality. For more materialist approaches the 'cultural turn', from 'things' to 'words' represents a further turning away from more traditional sociological studies of sexuality, which aim to fully appreciate the material context in which we enact and live out our sexualities, as well as the everyday settings in which gender is enacted, even 'performed' (Eves, 2004; Goffman, 1969; Jackson, 1999). It is important to recognise the tension in negotiating spaces, rather that the subversion of the values which it holds. Such an approach differs from and yet resonates with Butler's (1990); not so much about creating subversive 'new' possibilities (simply demonstrating that gender is performative) but rather with undoing the unequal social relations, which may result in an undoing of the boundaries, binaries and inequalities through which gender exists. It appears more appropriate to adopt a material 'reality'-based reading of performance and, in expanding Bourdieu's (1984) classed framework, Skeggs (1999, 2001) may offer a more useful illumination of both classed and 'queer' identity (Taylor, 2005a).

Written on the body

Drawing upon her longitudinal ethnographic research (1997) and her research on violence, sexuality and space in Manchester and Lancaster, UK, Skeggs (1999, 2001) highlights the contrast and tensions existing in scene spaces between a group of white working-class heterosexual women, whose identity is based on 'dis-identification' (from being working-class), and a group of lesbians who form their identity through visibility, recognition and territorialisation. Both identification and dis-identification are spatialised, revealing how identities impact upon space and vice versa and enable entitlements to be asserted and achieved: appearance and the reading of it serves to de/authorise certain identities and claims on space. Skeggs argues that leisure spaces act as sites for the maintenance and reproduction of complex power relations, rather than acting as a stage for enacting new lifestyle options. Again, this questions the agenda of a celebratory queer visibility, highlighting the ways that class is 'written on the body' and cannot be easily subverted or discarded (Kuhn, 1995), working to produce misrecognitions, whereby the subject is fixed in exclusion, rather than pleasurable reclamations.

Skeggs (1999) uses two types of misrecognition: first, there is the way that bodies are read through appearance as having no value, which sets limits on embodied capitals and movements through space. This second usage is taken from Bourdieu's account of symbolic capital, which is acquired by a successful act of legitimation, but which then appears and is misrecognised as natural or as an individual character attribute: this misrecognises the historical and structural formation of capitals. Skeggs (1999) extends this second usage by looking at the ways that working-class women are positioned as immoral and tasteless, because of their concern with appearance. Their 'excessive' femininity is then read as the truth of their being, veiling the social processes and structures behind this judgement.

To be misrecognised therefore implies a potential fixing in space and a fixing judgement. In Skeggs' study (1999) the feminine appearing bodies of working-class women were judged on the basis of excess and devalued ('big hair, short skirts, lots of make-up'): they were not recognised, acknowledged or accepted as being entitled to occupy scene space. Skeggs (1997, 1999, 2001) claims that appearance, and particularly the classed reading of this, is the central mechanism through which spatial and entitlement struggles revolve, as the means by which classed 'others' are misrecognised.[15] Thus, misrecognition has an embodied physicality to it, where bodily appearance, taste and disposition can again provide clues about the placing of bodies (Bourdieu, 1984). Being recognised as something, as worthy, enables claims to be made politically and inter-personally. It is dependent upon symbolic systems of knowledge and evaluation, while to be misrecognised 'is not simply to be thought ill of, looked down on, or devalued ... it is rather to be denied the status of full partner in social interaction and prevented from participating as a peer in social life' (Fraser, quoted in Skeggs, 2001: 295).

Skeggs (1997) shows how working-class women invested in heterosexual femininity as a kind of physical, bodily capital, a creative solution to 'blocked chances'. The struggle for recognition occurs across spaces and identities but 'only some groups can positively and resourcefully spatialise their claim for recognition and visibility ... and only some groups can legitimately and/or symbolically convert their visible claims' (Skeggs, 1999: 228). The process of misrecognition captures this conflict.

Different spaces and different actors within space impact upon, respond to and affect the performance of identity. Holliday's (1999) participants were sensitive to the demands placed on them by dress codes at work but became less self-conscious when it came to their 'leisure wear'. Nevertheless, they also felt that scene spaces also regulated their embodied performance and physical appearances, generating exclusions. Fashion becomes identity and not fitting in carries a premium. This re-emphasises the issue of access to capital, which determines 'who can wear what and thus who can be what' (Holliday, 1999: 481). Despite these recognitions, Holliday condemns those who criticise the scene as divisive, a 'manoeuvre which individualizes sexual subjects and divides queer community' (1999: 483).

Yet divisions are already in place and sustained by those with the cultural and economic resources who can regulate the boundaries of inclusion into scene space. In terms of embodied appearances 'The importance of dress as a signifier of sexual identity, and of looking as a social, identifying and sexualized activity ... is crucial for a recognisable identity and structurally central to the theorisation of marginal identities' (Lewis and Rolley quoted in Holliday, 1999: 489). Bodies and appearances are subject to evaluation and to a 'disciplinary gaze', as meanings, behaviours and actions are constructed in interactions, in the presence of other actors.[16] Furthermore, sexual subjects are not just, if at all, located in 'queer communities'; not so much a divisive manoeuvre as a pervasive reality.

Everyday space, everyday experiences

Existing geographies of homosexuality have largely concentrated on the open expression of sexual identities in residential and commercial space (Thomas, 2004). However, the negativity associated with being lesbian or gay forces many people to conceal their sexual identity at different times and places (Brekhaus, 2003; Mason, 2002; Valentine, 1993a, 1993b).

Attention to visible gay communities is problematised by the reality that most lesbians live and work in the straight world, where they face discrimination. Choosing to pass at certain times and places, especially on the street, can involve doing another kind of performance as lesbians try to avoid hostility and discrimination by negotiating asexual or heterosexual identities (Namaste, 1996; Valentine, 1993a, 1993b). Corteen (2002), for example, examines perceptions of safety and danger amongst lesbians, noting the strategies, such as the deployment of 'safety maps' in venturing through spaces and avoiding homophobia: 'A safety map is an ever-changing personalized, yet shared, matrix of attributes and relations that individuals employ to make their way in public and private space' (Mason quoted in Corteen, 2002: 265).

Studies such as the above note how lesbians perceive and experience everyday spaces, arguing that lesbians often feel 'out of place' in many environments, such as the workplace, because of its institutionalised heterosexuality. But just as sexual identity is felt, it can be argued that class, and particularly being working-class, can produce feelings of being 'out of place', informing experiences and perceptions. Sexuality, gender and class have an impact on the understanding of everyday space, as well as the ability to access space (Moran, 2000; Moran et al., 2004).

Rarely are working-class people's feelings about their own, often stigmatised 'communities'[17] explored (although see Steedman, 1986; Reay and Lucey, 2000; Walkerdine et al., 2001 and Howarth, 2002). Space is not only heterosexualised, but workplaces, housing and activities within space are also classed with the 'norm' being middle-class. Deviance from the norm results in judgements and discrimination – and the demarcation of a spatialised underclass (Campbell, 1993; Furlong et al., 1996; Kefalas, 2003; Morris, 1994; Murray, 1994). While the working-class are stereotypically seen as inherently more sexist, racist and homophobic I will challenge this view, with attention to those studies which warn of reinforcing these assumptions (Kadi, 1997; Moran, 2000; Raffo, 1997; Skeggs, 1997).

It is often difficult to be entirely at home in your surroundings, with classed – and sexualised – exclusions occurring. Southerton (2002) is concerned with social class identification and examines the spatialised boundaries of identification, based on three groups who live in the same town in the South of England but who differ in their volumes of economic, cultural and social resources. Capitals become embodied in the construction of 'professional', 'respectable', 'real' identities and the boundaries of identification (boundaries between 'us' and 'them') regulate who can fit in these places. The least affluent group, living in the least desirable area, expressed narratives of 'economy', 'custom' and being 'down to earth'. They had a firm sense of the 'reality' of the space as opposed to the perceived 'pretence' enacted by those outsiders who were 'a bit stuck up'. The second group can be recognised as the 'respectable' middle-class; 'fitting-in' meant being 'respectable', while the most affluent group used narratives of socio-economic success, promoting the idea that 'we' are refined, as opposed to vulgar. The boundaries of 'us' and 'them' deployed are affirmed and re-affirmed through embodied inter-action with classed 'others' with the process of becoming included requiring 'boundary work' (Jenkins, 1996).

Southerton (2002) makes a case for the reinforcement of class bound-aries, comparing his findings with Lamont's (1991, 1992) work on the impact of social mobility on networks and identifications. Mobility requires economic capital, but if the cultural and embodied capitals of individuals do not 'fit' then they can still be subject to exclusion.[18] Given the continuation of class processes informing positions, possibil-ities and identifications in space, Southerton (2002) concludes that emphases on freedom from structural constraints and self-reflexivity in the identification process are somewhat premature (Beck, 2000a,b; Giddens, 1992). Moving in from the margins does not necessarily put you on the inside and good fences may not make good neighbours. The formation of boundaries relies upon and recreates both classed and sexual inequalities and identifications.

Home is where the heart is?

The home, particularly for those who fear the personal and employment consequences of being 'outed', can take on a vital role as a lesbian social venue, in particular areas (Gabb, 2005; Twigg, 2000). Valentine's (1995) research, based upon 40 in-depth interviews with residents of a provincial urban area in the United Kingdom, chal-lenges the assumption that lesbians do not concentrate spatially.[19] Lesbian spaces are apparently there if 'you know what you're looking for', suggesting that while lesbians may not have recognisable mate-rial spaces, they are not without location. It would seem that there are spatial concentrations of lesbians but 'the neighbourhood has a quasi-underground character; it is enfolded in broader counter-cultural milieu and does not have its own public sub-culture and territory' (Adler and Brenner quoted in Valentine, 1995: 96). But where are these 'quasi-underground' locations, who knows about them and who or what 'controls' them?

While Valentine claims that heterosexism influences which urban areas lesbians chose to live in, choices 'that reflect the fact that lesbians have different lifestyles and hence different housing needs from many heterosexual households' (Valentine, 1995: 98; Weeks et al., 2001) these need to be reconsidered in terms of the housing 'choices' of working-class lesbians. Working-class women may not be able to capitalise upon existing social capital networks within communities and may lack the ability to relocate (Putnam, 1993; Weeks et al, 2001). Street spaces and city spaces have received more attention, than the 'private' spaces of home (Glennie, 1998; Leslie and Reimer, 2003), while consideration has to be given to the ways that housing embodies a set of social relations (Bell, 1991), with intersecting classed, gendered and sexualised components. In addition, the home as 'safe space' does not always hold true: it is not always a place of emotional and physical well-being (John and Patrick, 1999).

Black sheep of the family

Transformations in intimate and personal life are widely signalled (Giddens, 1992; Heath and Cleaver, 2003; Roseneil, 2000), apparent in the introduction of Civil Partnerships across much of Western Europe, which formally recognise same-sex relationships. Nonetheless, the cost of achieving these *sexual* citizenship rights has been a simultaneous connection and dis-connection between class and sexuality as only some lesbians and gays can articulate their 'rights', only some can be effectively incorporated into the mainstream (Taylor, 2005b, 2005c).

Various studies of lesbian relationships have pointed to evidence of 'sameness' and 'equality' (Dunne, 1997) at times suggesting that this group most typically achieves the 'pure relationship' (Giddens, 1992), exemplifying 'new' forms of intimacy whereby intimacy is not sought through couple relationships alone but rather through their 'family of friends' (Weston, 1997). Weeks et al. (2001) explore narratives and experiences of 'alternative families', based upon in-depth interviews with 96 self-identified non-heterosexuals in the United Kingdom between 1995 and 1996, and also suggest that a transformation is underway signified by new 'families of choice' based on democratic, egalitarian personal relationships. They examine discourses of 'resistance' and 'self-invention' in contemporary stories of intimacy and look at the ways these sentiments and ideas generate well-being, both emotionally and practically. In this respect they deploy the notion of social capital but in a different way from that developed by Bourdieu (1984), using it to highlight strategies of networking and community building and the generation of 'reflexive', self-consciously created non-heterosexual communities. The ability to relocate to 'friendly' spaces and to create friendship networks, is however, affected by material processes as well as by subjective, 'inventive' desires. The overt optimism of their account at times glosses over potential exclusion, materially and interpersonally, in friendship and family groups. A 'family of friends' may not be all that friendly, when the embarrassing classed outsider comes to tea.

There are those who contend that intimate relationships still do not transcend structural inequalities and, as such, cannot be thought of as undergoing radical alterations (Jamieson, 1998). In reviewing academic research on personal relationships, across Europe, North-America, Australia and New Zealand, Jamieson's account suggests a rather more complex and conflicting tale of intimacy 'transformations', problema-tising identity 'stories' against material processes: the life that is told versus the life that is lived, where stories are never 'just stories' (1998: 11).

Johnson and Lawler (2005) explore how class becomes an obstacle to successful, heterosexual relationships and, in contrast with Giddens (1992) Beck (2000a,b) and Bauman (1990), suggest that it is crucial how people experience and enact intimacy. On the basis of research in the United Kingdom with 24 heterosexual men and women between 16 and 80 years, Johnson and Lawler (2005) uncovered the emotional and emotive, rather than purely material aspects of class, affecting how indi-viduals feel about one another. They explore how people construct and determine who are worthy compatibles, who know the 'right' things to do and say socially and conversationally, who can partake in 'proper' leisure practices, all the time being culturally tasteful as opposed to une-ducated, brash and overly sexual ('tarty'). When considering aspects of classed in/compatibilities Johnson and Lawler (2005) demonstrate that love really cannot conquer all; while working-class women could be the basis of desire and sexual attraction, they were most definitely not 'the type of women' to form lasting relationships with; after all, surely they were only their sexuality? The class schema for evaluating the 'right' sort of people who we feel 'at home' with is explicable through Bourdieu's 'habitus', generating forms of non/compatibility and dis/tastes. Our positioning in social space, and the intersecting dimensions of class and sexuality within this generate 'sympathies and antipathies, affections and aversions, tastes and distastes', impacting upon construc-tions of closeness versus distance, the material and emotive factors within intimacy (Bourdieu, 2000: 150).

Nevertheless, the experiences of working-class lesbians are absent from much theorising about personal relationships. Multiple inequalities and challenges within lesbian relationships are glossed over by privileging accounts of reciprocity and accountability; commonalities are said to be produced on the basis of sameness, that is shared gender, but there is little attention to the way in which differences of class can effect, enhance, disrupt and fracture relationships.

Emotional capital may well be more easily achieved in circumstances of privilege but this does not mean that working-class lesbians are without emotional worth (Illouz, 1997; Wilkinson, 1996) – rather the combined cultural, economic and emotional capitals within relationships are worthy of attention (Reay, 2004). While there has been attention to the gendered division of emotional work (Duncombe and Marsden, 1993) within heterosexual relationships, this often retains a middle-class bias, as highlighted by Wright (1996), and the emotional investments within working-class relationships are ignored. As well as looking at sexual relationships, I explore friendship and family relations. Depictions of working-class families seem to be caught between a binary of romanticisation/ pathologisation, with a strong tendency towards homogenisation and stereotype (Raffo, 1997; Rubin, 1976). The pathologisation of working-class families continues in notions of 'underclass', which Murray (1990, 1994) uses to refer to fatherless families and which is arguably sustained in much UK and US social policy and everyday discourses (Byrne, 2005; Carabine, 2004). Similarly, as Jamieson (1998) argues, extreme gender divisions, which continue across social classes, are still considered to be more typically working-class. I examine the experience of growing up working-class, in working-class families and communities, not to reinforce such stereotypes but rather to contest them and to realise the worth in examining working-class lives – lives lived not idealised.

What have I started?

So far I have reviewed the ways that class and sexuality are, and are not, discussed. I have noted the difficulty in defining class, given the various categorisations and classifications used. Yet my concern is not so much about what class is, or could be, but rather with the meanings and experiences of being 'working-class'; what class does. I argue for the continued validity of class identifications suggesting that the ability to be 'ambivalent', 'self-reflexive' and 'mobile' with regard to identity claims is a particular classed resource. Simply voicing an interest in class can be contentious, whereas my concern with sexuality is sometimes seen as the 'interesting' and redeemable part of my research (Taylor, 2005a). There is often less controversy aroused, although exploring sexuality is not an easy thing to do either. For example, even those who examine the intersections between race, class and gender have omitted sexuality (Anthias, 1998, 2001).[20] The 'working-class' 'lesbian' occupies the ignored space in between these terms.

I have indicated persistent classed, gendered and sexualised processes across various social spheres. Attention to these has been disappearing, not considered relevant to lesbian lives, or not fully grasped by theoretical focuses on the structures of capitalism and the 'political economy of sex', where actual people rarely appear. I have argued for the inseparability of class and sexuality, as a corrective to analyses that examine one or the other, and I aim to follow this linkage through in the following chapters, not to suggest a causal relationship but rather to highlight the relevance to those who occupy and negotiate both categories. In so doing, I combine different theoretical frameworks and draw upon empirical studies in order to convey the multifaceted aspects of class and sexuality intersections.

Double jeopardy: theorising class and sexuality

This book explores the economic, cultural, interpersonal and embodied aspects of class positioning and dis-identifications, taking class and sexuality 'beyond' the economic alone. While materialist approaches analyse the structural conditions of capitalisms, and the operation of sexuality within such systems, classed individuals are absent from many accounts: I do not individualise class processes but rather seek to examine how class is negotiated in everyday life. In deploying and departing from Bourdieu's (1984) theoretical model of classed habitus and classed capitals, I analyse the multifaceted nature of class as an entrenched disposition, embodied in cultures, lifestyles, tastes and appearances. Class is more than economics, more than the materialism still discussed at the structural level ('capitalism'). Class attaches itself to classed individuals and in so doing class becomes apparent in everyday interactions. In retaining and explaining the relevance of classed 'capitals' and classed 'habitus' throughout this book, I aim to highlight both objective and subjective class positionings: access to capitals affects and structures movements through space and affects access into acceptable, respectable or 'spoilt' and devalued identities (Skeggs, 1997; Reay, 1996; Bettie, 2003). I examine class as produced through social, cultural and economic practices, negotiating the dichotomy between 'old' un-gendered economist analyses of class and 'new' culturalist class analyses which, at times, polarises rather than intersects the cultural, social and economic.

I also seek to extend such a model by considering the significance of gender and sexuality – as well as class – to identifications, movements and resistances. In doing so, I seek to theoretically establish the inter-section of class and sexuality, empirically highlighted by working-class lesbians' life experiences: sexuality is also a structuring force, as well as an identifier and point of identification, an emotive issue fostering material, embodied and cultural inclusions/exclusions. Here the concept of 'habitus' and 'capitals', applied to class, becomes useful in thinking through access to sub-cultural spaces (ie: scene spaces) – whether this access is legitimised and what the classed and sexualised aspects of this are, as structuring, interpersonal and embodied processes and forces. Integrating, and thus furthering, Bourdieu's model with existing theories of sexuality will reach beyond the impasse created by dichotomised materialist/queer theorisation of sexuality.

Skeggs (1997) and Bettie (2003) illustrate the gendered and sexualised components of classed capitals. However, working-class lesbians were further removed from the category of 'respectable femininity' on two counts – their class and their sexuality counted against them. Nevertheless, there were powerful resistance and pleasures within this and, as such, I offer a challenge to the theorisation of class identity solely around notions of 'escape', 'avoidance' and dis-identification (Bettie, 2003; Lawler, 2000; Reay, 1998; Skeggs, 1997). In pointing to the empty spaces between materialist, queer and 'transformations of intimacy' accounts of sexuality, my intersectional study makes theoretical developments, based upon empirical findings, furthering the dual consideration and intersection of class and sexuality as a material, cultural, subjective and embodied one.

Struggling to get out of the starting blocks: the beginning

As someone who defines as a working-class lesbian, I wanted to know more about other women's experiences – to try and answer the question of what it means to be both, by asking people who are. My motivations are personal, political and sociological; academically, I could position my research as fulfilling a 'gap', yet I would not want to position myself, my research and my participants in this space alone (Taylor, 2005a; 2005e). Elsewhere I have demonstrated the empirical interconnections between sexuality and class, while drawing upon my own subjectivity, identifications and experiences in order to provide a personal and aca-demic 'prodding of the gap' between sexuality and class, locating myself by discipline, experience and identification and by prevailing academic trends and dis/contents. When I started my research I wanted to explore how class and sexuality affects all aspects of life, from education to club-bing, from relationships to shopping, and all the bits in between. I was, perhaps, becoming some kind of sexuality trainspotter – but this awak-ened concern in me did not, of itself, create the group which I was to study. Questions were constructed to investigate how sexuality and class permeated women's lives; interviewees were asked to discuss their own experiences in the context of growing up, schooling, job opportunities, family and community. I collected past information about childhood, family structure, attitudes to school, school type, education history and family attitude to education. I also asked about the economic and material circumstances of their childhoods, including locality, school leaving employment expectations, parents' education and employment and their own assessment of their social class background. In addition I gathered current indicators of employment status, neighbourhood, housing and income level. I asked about experiences of 'coming-out', about relationships and participation in scene spaces.

More thorough methodological accounts have been produced else-where (Taylor, 2004a, 2005a, 2005e) allowing this section to be rather brief. Fifty-three women who identified themselves as working-class and lesbian, from Scotland (the Highlands, Glasgow and Edinburgh) and England (Yorkshire and Manchester) took part in my research, through a combination of one-to-one interviews, paired and group interviews. Interviews were conducted between 2001 and 2002, across the different localities. The average age of respondents, ranging from 16 to 64 years, was 34 years while the largest group of interviewees were between 20 and 25 years (14 women) and such diversity allowed the continuation of classed experience and class identification across life courses to be revealed (see Appendix for a 'thumbnail' sketch of each interviewee). To agree with Youdell (2005) the data that I present here has been generated, co-produced and interpreted, rather than simply collected, which is not to blur or diffuse what is said but rather to acknowledge constructed, competing – and enduring – 'voices'.

Savage et al. (2001) view the strategy of asking questions on class at the end of the interview as advantageous, highlighting that some research may be criticised for using loaded questions, which then prompt them to reply in 'classed ways'. However, this again illustrates the particularly contentious nature of researching class; there is often an assumption that the researcher has an (unjustified) pre-set agenda, whereby beliefs are rigid, inflexible and imposed. Through prior reading of advertisements and/or articles, in lesbian and gay publications and spaces, all women who took part in my study knew that the central focus of my project was to detail the life experiences of working-class lesbians (Taylor, 2004a, 2005e). Having introduced class upfront was neither negative nor predetermining of the agenda and outcome. I do feel that working-class women's accounts of what class is, means and does are vitally important as it is not just the prerogative of academics to decide what the 'proper' meaning of class is – or to decide upon whether it exists or not. The term 'working-class' is prevalent throughout the women's accounts and I do not believe that it would have been used so extensively to describe their own experiences had it been imposed.

I transcribed all taped interviews myself, mostly soon after the actual interview took place, making notes on where we had met and how I felt it went. To simply state this seems to hide the difficulties in transcription, not just that it is an extremely time-consuming and difficult task, but also the issue of translating spoken words into a written form, with pauses, full stops, commas and exclamation marks, so as to render them understandable. In making interviewees' phrases 'understandable' and 'tidy' I felt that I was, at times, performing a kind of classed translation. And while I could generally pick up on Scottish colloquialisms (I use these myself but learned to straighten them out on the written page) some phrases used by respondents from Yorkshire and Manchester took more figuring out. I was 'insider' and 'outsider', a mediator communicating working-class voices to a middle-class audience and I was unsure what I should do with these colloquialisms and idioms: omit them? Translate them by submitting a 'proper' version? Use them as evidence of working-class authenticity?

Often the researcher and the researched will be using different languages and speaking styles that represent cultural, ethnic and social backgrounds and working-class women may lack the kind of 'authorial exhibitionism' (Skeggs, 2002), which comes with having legitimate 'linguistic capital' (Bourdieu et al., 1999). Accordingly, 'it is important to engage with the "politics of talk" and to recognise that what counts as language, who uses it ... what it can mean and do, are not merely part of a neutral and given reality, but are products of power relations and struggles' (Mason, 2002: 237). I have tried not to translate working-class women's words but I have perhaps reduced a diversity of accents to my way of speaking and writing. I have necessarily and at times uneasily used an academic framework to interpret and understand the experiences of working-class lesbians. Such a framework is now part of my 'cultural capital' but I do not aim to reinforce distinction between what 'they' said, knew and experienced and what I, as researcher, should say and write. This is the constant struggle in investing and dis-investing in varied discourses of knowing.

The issue of transcription is not separate from data analysis, it guides what is going on, what can be voiced and what can be heard. Having transcribed all interviews I read and re-read them, noting commonalities, themes and differences – dramatic, powerful, sad, funny and painful stories stuck in my mind and forced attention towards them. The analysis has never been, in my mind, separate from the individual interviewees who spoke the words, provided the data; as I poured over their accounts I could still remember the way it was said, the tone, irony and humour often present. Often I would laugh aloud when re-reading transcripts, often I would be saddened and upset, always deeply affected by what was told.

I started analysing the data by making it 'tell stories'. I coded the data into themes and stuck these on the wall, often taking up the entire wall space of my office (and that of my room mate who was often horrified on entering the office to be greeted with 30 pages of A4 sheets blue-tacked on the wall, variously highlighted, post-it noted and moved around). By literally looking at the data I could see the themes emerging and I then turned to my computer to 'cut and paste'. However, it was with care that I did such separation, linkage and deletion always looking back up at my colourful wall display. Divisions, cuts and pastes were not undertaken in a haphazard jig-saw manner but carefully considered; I started with my data and linked respondents quotes together to tell a (varied) story, a story which I would return to, moving back and forth between my data and my analysis, building this picture up rather than selecting quotes to embellish a pre-existing account. Each stage of re-drafting, of which there were many, involved more consideration of what was to be included and excluded.

The approach which best describes my technique of data analysis is 'grounded theory', the goal of which is to facilitate a rigorous definition of categories through the process of analysis, enabled by the strategy of coding data as themes emerge. Grounded theory is a good, inductive, starting point for theory construction, differing from more deductive approaches where guiding theories are utilised at the beginning to pro-vide the categories of analysis. Yet this is rather a false opposition as the process of data collection, asking questions and finding answers, analysing and theorising were all interwoven: theories were tentatively formed from the data, tested and revised against the data, but this process also relied on the in/adequacies of pre-existing literature and theorising on class and sexuality.

It should be noted though that the existing theory, while still drawn upon, could not satisfactorily explain the data collected. Hence, as Skeggs suggests, I have drawn on 'different theories, using them when appropriate, ditching them when not, reworking them to construct explanatory frameworks' (1994: 82). Analysis has emerged from the data and although I could have arranged the data differently, coding it thematically enabled me to keep in touch with topics as they emerged and became self-evident. The women in my study provided rich data and I have strived to let their voices speak, while also providing enough context so that they can be properly heard, a necessary relationship between theory and data analysis. The second chapter seeks to do just that, acting to set up issues which are developed in subsequent chapters.

2
Class and How to Get It

Class is not something that was but rather something that very much is. This chapter charts the meanings of class and establishes its relevance to the lives of the women I interviewed, challenging the idea that class no longer has salience. If someone has proven this to be the case, they seem to have neglected to inform most of these women. They are living in a world that is more classed than some of the above theories would allow for. Who do we believe? The writer or the written? Given the absence of the opinions, views and experiences of working-class lesbians in academic literatures and debates, I will foreground interviewees' everyday sentiments, biographies and stories; their articulated sense of the intersections between class and sexuality which are revealed as both profoundly personal and sociological.

Notions of 'fluidity' and 'mobility' (Urry, 1995, 2000a) do not explain continued social inequality and are of little use to those experiencing what they see as day-to-day reality. Even as class was traditionally defined by sociologists, questions of experience and exploitation were often erased. The employment aggregate approach, for example, says little about how class is played out in everyday life. The crucial question becomes how many classes there are, rather than what class does, de-politicising the analysis, as Reay (1997) warns. With class definitions becoming more 'complex', 'diverse' and 'fragmentary' (Pakulski and Waters, 1996), as class boundaries are 'opened up, made more fluid' (Walkerdine et al., 2001: 38) and as class membership becomes more uncertain, self-definition can be, as Walkerdine suggests, a painful process. But even if class influence is hard to tease out, this does not justify the abandonment of the working-class. What it means to be working-class may be different in every case, but not so different that recognitions or connections cannot be made (Mahony and Zmroczek 1997).

38

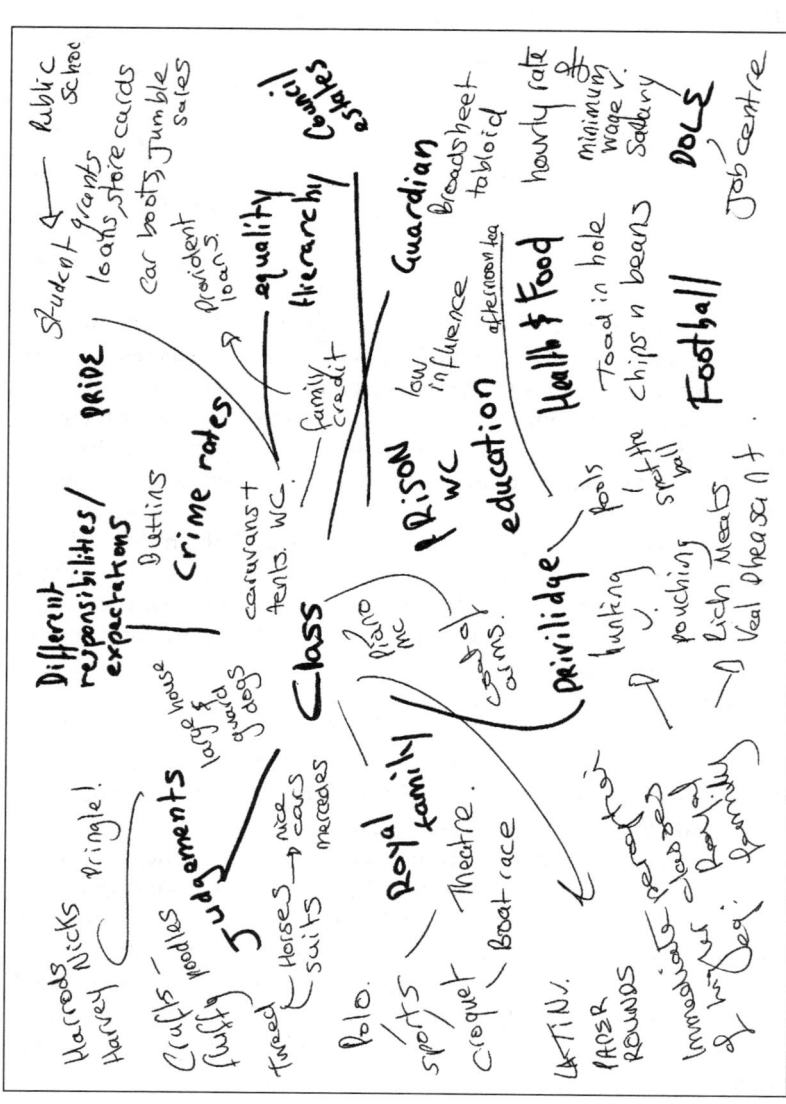

Figure 2.1 Young Person's Group.

Class is not only still with us; it affects lifestyles, communities, emotions, experiences and needs: it entails much more than, but includes, economic circumstances (see Figure 2.1). It is not just something you are but something you do, something that constitutes, contains and comforts.

This chapter looks at the multiple meanings of class and the ways in which interviewees 'got it', that is, came to know themselves as working-class and the experiences, attitudes and feelings which such identification entailed. Their recognition of inequality dispels ideas about the irrelevance of class to identity formation and economic marginality. Their embedded working-class experiences are related to their own and their parents' employment (or unemployment), the patterns of identifications produced as well as the emotional, physical and embodied markers of class, which all point towards the impossibility of being classless.

Rarely, if ever, do working-class people's views about what constitutes middle-classness get heard; here this silence is confronted, especially evident where respondents challenge middle-class 'superiority'. Nevertheless, many women in my sample occupied much more vulnerable positions than a neutral middle-class position would enable; these vulnerabilities can be seen at times when some women seek to prove their 'decency'. At the same time a middle-class position was often avoided and for those few women who had moved somewhat, in terms of career progression, this was at odds with their entrenched working-class experiences – their 'pasts' were not erased by their 'presents'. I focus primarily on the meanings of class, given the political and academic controversy and contention surrounding this term, while making connections and intersections with sexuality throughout and again in the final section 'Out-classed?', signposting the issues to be raised in proceeding chapters. It will be seen that interviewees have powerful understandings of the existence, process and effect of class and sexuality – understandably so since they are lived experiences.

Heinz 57 – the variety of class

Women's accounts and ideas challenged the simple equation of class with one singular (disappearing) phenomenon. When discussing class, most women detailed their material realities, describing their own adverse economic situations and those experienced while growing up; the influence of 'past' (financial) experience affected current positions. As such, the women in my sample cannot be viewed as occupying 'uncertain' or 'mobile' class positions (Urry, 2000a, 2000b). They know where they are coming from, they get what is going on. Variety is not uncertainty and to some extent certainty would be naivety; as Jane says, 'I mean working-classness, I wouldn't say is just one thing. I would say that it's a mish mash and a variety of all of your different identities mixed into one.'

The multiple and all-encompassing characteristics of class connects its economic, cultural and emotional facets (Skeggs, 1997). Although Grace states that 'I couldn't define why I would class myself as working-class,' she then recounts a series of constraints, expectations and experiences across social sites, which she directly relates to class:

> I suppose it's more about a state of mind rather than anything else. I couldn't define why I would class myself as working-class other than I was brought up in a council house scheme. I didn't necessarily know what working-class was but I knew that's how people saw us, do you know what I mean? But I couldn't pin my finger on why that would be or what that was about other than sort of living in a certain part of a town or – and maybe at school as well, kind of knowing that the teachers wirnae pushing us as much as maybe they pushed other kids on the private estates and stuff. And maybe not really thinking about that as much when I was at school but after I left school, thinking, what was that about? (Grace)

Grace's statement swiftly and succinctly summarises a great deal of sociological thought on class and its enduring importance in terms of identity and resources, from the classroom to locality. Grace's consideration, it would seem, does not produce the sum of what class 'is' as an essential, fixed thing. On one occasion financial circumstance and the structuring importance of this will be paramount, while at other times the emotional 'reminders' (both positive and negative) of classed associations, whether through 'past' family life or/and through interactions with classed others, will take precedence. Doing class would seem to change from day to day, from incident to incident and constitutes a various process as opposed to a fixed set of criteria. 'Realisation' and expression of class processes and experiences was no simple matter, particularly given the prevalence of discourses on 'classlessness'. Their accounts can therefore be seen as strong, multiple and varied challenges to this erasure; 'how can class not exist if we say it does?'

As well as illustrating the importance and effect of class across different locations such as school and workplace, many women simultaneously asserted the 'obviousness' of their own class position, while reflecting on past experiences with renewed realisation. There was often a struggle to articulate current meanings because of the 'obvious' nature of their class; how do you make somebody get what you have always just got? The 'subconscious' level of class identification, as Amy put it, sometimes makes it hard to assert the meaning of class in concrete terms:

> I never really thought of anything other than working-class, it's what I've always been, it's what my parents are. I never think of any other classes, it's just 'I'm working-class because I am' ... I don't think there's a need for it to be there but to me you *are* put into a bracket and that's where you are. (Amy)

The dry and abstract classification tables miss out any sense of what class means for working-class people and overlook the tensions, uncertainties, as well as pleasures, within this: class is not just a set of statistics, a series of boxes to tick, it lives and breathes. The 'obviousness' and multiplicity, as expressed above by Grace and Amy, as well as the emotional ways that class is 'just' felt, all make class processes difficult to claim and explain.

But to reflect on class involves dealing with all these aspects and these may not be easily expressed, even if they are felt. Here Lisa and Kelly are reflecting on the meaning class has for them and their awareness of this. Lisa becomes frustrated because of the insistence that she articulate her experiences through the 'language of class'. She knows about the relevance of class in her life but is made vulnerable through her 'admission' that this sometimes operates 'subconsciously', without being immediately recognisable or easily expressed. When Kelly attempts to impose an understanding, which includes the inability to express the language of class, to use the codes, Lisa becomes defensive. It is her class, her language and her self that has never needed to articulate:

> L: Yeah, oh yeah. I never thought of that, but yeah, subconsciously I was conscious of it, if you know what I mean.
> K: I think the thing is you've not had the language to put onto experiences.
> L: I have I've just never considered it that much.
> K: You're aware of it. It's obvious that you're aware of it and you think about it, you've just not articulated it.
> L: I've just never thought to articulate it.
> K: Or had the names to put to it.
> L: I have had the language for it.
> K: No, I'm not saying you don't have a language, Lisa. (Lisa and Kelly)

What is interesting is that it is not the lack of 'a language', which Kelly thinks has prevented Lisa's articulation of class but rather '*the* language', implying a specific linguistic code for the expression of class. We all have *a* language, but how many have or indeed need *the* language? Class can be difficult to convey precisely because it is something that is felt rather than theorised, which exists not only at the structural level but also at the personal and emotional level, as told by Jane, 'It's, well, for me it's about, it's felt a lot of it so it's gonna be quite difficult to articulate a lot of things. I think a lot of it's about emotions and it's stuff that's felt.' Kelly also speaks of the pain involved in witnessing her mother's struggle, something that, she argues, does not get acknowledged:

> You [Lisa] touched upon it earlier, you know, when I first got my packed lunch box, it seems a little thing but it's actually quite painful. And you spoke about your mum putting extra money in her pocket, you know, and you worrying about your mum and her feelings and wanting to tell your mum 'I understand that you're doing everything you can for me, I'm not going to put more pressure on you.' ... For me also my mum working nights at that factory she was always tired, just growing up like that, trying to live from day-day. That's what I'm talking about and that doesn't very often get acknowledged. (Kelly)

The validity of such pain is not often appreciated, it is often easier to characterise the individual as flawed, over-sensitive or aggressive. Sonia takes the blame for her anger when she states 'You know, it's not a chip on a shoulder, sometimes it's a fifty pound bag of spuds, you know. But you just have to accept it about yourself.' There is a simultaneous process of challenge and conformity, of blaming the self. The problem lies with the one who has got it, after all they are the ones 'mouthing off'.

Another form of dismissal is to try and 'shame' people, asking 'what do you *do*?' to try and find out what you *are*. The Manchester group discusses the frequency and implication of such a question, challenging and rejecting the class basis for this:

> I get embarrassed by people who try to put you in a different light and it embarrasses me 'cause they're acting like somebody and they're putting it on for other people and I find it really very embarrassing. I don't find it upsetting for me, I find it embarrassing for them. (Doris)

Doris reverses the expected embarrassment, reclaiming positive value for herself despite the expectation that she should be ashamed.

Processes of dis/identifying are subject to their own negotiations and recognitions, 'accomplished' through work and effort. Sometimes you have to work to get it, in all senses of the words.

Identifications also occur through recognition of what they are not (middle-class and straight) which highlights the comparative aspects of identification and identity. Our identifications also require validations from others (Jenkins, 1996); it is not enough to assert an identity if nobody else notices, if nobody else confirms this, either by similarity or difference. Some women mentioned the differences and inequalities between classes or between themselves in the case of paired interviews and focus groups, comparing, contrasting and in/validating:

> You were brought up in a different type of working-class than me, completely different. The environment that I was brought up in, completely different. You were brought up in a nice house, your parents didn't have much money but more than mine. (Lisa)

Lisa and Kelly negotiate their shared and different experience of working-class existence, which again is indicative of the variety that the term and the social experience embodies and signifies. However, as Lisa's redress expresses there is something more gripping about class which cannot be explained through 'variety' and 'difference' – and Lisa's words as well as emphatic (and perhaps accusatory) tones demonstrate this; the injustice felt through living out classed inequalities. There is a process of comparing and contrasting, even with someone who Lisa 'knows' and describes as working-class. Although this could be dismissed as friendly banter, the competitive edge is hard to miss. The aim of the exchange is not to elevate their respective backgrounds and positions, to claim a middle-class privilege, but to establish 'who had it worse', who has got it and who would only like to have it. Mis/understandings, denials and conflicts also occurred within the focus groups, which included middle-class as well as working-class lesbians. Here the tensions were greater as women sought to 'out' the other in class terms, and reveal their (middle-class) 'privilege'.

K: Well I think we're all in the same position, whether you're middle-class or working-class or upper-class or lower-class.
D: Yeah, but you're middle-class.
K: I never said I was middle-class, I said I came from a middle-class area.
C: It's a bit harder in the rural areas.

K: It is. The only reason I say middle-class is that my mum and dad have got money.

D: So that would make you middle-class.

K: No but I don't classify myself as middle-class 'cause I don't have money, I've been on the social, I work in a factory and I'm not a snob. So as far as I'm concerned I don't have a class, I'm just me ... But the area I come from is a middle-class area. (Kay, Doris and Cathy)

Kay responds to the 'accusation' of being middle-class by asserting her present lack of economic capital, as well as outlining her own attitudes – a middle-class position is rejected when she states she is not a 'snob'. Although her parents may have been 'one of those', she is nothing except herself, middle-class by heritage but working-class by association, working at getting it although aware that she cannot fully claim it. These tensions and dis/identifications were managed within the groups and were, to some extent, resolved based on shared experience in terms of sexuality, even if class commonalities were rejected. None of us are only our class or sexual identities – these are experienced across different sites, as noted above in the difference between urban and rural experience, which have an effect on situating identity in terms of location and history as well as multiple other factors.

The women in my sample were, perhaps unsurprisingly, very class aware. In fact it is both remarkable and unremarkable that working-class people are able to speak about the meanings of working-classness. Class to them was clearly not an irrelevance or an out-dated concept; it was active in their lives and identities.

We all stand together?

The persistence of working-class attitudes strongly contests the supposed irrelevance of class in terms of self-identity and beliefs (for example, Urry, 2000a, 2000b; Pakulski and Waters, 1996). For many of the women in my sample, a working-class attitude is connected to the objective experience of being working-class, living with and managing poverty, unemployment, ill health and poor housing conditions, engendering empathetic as well as politicised understandings. Their identifications with positive 'working-class' attitudes are compared and contrasted with the believed 'taken-for-grantedness' of the middle-class. There was often a rejection, refusal and dis-identification with what were felt to be 'middle-class' values, and opposition to the 'polite air' of middle-class people who were repeatedly ridiculed for their 'airs and graces'. While most made qualifiers about their statements, as Sonia does in this following account, there was less of this when discussing material privileges and the corresponding un/reality of different classed positions: 'I'm not saying, you know, it's a wonderfully working-class background but I think it's more upfront when you know where you stand. I absolutely do. We're working-class people ... Again, that's stereotyping but that's my experience'.

Stereotypes are widely circulated and utilised by all classed individuals, it is what we do to make sure that we know who the other is, to construct a known truth, be it true or not. Yet there is a felt difference and inequality responsible for generating these 'stereotypes' of middle-class individuals, generated though encounters with classed 'others'. Working-class lesbians still have to deal with the legitimised, typically negative, characteristics associated with working-classness: a stereotype worn proudly at home can easily be turned inside out within society. Interviewees constantly negotiated, revised and even perpetuated these beliefs. In a classed society, no-one can speak of class without reference to these terms when dis/identifying themselves. Yet while many women ridiculed the 'pretentiousness' of the middle-class very effectively, they often lacked wider social legitimisation for this belief; in contrast, middle-class stereotypes of working-class people are generally received as the 'truth'. Many of the women I interviewed negotiated this 'truth' (Skeggs, 2004), highlighting its currency in their own statements as they managed and spoke of their own beliefs, attitudes and identities. According to Mandy, 'I think in a lot of working-class areas people, despite obviously some problems, people are a lot friendlier because they help each other out and stuff and its not so much backstabbing I don't think.'

Despite, or because of, some 'obvious problems' class was described in terms of political attitudes or beliefs. Associations were made with parental involvement in, for example, trade union activity and the miners' strikes[1] which highlights the continued effect of these, thought to be resolved and indeed 'old fashioned', disputes. The past, it would seem, is not put to bed but is still banging about on the backstairs. This necessitates a re-evaluation of the concept of 'classlessness' present in political and academic debates, which often point to the demise of these sectors and activities. Although the political voices may not be quite as loud today, they are still there along with the persistent echoes of past generations. For example, many women spoke with conviction about the value of 'solidarity' and 'commitment', as well as a support for the (working-class) 'underdog', as Grace exemplifies:

> I suppose me and my family and my friends and people that I know ... have sort of quite strong social beliefs, I suppose, in terms of

looking for equality for people and wanting everybody to succeed or have fair – well, equality of opportunity in terms of having access to stuff and the same chances, I suppose. And, eh, I suppose a sense of kind of a support network as well 'cause at the time I was growing up, I was about 11 during the miners' strike, so that whole kind of thing going on round about the dispute and sort of everybody pitching in and helping out, you know, although it wisnae their fight. Or well, it was but, do you know what I mean, not directly affected but the way it affected all the families and all our friends and things at that time. (Grace)

As the women's accounts make clear, class is a major aspect of their political associations and investments. This challenges the pervasiveness of 'new' forms of cultural pluralism and cultural fragmentation, which are seen to mark the end of any direct association between class, culture and politics (Beck, 1992; Lash and Urry, 1994). Pakulski and Waters (1996) typify this position when claiming that class divisions and class struggles are replaced by fluid and continuous status inequalities: 'struggles around such diverse forces as postcolonial racism, sexual preferences, gender discrimination, environmental degradation, citizen participation, religious commitments and ethnic self-determination. These have little or nothing to do with class'. (1996: 26). Tell that to the women I interviewed, as nobody seems to have informed them so far. Interviewees' political attitudes and indeed activism were instead constituted through the uneasy, yet profound, intersection between class and sexuality, which they could not separate out, in the clumsy manner which occurs above (Taylor, 2005c). Jeannette speaks of the importance of standing alongside your own side, returning to the overwhelming emphasis on political empathies:

I suppose it's about value and hard work, honesty, commitment, standing up against exploitation, solidarity with other people from the same, who are experiencing the same forms of oppression as you. So you know, whether that be class, economic based or whether it be to do with gender or whether it be about sexuality. (Jeannette)

The emphasis on empathetic understandings as a basis for political investments, as demonstrated by Grace and Jeannette, perhaps allows only certain associations and political identifications to be made. But working-class women rarely gain recognition for their struggles, constructed instead as exhibiting the 'wrong kind of resistance' (Lawler, 2002; Taylor, 2005c). As a result, Lawler suggests that the only voices that will be heard and recognised are the ones with cultural, symbolic and material privilege. Those who shout loudest are often known as the rabble, those who shout slightly but with clever words are often seen as right.

Working-class work horse

As well as investing in political beliefs and values, many women also had investments in belonging to certain families, communities, workplaces and areas, through personal and parental association. The sense of belonging was not easily achieved, rather tensions were again apparent, affecting and producing dis/identifications, relevant in terms of class and sexuality: disassociations as well as associations were made. All the workers are by no means equal and those that do not work are definitely not. In relating and critiquing their working-class lives, working-class lesbians run the risk of contributing to the general societal denigration of the working-class. Discussion is difficult if you speak in fear of bad mouthing yourself.

Parental employment is relevant and consequential to the women's own (employment) positions and experiences, recurrently accorded significance not just as a material marker but also because of the historical, cultural and emotional associations – as 'part and parcel' of a working-class position. A wage slip can say much more than just how much you were paid that week, as Faye and Michelle demonstrate:

> Not just income based, but I think without that history I wouldn't have the low income anyway – the income is part and parcel of it, if you don't have the income it's because you've come from somewhere else. (Faye)
>
> My dad was a road sweeper, my mum was a lollipop lady, we lived in a shitty area in Fife, you know, Fife, what can I say? You couldn't get more working-class, real working-class stuff. (Michelle)

The emotion aroused when describing parental employment reveals that these occupations are more than classifications. It matters what you do, what your parents did, for good or bad they say something.

The financial aspects of being in poverty are emphasised alongside the subjective experience of knowing that what you were/are is not valued. Hard work is infinitely harder if it is seen as worthless or less worthy, but jobs were also accorded value on the basis of their 'common' and 'normal' characteristics. May recognises that she is classed through her job (production work). She identifies as working-class and talks about the meanings this has for her in the course of the interview. In the following account May indicates an awareness of being judged while diffusing its significance as a class encounter:

> I'm not often asked what class I am anyway 'cause I think it's, people just assume that I'm working-class, which is what I would call myself if someone asked. I think it's more to do with, for me it's purely status I think. It's to do with how much money you earn, what your background was ... So it's purely status, it doesn't mean anything to me. (May)

Despite the above pronouncement, some women still sought to prove their 'worth' and 'value', and invested in the concept of a (working-class) 'work-ethic', even when experiencing unemployment. This may be viewed as an avoidance of stigma, a rejection of the 'laziness' generally associated with the unemployed. Although emphases on individual responsibility detract from class processes, I would suggest that poverty and unemployment are still experienced at the level of the individual – and women often reflected on the unfairness of the situation, more so when considering their own 'hard work'. If you are constantly getting knocked, it hurts and that is quite individualising. Occupation is often seen as an indicator of innate talent or as evidence that an individual has worked really hard and is 'deserving' (the opposite is then said of the unemployed). This notion appears in the following conversation between Vanessa and Lauren and is felt rather than expressed in concrete terms:

> V: I think I was brought up ... that you strive to be the best of your sector and you study, you try to be the best at that kind of thing, em, make your way to the top. People strive to be as comfortable as they can be.
> L: That's about class.
> Y: How come?
> L: I don't know. (Lauren and Vanessa)

It is obvious and unknown.

The impact of poverty upon many women in my study was extensive, affecting lifestyles, opportunities, health, housing and many other things. Many struggled with basic needs, but their desires and 'wants' also need consideration, given the relevance this has for feeling 'normal'. For example, Kirsty speaks of the difficulties of being a single-parent and living on benefits. It is worth noting the items (food, transportation, clothes) that she lists as essentials, given that single-parents (especially mothers) are often portrayed as 'scroungers' and beneficiaries of a lenient system. The price of an adult return to town on the bus is hard to see as a frivolity. Her lack of these 'normal' things lead her to distinguish between the 'working-class' and the 'lower than working-class', which she then positions herself as,

> I mean it doesn't make you feel completely better having a bit more money. You don't suddenly, your mental health doesn't suddenly improve overnight but it does feel good if you're feeling bad to be able to go shopping and spend 50 quid on clothes, you know (laughs) that's nice ... And to be able to, you know, go to another shop and get nice ribbons for your child's hair so when she goes to school, she looks like the smartest child in the school. That's important. I like that. These things are important. (Kirsty)

Who can afford to reject such things? (such as children's ribbons), and for whom does the inability to buy such things constitute failure and shame? (Bowring, 2000). Kirsty, like many of the women, makes clear the continued classed links between un/employment, needs, wants and shame. These everyday 'differences' were consequential. It is not much fun looking in the mirror and being reminded that you are one of those who can't, even if you wanted to (and you probably do).

Have you got any ID?

'Identity' has become a key term of debate, with proclamations of the emergence of 'new' identities and the 'transformation' of existing ones (Jenkins, 1996). In terms of class, many writers see the 'ambivalence' of class identities as key to renewed class analysis. However, there are continued class identifications and 'ambivalence' does not capture the ways different class groups 'identify' or 'dis-identify' (Bradley and Hebson, 1999; Savage et al., 2001). Identifications operate in everyday interactions with others, who may affirm or challenge class identity: what if nobody agrees with you, or even gives you the time of day? Talk is cheap; the stamp of approval can be more costly.

Many women stated that class was an important and on-going part of their identity, something that they were aware of on a daily basis, rather than something they were 'ambivalent' about. As Jude shows, her identification is particularly important when coming into contact with members of different classes:

> My class is part of my identity still, yeah, because it's not something which you define in terms of your background. It's something that

you live with everyday and something that you are *reminded* of every-day, particularly when you come into ... em, contact with people who are middle-class or upper-class. (Jude)

Others sometimes spoke of their class position as neither a good nor bad part of their identity – rather it 'obviously' 'just is'. However, this claim seems to put forward a certain neutrality, missing from their other accounts. Working-class lesbians were aware of the negative associations and stigma attached to being working-class but the importance accorded to this varied. Here, Amy suggests that her class identity does not cause her any 'problems' (although her class position does: later Amy speaks of having no money, of being unable to move from her council house and of the issues that occur in her relationship, which she herself ascribes to class):

> I don't think it's wonderful or bad to be, any sort of class you're in. I mean I don't go about going 'Oi, I'm working-class' but I don't feel bad about it either, it's just a part of me, I suppose it's a part of my identity but it's not something I linger on or think about. Obviously it disnae cause me any hassles. (Amy)

Depending on the situation, different parts of our identities may come to the forefront – but with class this can sometimes be suppressed as an attempt to 'fit in'; constantly kicking at the boundaries becomes painful and no-one is immune to the stereotypes surrounding class. Lisa apparently suspends her identification as working-class when she states 'I hate the fact that people just sit, especially working-class people, glued to the TV.' When and where can (positive) identifications be made?

May speaks of 'labels', highlighting the difference between self-ascribed labels and those 'offered' by others. Many women were also labelled in terms of their embodied appearances and accents, the visual and heard signifiers of class, which they could be placed by – and place others by. These embodied signs demonstrate the continuation and inescapability of class. How is it possible to escape from that which is apparently revealed through every recollection, every confidence? Class contains many embodied aspects to it; presentations, dispositions, styles and accents, which make us physically recognisable as classed individuals. These become noticed and recognised through social interactions where daily displays are enacted, produced through the habits learned within specific classed locations – the classed habitus (Bourdieu, 1984). Angela demonstrates the all-encompassing aspects of class as a 'social experience', which cannot easily be moved away from, for there is an embodied physicality to it. Hers is a profound pronouncement on the all-pervasive nature of that which you are:

> I am still very much working-class. I believe that class is a social experience and not simply what you earn. It can be what you eat, what you drink and what you wear when you drink it. All of my experiences are filtered through a working-class lens. (Angela)

It is difficult to prevent the reproduction of inequalities in the transmission of physical capital, which ultimately reduces or compounds other capitals, including economic ones. The circulation of physical, embodied capital has effects at the interpersonal and structural level (Bourdieu, 1984; Skeggs, 2004). But being looked at also involves looking back.

Looking up?

Perceptions of what constitutes middle-classness included positive and negative associations and characteristics, and were constructed through contact with people who interviewees described as middle-class. Such people were believed to have material resources and comfort, a 'nice' existence, free of struggle and perhaps cushioned by inherited wealth. When asked what her description of a middle-class person would be Kelly states that being middle-class is about 'being brought up living in a family where you're not constantly living on the breadline or worrying about it. A nice house, a nice car, enough money to have those things.' The words 'nice' and 'comfy' were often used in relation to economic position as well as in referring to (related) middle-class lifestyles. Such comfort was believed to ensure a degree of 'safety' and 'control', elements which many women felt were often missing from their own lives. To be middle-class is to not have to hide behind the sofa when the rent man comes, and indeed to have bought the sofa you are not hiding behind, new.

There was often a degree of envy produced through comparison with middle-class privileges, both in respect of financial well-being and also in having access to 'normal' things, including 'respect'. This suggests an awareness of a class norm in operation, as well as their distance from it. However, as previously noted, working-class identities were not always experienced as uncomfortable or unpleasant – identifications were produced through comparisons with classed 'others' but their identifications cannot be reduced to this alone due to the multiple ways that most women recognised themselves and were mis/recognised. Kelly and

Lisa discuss the complexity of this: Lisa feels her class 'consciousness' was not fully or only informed through contact with middle-class individuals and indeed highlights such a view as patronising. Responding to this, Kelly then modifies her claims that such contrast is not only brought into being through middle-class difference, but also by daily 'reminders' occurring in multiple social contexts:

> What I'm saying is that you can identify as being working-class but, if you're working-class even if you've never been anywhere else or whatever, you'll know you are working-class 'cause you'll have seen people who are different to you and you'll feel like you're different to them ... I don't think you have to necessarily move out of the area to be able to do that, I think you can be down the shops and see someone who is different to you. You can be aware of your class but to be *really* aware you have to see your difference, being compared to. (Kelly)

Many women distanced themselves from middle-class positions through describing the negative characteristics that they ascribed to it – as well as being a source of comparison and envy, it was also a source of disdain: middle-class, middle-of-the-road, distinctly mediocre. Middle-class people became the embodiment of these positions, as 'conventional' and even 'ignorant' in so far as their perceived comfort was felt to protect them from working-class existence, evoking critiques of 'smug' self-certain 'arrogance':

> Em, you think of the range rover and the 2.5 kids and em, yeah, a stereotype which is actually a number of people's reality is like parochial, a bit smug, a bit narrow minded, a lack of awareness of what life is like for the majority of people on this planet. Em, I wouldn't say I've got an awareness of what life is like for everyone on the planet but you know what I mean (laughs). (Fiona)

Like Fiona's last minute qualifier, many women were aware of 'generalising' and 'stereotyping', aware of the limitations of their own accounts. Jill, for example, describes her own assumptions as a form of 'inverted snobbery', but continues to make them nonetheless:

> Money and privilege aye but I suppose money gets you the privilege, so at the end of the day it still comes down to money for me. I know plenty of people who're really schemie and pretty bammy but at the end of the day they'll have plenty of money, they're supported. I might be called a snob for saying that ... . I don't really care (laughs). (Jill)

It is not enough to display or enact apparently 'working-class' characteristics ('schemie') as these can be held simultaneously with middle-class
capitals; in such an event working-classness is denied. The contradiction
generates anger and annoyance as well as feelings of discomfort,
expressed by Jill's sentiment that she could be called a 'snob' (and perhaps
positioned closer to 'middle-class' as a result). Sometimes these tensions
led to 'avoidance' of class, where middle-class associations were especially avoided. Such avoidance has a classed base in itself and is rather
different from uncertainty.

Not with a barge pole: avoidance of the middle-class

The idea that 'you are what you do, where you live, what you would like
to do' was a commonly invoked identity claim. A few women had
'moved' somewhat as a result of career progression (Sharon, Angela,
Jeannette) and were, at times, uncertain about naming class. Yet, at the
same time, they repeated their working-class identifications and reiterated
entrenched working-class experiences, a case of 'you can be what you
say you are'. The avoidance of class meant that some women effectively
avoided being 'labelled' as middle-class. Although this can be theorised
in terms of a rejection and dis-identification with middle-class 'otherness'
I would suggest that the complexity and rejection felt and voiced here
says more about the all-encompassing aspects of class, about how
women still identify as and feel working-class.

   There were various ways in which (middle) class was avoided – and
for different reasons. Sharon and Angela felt that their own class position had changed somewhat, although they were reluctant to re-name
themselves as middle-class. What then happened was a playing down
of the material objects that they had acquired while re-stating their
entrenched childhood – and adult – experiences and attitudes.
Alternatively, 'differences', which they had already named in relation
to different classes, were diffused. Class was accorded a much more neutral status here than other parts of their interviews suggest (see Savage
et al., 2001).

   The refusal to be re-named as middle-class stands in contrast to the
notion of aspirational class mobility, whereby middle-classness is
viewed as an enviable position. Wanting to have a nice car is obviously
not the same as wanting to be the kind of person who would sit in the
driving seat. But what consequences do such refusals have for the individuals involved? What ways do they (not) 'move'? Angela is able to
refuse middle-class existence from a relatively secure (financial) position
('just *material* things'). However, her (new) 'objective' position contradicts

her 'subjective' beliefs and also serves to marginalise her 'past' 'objective' experiences. The tension between strongly identifying markers of middle-class existence and rejecting them as insufficient, when applying them to conceptualisations of self-identity, is evident. Angela's tone is defensive and a middle-class mind set is something to be avoided at all cost, although it is apparent that this is affordable:

> A: I wouldn't, I wouldn't define a middle-class person ... I suppose when I was growing up my definition of middle-class would have been somebody who lived in a bought house, that type of thing, who lived in a nice type of area, who had a reasonable level of income. But that doesn't cut it for me.
>
> Y: Why not?
>
> A: Eh, because those are just *material* things. I think it's about attitude, I think also a part of why I define myself as working-class is because I don't look down on anyone and I think sometimes people who define themselves as middle-class or upper-class, they're putting themselves above, on a level above other people, I would never do that. (Angela)

Angela argues that her 'attitudes' remain working-class and, as such, she has not moved to a middle-class position.[2]

Some 'choices' were much more compelling and enforced, rather than 'preferred'. Many women 'lacked' both the 'objective' and 'subjective' signifiers of middle-class existence, but what is interesting is the way that these signifiers were rejected anyway; middle-classness held negative associations for many women who then felt they never could be, nor want to be, middle-class. Dawn doubts she ever could be what she imagines middle-class to be:

> I'm not ever really going to be em, middle-class, I don't think. Em but then I think that's to do with what I think middle-class is, you know, a lot of that is two kids, a dog. I have a very set image of what it is and I don't think I'm ever, well I'm obviously not going to be that but you know what I mean. (Dawn)

Dawn's 'obvious' departure from middle-classness seems to hint at and combine both her classed and sexual distance from the norm, although working-class lesbians can have the 2.5 kids – but perhaps not the range rover, which Fiona described earlier. Avoiding the markers of class requires knowledge of what class is and does and indicates how some women felt about their own class. Sally, for instance, speaks of 'feeling sorry' for people who live in council flats – as if this was far removed from her own situation, which it isn't. There are different ways in which individuals avoid and distance themselves from social class, whether the rejection is based on resisting pathology, displaying the 'correct' attitudes (either 'working-class' or 'classless') or 'denying' class privilege. Again, these complex dis/associations produce feelings of shame and guilt. It is important to remember the 'objective' 'impossibility' of moving towards a middle-class position felt by many working-class women – their subjective refusals were often held in conjunction with this realisation; 'can't, won't, really don't want to'. Even those who had 'moved on' were determined to remain working-class, powerfully challenging notions of mobility and confronting their own 'avoidance'. The avoidance of the middle-class is fierce and working-class teeth are bared, no matter how long ago those teeth were cut.

Moving on but staying put

There is a tension in being true to oneself compared with the possible perceptions others may have of you, the tension between 'staying put' and being 'moved on'. Amy indicates a lack of opportunity to become middle-class – not that this is desired. The middle-class in her account seems to be an alien land, populated by strangers who do strange things:

> I don't think, it disnae matter how much money, I would still consider myself working-class. I don't think I could get that uppity bit about me, it would be pretty difficult. I mean it's been instilled in me for years 'You vote labour, you dae this, you dae this, this is what working-class people dae,' so I don't think it would change. I'd never ever go up there, I don't know if they think they're more clever to be middle-class 'cause you have to have the nice job to have the nice money so you must have some brains or something! Em, and I don't know if I would ever be that clever. I mean does it bring it all back down to money or I mean how do they get their money and stuff like that? But no, never think about being anything other than being what I am! (laughs). (Amy)

Amy's account reveals the ways in which mobility can, and cannot, be achieved. For Amy this involves becoming more 'clever', but at the same time she is aware of the power involved in defining what and who is 'clever'. Amy does experience changing circumstances but the 'movement' is not so great as to constitute a change of class position. Instead her continued experience of relative poverty is indicated, which continues to act as a barrier to upward mobility, as do her instilled attitudes and beliefs: 'move to the middle-class? I'd much rather go somewhere nice instead.' Outlining possible movement, Amy still highlights (and dispels) the stress involved in managing her financial position:

> When I lived in Garrowby and I never had a job and I lived in a council house and everything, I used to say I was skint when I had about £3 in my pocket and that was me skint but now if I've got £20 in my pocket I'm skint. That's a really funny thing to try and get round in your head and it's, I don't know where that comes from but it's so bizarre when I think back and I'll go 'I've got no money' and I've got £10 quid or something and I'm going 'I've nae money, what am I going tae dae?' and six years ago I was sitting with £2 going 'What am I going tae dae?' Get a life! (Amy)

Again, even though Michelle feels she has moved in some respects she is aware that she remains 'vulnerable':

> I've got a voice, I've got a *choice*. I've empowered myself, I've made the decision not to stay *there* [Fife], I've kinda taken the step up ... My landlord could chuck me out at any moment and I'd be back to fucking homelessness, nothing to clutch onto. (Michelle)

Mobility was often associated with (flawed) aspirations or 'pretence', while working-classness often represented a more 'real' location, something about themselves that many were content with. The reported comfort and sense of belonging within working-class communities and areas, as more 'real' locations, also problematises notions of mobility and 'moving on'. There is no point in packing up and moving on up if home is where the heart is. Nevertheless, their sense of comfort was fractured by 'insiders' and 'outsiders' as they managed the pathologised representations of working-class locations and the normalised expectations that they should 'move' and 'get out'. The stigmas associated with working-class status occasionally fuelled attempts to prove 'worthiness' or 'decency', while the intersection between class and sexuality meant that decency was sometimes rejected, sometimes accepted and always precariously negotiated.

Somewhat better than the rest?

Different classed judgements (from differently classed individuals) lay different and unequal claims upon establishing a position 'somewhat better than the rest': the effects of such claims also differ across class. The significant concern amongst interviewees to show or prove 'decency' can be seen as an avoidance of the pathology typically associated with working-class women (Skeggs, 1997) – and lesbians. However, by utilising such discourses some women in my study may be accused of perpetuating the very processes which render working-class lesbians deviant or 'undeserving'. In contrast, I claim that such a theorisation serves to further stigmatise respondents by allowing them to appear as 'unconscious' dupes. My intention is to reveal the ways in which class circulates and with what effects: working-class women actively negotiate and challenge interpersonal and structural processes while also being constrained and circumscribed by these.

Several women did express pragmatic desires to 'move', or to be better off, while critiquing the pretence involved in 'bettering yourself'. Women often wanted to escape the poverty connected with their working-class positions, as well as the negativity associated with this. Many were concerned to prove their worth and decency – these defences were made in recognition of the fact that they did not inhabit 'valuable' locations. Accordingly, there was a concern to prove they were not careless or reckless, that they did not engage in 'dole scrounging' or crime. The classed effect of this was that stereotypes about working-class behaviour continued to be circulated; in proving their decency some women compared themselves with 'indecent' (working-class) 'others', bringing into question the forms resistances and identifications can take.

Kirsty, for example, attempts to display her 'decency' through caring standards – revealing the structural constraints she has to negotiate (along with middle-class women); their worth, measured in mothering and other caring capacities, is also that which renders them potentially 'exploited' (Skeggs, 1997). But for Kirsty, class position is more than simply an 'add on', rather notions of 'proper' parenting are produced through these classed hierarchies and Kirsty distances herself from the 'bad' parenting practices of the 'others': 'I only have to, you know, look out my window at the lower than working-class. It's the people that are sat in the pubs drinking all night while their children are, you know, running around the streets 'til 10 o'clock at night and not bothered.' Nonetheless, being 'decent' also worked to displace middle-class judgements, re-working typically classed judgements – decent is as decent does:

> D: It's about decency. You're talking about people in frocks acting posh, but I am decent, I was brought up decent, it's as simple as that.
> C: What do you mean, what's *decent*?

D: Being brought up decent, like I remember my mum saying 'Well
you may be working-class but you are decent.' (Doris and Cathy)

Rita shows that, for her, being 'classy' involves being 'decent', her
account therefore produces challenge but also a degree of 'conformity';
it is difficult to assert worthiness without comparison to normative
standards. Decent is as decent should do:

I feel that class isn't necessarily money 'cause I know that there's a lot
of people call themselves pretty high class 'cause they've got a lot of
money and they're not, they're beneath me. Things like having
manners, how to talk to people, how to be when you're out, that's
what I call decent class whether you've got decent money or
not. ... That's how I define it ... somebody who is a decent person
and has got manners and knows how to act in public, how to treat
people, etiquette. That sort of thing. It also helps if you've got
money! (laughs) ... There's nothing worse than someone who has no
class and no taste and having a pile of money 'cause someone who's
got no money, like myself, who's struggling, I still have class. (Rita)

Rita is out about her class, but many respondents spoke of those in the
middle-class who did not want to 'come out' about their class position.
Rather than being concerned with their 'decency', dis-identification was
believed to occur through guilt and denial of material privileges. This
was evident in encounters some of the women in my research had with
middle-class individuals who, in conversation, were perhaps trying
to empathise with working-class lives. However, instead of making
connections, greater distance was the outcome, as less means more to
certain people:

If I say I've got no money I mean I've got no money but I think when
middle-class people say they've got no money they might be down to
their last few thousand in the bank or whatever. If I'm penniless, I'm
penniless which I am most of the time, it's just a constant struggle.
There were times in London, em, I didn't used to open the door. I was
terrified to, I had to tell the kids to hide because I was in debt, it was
the TV license people coming or, do you know what I mean, just constant. That was an awful thing to have to put my kids through, how
do you explain that to you children, you know. (Mavis)

These accounts show the complexity and resentment behind class
processes, including comparison, envy, hostility and guilt. There is a system

of establishing who is working-class, rather than a guilty 'fake', somebody who should, and probably does, know better than to claim they are 'one of us'. But there is also an avoidance of being too overtly 'working-class', while continuing to identify as such. There is a classed characteristic to being 'uncertain' and 'ambivalent', absent from the women's lives (Savage et al., 2001). Instead there are continued economic and emotional 'reminders' of class positions, mediated too by sexuality.

Cathy notes a certain tendency to displace and refuse class by rejecting labels. This process is markedly different from the occasions when some women (temporarily) reject the label – with different reasons and effects. Numerous assertions of the continued relevance and effect of class inequalities were powerfully and often angrily made. To deny the existence of class is to deny the validity of those who identify as working-class and that is quite a big thing to take away from somebody when they are rather keen on keeping it.

Out-classed?

Like working-class status, lesbian identity can be marked in a series of negative ways, from which working-class lesbians had to construct a positive identity. The women were not 'poor' or 'vulnerable' individuals, incapable of establishing a positive sense of self, as dramatically shown by their accounts. Nevertheless, their structural position as working-class lesbians meant that various inequalities and discriminations were endured. For example, many women were aware of the gender inequalities affecting possible incomes – similarly, they theorised and rejected heterosexual 'privilege', remaining both aware and sceptical of it at the same time, as Fiona laughs and comments: 'There's the thing that you can be losing a certain economic security there basically you're not going to be able to do that thing, if you want a child you're not going to have a guy to support you. I mean even that's a bit of a hit and miss, I mean how much support are they *really!*'

It is difficult to deny its existence, but that it exists does not mean it is desired. This parallels the awareness and rejection of middle-class 'privilege', discussed earlier in this chapter; in both cases the practical elements are, for many, considered desirable (for example, having more money) – but on a subjective level, all women rejected these positions. It would be nice to have the bag but not the baggage.

As working-class women they too had to negotiate gendered expectations and discriminations and their lesbian status did not exempt them from this. However, in this example the comparison is made with heterosexual relationships and challenges are made to this socially validated norm, the classed specificity of which is also highlighted:

> *E*:   She's married, she has kids, first child, second child next year. She isn't working, she's got a meal ticket and she sees herself as a proper hostess, very much, yes. That's what mummy's done and mum's just had baby after baby and daddy's given them a home.
>
> *C*:   If a working-class woman does that she's seen as a complete trollop, isn't she?
>
> *D*:   Exactly! (Emma, Cathy, Diane)

Cathy and Emma seem alert to the classing of 'respectability' (Skeggs, 1997), recognising that while some move up, others move down, in social estimation as well as in financial terms. Many women spoke of the heterosexual and classed expectations of them. These processes form multiple oppressions through which class and sexual identity is negotiated and experienced. These do not go away when either class or sexuality is 'achieved'; rather they continue to be present in everyday social encounters, as Kelly suggests:

> For me it's more difficult being a lesbian, being a working-class woman. I can't actually say that 'cause I've never been middle-class, but in terms of relationships with my mum it's like, the expectation of my femininity, it's like that hyper-femininity. If you go down my way it's all of the women in short skirts, working-class women. (Kelly)

Kelly, like many other women, did not invest in the 'respectably heterosexual' classed form of femininity (Skeggs, 1997) refusing to trade their femininity and appearance on the marriage market, but they were still misrecognised through femininity and class. They were often still positioned, classified and located via class and sexuality, where the reading and fixing of lesbian and working-class status often diminished entitlement upon social space and entitlement to be properly recognised as worthy of respect and esteem. Misrecognition worked on an interpersonal and material level, where judgements, mis-readings and devaluations affected access to resources including the means to assert identity and have that identity validated.

Class mobility was indeed affected, but more constrained, by sexuality than Dunne (1997) suggests. Also, 'mobility' was often not presented as a positive option ('dragged up'!), instead implying a degree of dependency, as Cathy suggests:

> You talk to mainstream women and class you end up talking about 'Well, it's who you marry.' I think that's the thing with lesbians, that's what's different, a woman can change her class by marrying the right fella, that he can kinda drag her up into whatever class 'cause she then belongs to the husband and joins his family or whatever. For lesbians that's different, you don't have that even if you end up dating a middle-class girl. (Cathy)

Cathy's greater distance from societal norms, given her sexuality, would seem to explain her lack of concern with being 'upwardly mobile', something which she cannot 'deal with' given other pressures: 'I don't think it's as much of an issue in the gay scene in terms of being upwardly mobile and middle-class and stuff like that. It's a different level of survival, you're just trying to get by as gay.' But this does not mean that being *working-class* becomes irrelevant; 'getting-by' is instead influenced by both sexuality and class. The women I interviewed can be seen as insightful social commentators capable of managing and theorising class and sexuality as social structures – they also position their own lives within these structures, through comparing and contrasting prevalent beliefs with actual lived experience, relevant not only to class but also to their experience as lesbians. Cathy persuasively challenges the 'myth' of classlessness, relating this to a climate of individualism and apathy within the lesbian and gay community:

> There's this myth going on that it doesn't matter who you are, they are just labels, it's not important, you know, it's all in the past, it doesn't matter we've got equality and it's the biggest load of shit. I'm not falling for it. It really is, it's like this thing that class no longer exists, we don't need lesbian and gay pride anymore, all you have to do is live your life there's no need for all that and it's like 'Yeah, we'll have ten years of this, of being completely isolated' and having been told that you just have to cope, then in ten years time there'll come another cycle and it will matter but you'll just have to go through that ten years of doing your own thing and living your own life. (Cathy)

The accounts of working-class lesbians begin to reveal the impossibility of being classless, in all its variety and complexity.

To conclude this chapter, which has outlined the key issues to be developed throughout this book, the ways in which class is felt, experienced and identified with, against complex denials, refusals and judgements, proves its continued existence and effect. The emotional underpinnings of class expressed by the women in my study also prove its continued salience as a factor in identity construction and negotiation. This challenges those theorists who announce the demise of class and disregard it as a factor informing experience. Class conflict is not situated in the past, rather the women's 'pasts' and 'presents' are mediated through class structures and classed encounters throughout a variety of social sites.

Following chapters will develop the connections between class and sexuality, demonstrating their continued relevance to those who occupy both positions. The next chapter examines how class and sexuality are initially encountered, 'realised' and resisted, by focusing on the women's experiences of growing up in working-class families and communities and the ensuing disadvantages and devaluations incurred. These external judgments related to and were reinforced by other social institutions, notably the schooling system, which is also discussed in the following chapter.

3
Close Encounters of the Classed Kind

Class, gender and sexuality come together in everyday family life, in the characters, incidents, stories and tensions that characterise, shape and disrupt day by day; a sense of identity and belonging, and a recognition of value and estimation, gradually but often forcibly and vividly emerge. These subjective senses and material realities are based in the home, within the broader 'community', the placing of and negotiation between members of households, and the ways in which these hierarchies are confirmed, challenged and refused. Schools also operate as institutions which inform and mediate parenting practices, localised feelings of not/belonging, subjective and material im/possibilities and interactions and distinctions between community peers.

Many interviewees spoke of initial 'realisations' of class processes and inequalities in terms of growing up in specific families and communities and the experiences that this entailed. For example, all respondents faced financial hardship in childhood as a result of parental unemployment or low-paid work and often went without basic necessities, enforcing an awareness of disadvantage. In recounting stories of working-class life, Rubin (1976) uncovers feelings of pain, shame and deficiency; her interviewees recalled memories of life as hard and 'mean'. These feelings and responses were common amongst the women I interviewed, pointing to the ways in which class was realised, enacted, challenged and 'accepted' in everyday life. While working-class women may be caught between romanticizing and pathologising experiences as they retell their 'stories' (Raffo, 1997; Rubin, 1976) the acute awareness of these binaries and the enforced reflection into how others see them, and their families, produced a sense of certainty, a case of 'you are what you know yourself to be'.

The pathologisation of working-class families continues in the notion of an 'underclass', which Murray (1990, 1994) uses to refer to those families without fathers. Similarly, as Jamieson (1998) argues, extreme gender divisions, which continue across social classes, are still considered to be more typically working-class (Lareau, 2003). Women in my study spoke of their families and the gendered inequalities in operation, but the ways in which these are considered problematic, or not, can be explained through class. Their empathies and resentments were generated through an awareness of how difficult it was for their parents to manage, albeit in gendered ways (Jamieson, 1998; Lareau, 2003; Rubin, 1976). 'Happy families' and indeed unhappy ones are not contained within or constituted through this singular unit. Still, images, or imaginings, of 'the family', like the working-class community have also contributed to notions of a mythical past in which people were more willing to help each other (Bulmer, 1986). When everybody is stuck in the same boat, the least you can do is to lend a hand. This becomes more difficult when the boat starts to decay and people realise their feet are getting wet.

All interviewees were highly aware of shared vulnerability within their classed communities and the enduring emotional and material effects of communal decline. Moreover, they sensed that some were more vulnerable than others, even within a shared working-class location. As Jamieson notes, even in 'working-class communities there were (as there still are) people who fell or were pushed through the close-knit net' (1998: 82). But rather than citing this as evidence of the non-existence of 'communities' they indicated instead the ways in which gender, class, race and sexuality were enacted and realised within their communities.

My old man's a dustman ...

Parental employment predominantly consisted of unskilled or partly skilled work, vulnerable to economic fluctuations and sector decline.[1] This generated an awareness of disadvantage and fuelled feelings of anger and resentment. Given direct economic hardship, class was experienced on an immediate, material level and often did not have to be theorised or explained. The consequences of unemployment included family and community 'stress', which can so easily be individualised without appreciation of the repeated difficulties faced by working-class people. While notions of individualism work against class 'consciousness' and identification with classed 'communities', many women I spoke to managed and challenged prevalent views of themselves as unsuccessful, poor and disadvantaged individuals, rather than as members of structurally disadvantaged groups. The women were able to disrupt, with humour, the simultaneous romanticisation/pathologisation of their family circumstances.

I use Alice's father's experience of un/employment to exemplify economic hardship and vulnerability not because I find his line of work obscure and fascinating (I am aware that it may be read as such), but because his experiences were not untypical amongst the women in my study; many spoke of their parents working in dangerous, harsh and monotonous conditions:

> The most desperate thing he did was work on a maggot farm near where we lived, I'd never heard about it. He said he was really desperate he'd do anything and his friend said 'Ah, you'd not do the maggot farm'. My dad thinks he's quite hard and he's done some really horrible jobs so he said 'I can do that' ... He comes back about dinner time and we thought that was very early and he was stinking, the stench! My dad came in and he just looked like, like a dead person. He was absolutely white and shaking and he stank of ammonia! He was really in shock. (Alice)

The physical and emotional effect of this type of work, undertaken to avoid poverty, is clear, heightening 'awareness' among all family members. It is hard to ignore poverty and hardship when you can quite literally smell it walking in the door.

Poverty can produce adverse effects for all concerned but, as the women uncover and resist, working-class existence can then become synonymous with 'bad things'. I am concerned with highlighting the conditions and experience of poverty without passing judgements on those 'poor individuals'; judgement is instead directed at wider political and social structures that create these conditions and restrictions. Jo's account, echoed by many respondents, highlights the (gendered) effect of the devastation of heavy industry, as well as the inability to challenge these processes. The story of one becomes the story of a community, of a sector of society – a narrative of loss:

> That was our community, you know, it affected like so many men losing their jobs and what did they do? Nothing. So they just got depressed or drunk or whatever. (Jo)

Immersion in such situations can create empathy between neighbours but as Grace reports, bearing witness to communal poverty ultimately rendered her father unemployed and ill (he had a nervous breakdown).

Her father's bread van went out of business as he was unable to charge people for food; knowing that they could not pay upfront he offered food on 'tick' and never received payment. Working-class 'co-operation' and 'trust', engendered through shared community, is not unproblematic, but it is worth emphasising the structuring of this, rather than present individuals as untrustworthy (Bulmer, 1986).

Many women spoke of the lack of material resources and access to 'normal' things during childhood, particularly clothes and toys, producing an awareness of their relative poverty while growing up. Others defended their position as basic though adequate; this 'adequacy' usually involved enormous work and effort:

> My father, who'd worked all his life in the shipyards, who worked tremendous hours, had to work overtime to keep us from poverty, and we did live in poverty. As a child I remember having to go to school with holes in my shoes and having to put cardboard in them. I remember not having gloves in the winter and my hands being freezing cold. So we did live in poverty, em, we never starved, we always had food it may not have been the best food you know, gristly mince and stuff like that. (Mavis)

Interviewees encountered class and its manifestations on a daily basis – they were on first name terms. The lack of a specific pair of trainers or the latest fashion item may not seem to be of crucial importance when considering the broader nature of class inequality but these items create feelings of inclusion or exclusion (Bowring, 2000) and formed a significant part of many women's class 'encounters' and realisations. Material indicators 'reminded' Mavis of her social position, being reinforced through comparison, although hard to ignore. Comparisons often generated 'difficult' emotions; Kelly used to feel ashamed and embarrassed by her packed lunch box, as this seemingly trivial item symbolised class difference:

> But at school I can remember at school being ashamed of my packed lunch box … I used to hide it under the table 'cause I was embarrassed. My mum used to work at a crisp factory and sometimes I would get crisps but other times my packed lunch used to look a bit sparse or a bit embarrassing. You know, it wasn't the fact that I wasn't fed but it was *what* I was fed. Things like trainers, things that did matter as a young person. But the packed lunch I can remember, I've told people and they've laughed at me. (Kelly)

It is clear that these items, which may be dismissed as trivial and materialistic, have meaning nonetheless, highlighting the significance of wants as well as needs (as Lisa says, 'When I was a kid I would have died for a pair of trainers'), particularly when the lack of desired objects classes you as a flawed individual unable, for example, to dress 'properly'. Normal things included going on holiday, which many women never experienced in childhood. Despite these negative classed 'reminders', positive class awareness was reached on the basis of re-assessing judgements and rejecting 'norms', 'materialism' and 'pretence'.

Working-class families are typically derided for their pathological manifestations (Lareau, 2003; Reese, 2005). For example, the construction of femininities and masculinities, in terms of mothering and fathering roles, often do not 'fit' for working-class families: 'She isn't the dependent, helpless, frivolous child-woman because it would be ridiculously inappropriate, given her life experiences. He isn't the independent, masterful, all powerful provider.' (Rubin, 1976: 178). Thus, there is a tendency to eulogise working-class mothers as heroines or criticise them as victims (Lawler, 2000). In my study, a lot of women spoke of 'creative mothers' who somehow absorbed the impact of poverty, who took the rough edges off and made life manageable, while fathers' identities as 'breadwinners' were ruptured by sector decline, and consequent unemployment displaced the sense of pride available to working-class men through manual work. Different family members had to negotiate feelings of shame, embarrassment and responsibility for different gendered reasons.[2] Many women's understanding, realisations and empathies often contained a gendered element, and their critique of gender inequalities also formed resistances to the heterosexual expectations of them. These realisations and resistances continued to impact upon current identities and identifications as initial class encounters were reproduced across time.

Class understandings were often produced through an awareness of mothers' attempts to 'hide' poverty. For example, Lynn's mother attempts to create a respectable, decent appearance, the efforts for which are also hidden:

You couldn't afford new clothes, my mother went to the Salt Market[3] to find clothes, I mean she worked extremely hard to hide the poverty, she worked extremely hard. The Briggate is still open and women couldnae have survived without the Salt Market. My mum would take us to the co-op to get our shoes measured so she knew our size and she would hunt for Clark's shoes in that size, oh aye, and she would only buy the best jumpers second hand. She couldnae have survived without that. (Lynn)

The language used by Lynn is emotive and the desperation is still audible within her repeated assertion that her mother could not have survived. Feelings about such limited resources were powerfully expressed; sometimes the empathy felt towards their mothers who 'did their best' had a gendered aspect, as women remembered 'demands'of brothers in contrast to their own acceptance of the fact that their mother had to cope.

Mavis's account, like that of other women, serves as a reminder of the enduring effects of memories and the ways these impact upon present selves. The past is always with us, keeping an eye on our bank accounts. Enduring the effect of poverty and unemployment is stressful, working to create family tensions. Here Alice's father's frustration is understood and critiqued – Alice's father defined himself as the breadwinner but his evident anger at not being able to fulfil this role negates the anger and suffering of other members of the family. Alice's awareness is then produced through resentment, anger and hurt. The experiences narrated here seem to have an enduring impact:

I really didn't like him for a long time … there was a tension with him constantly being made redundant … he lost all his self esteem, everything he's worked towards was just taken away, he became really quite bitter and quite frustrated. He was on the dole for a long time … No friends, no support networks, no job, no identity. He did become very bitter and quite aggressive, there were just endless arguments about money and work. It was very tense for quite a lot of years. (Alice).

Nevertheless, the creativity in coping with and managing poverty was, for some, positive; lessons were learned about the value of money and the importance of independence: 'I think it certainly taught me the value of money and I hate wasting things' (Lisa). For some poverty was just a matter of fact, even if it was painful. Nevertheless, aware of the romanticised version of working-class life, Sonia ironically comments that although her background was 'poor' she still experienced pleasure; realisations and assessments were produced through positive as well as negative experiences:

My mum was a widow and I lived on a council estate all my life. Free school meals, clothing grants. And we never, there was never a lot of money but it was like, you know, an old country western song, we had love! (Sonia)

Similarly, Jeannette argues that poverty, although experienced, was not the defining condition of her childhood (perhaps again as a result of her mother's efforts):

> When I was growing up, although we were poor, poverty didnae define me when I was growing up because most of the people probably round about me weren't that much better off and my mum worked really, really hard at making sure that what she had went around and was enough, despite my father's best efforts to piss it all against a wall, you know. Poverty was not – although it was something that was always there, it wasn't necessarily something to be scared of. (Jeannette)

Poverty was not something that was mentioned on the news; it lived in their back bedrooms and was often invited for tea. It was not feared as something other to their existence, instead everyone was 'in the same boat'. However, there are times when 'fitting into' classed communities and areas is disrupted, sometimes with amusing effects. Here, Lynn is conscious that her new appearance did not fit. The label matters, especially if you did not buy it yourself:

> I know when my father worked there were women in the office who kinda passed the time and gave us their kids' clothes, like it came to us in a big basket and they were beautiful ... We got their toys and it was like 'How could they need so much?' and it was matching clothes, right, so we were out to play in like Parkhead and we had these matching clothes and tights (laughs) nobody else had them, posh dresses. (Lynn)

In families and communities, attempts were made to claim and regain 'dignity' despite poverty and unemployment (see Figure 3.1). Sometimes these took the form of distinctions and differentiations within working-class communities based on job status and other signifiers of social worth – race and gender inequalities were also played out here as people asserted their worth in comparison to the 'other'. These factors enabled an awareness of social divisions, assumptions and expectations and the pain and pleasure in disrupting, resisting and enacting these.

Figure 3.1 Anna's map.

Jury of your peers

Many women grew up in 'politicised' environments as many of their parents were – or had been – involved in trade unions and had very definite views about employment rights and social divisions, which then impacted on their own class 'consciousness'. Political understandings were also generated through a sense of empathy within classed communities as neighbours faced adverse conditions and common concerns. The connections between political beliefs and class position are complex and working-class people have been simultaneously represented as apolitical and apathetic as well as potential 'revolutionaries' (Skeggs, 1997). Likewise, they are often presented as inherently more sexist, racist and homophobic (Moran, 2000; Skeggs, 1997). There is a danger in reproducing these stereotypes as I describe the women's accounts of their family situations, and family/community beliefs. Recognition of injustice informed many women's political beliefs and class 'consciousness', but political, social and emotional solidarity within working-class families and communities was also fractured by gender and racial discrimination and by the perpetuation of classification hierarchies and distinctions within classed communities (Bettie, 2003; Jamieson, 1998). Women experienced and challenged inequalities within these immediate locations, although inequalities were not solely produced or located there.

As Robinson et al. (2004) note that home space is both a resource and a constraint, a place where knowledge is transmitted and resisted, even in the avoidance of explicit sex talk, and where gender and sexual identities are 'performed', even as sexual practice is marked as illicit. As previously mentioned, many interviewees spoke of gender inequalities existing in their families, as in broader society. Lynn links gender stereotypes and divisions to the sectarian divide which is a feature of her locality (Glasgow):

> About how it was up to girls to say no, like it wisnae the guys' fault if the lassie got pregnant, it was the women's fault. I would say 'But it takes two', 'No, it's the woman.' My mother used to go a ton on that, all one sided. At school there was always sort of sexist comments, it was just around so much. It was very … not pro-woman, quite the opposite. But it became part and parcel I suppose when I was growing up there. Almost like the Green/Orange divide, you know Celtic/Rangers, Catholic/ Protestant, it was all part and parcel of that kind of culture. (Lynn)

As well as sensing a degree of similarity with people living in the same area, being 'in the same boat', several women noted the differences and inequalities within this, of knowing where they were placed and where they would place others. Sukhjit speaks of the racialised hierarchies within class – and the class hierarchies within race, adding that such inequalities are perpetuated on an interpersonal level as a way of 'bettering yourself' against the 'other':

> There's hierarchies within themselves isn't there about where your parents are working, were they unemployed, were they, you know, how shit was their job. So there was a lot of stuff in the community around being labelled 'cause there was a really strong need to find a way of living in crap circumstances, to be better than someone else ... My parents came over in the late '60s' from Pakistan from a rural village, although there might have been other people who migrated at the same time they sometimes came from different places, so there's a whole different class structure, so it's like class on top of class in some ways ... So it felt like not only was I part of a working-class community in Bridgetown but also in the wider system wherever I went, where Asian people went there'd be judgements about 'You're working-class and *' ... It's still banded around the term but we used to be called MP's, which is the region in Pakistan my parents are from. Nowadays you just get called the typical 'Paki' by other people 'cause they don't necessarily understand the subtleties of that, the class system ... So I struggled with that as well ... I always felt at the bottom of the hierarchy, or that I felt I was being put at the bottom, I don't know that I necessarily felt that I was at the bottom. (Sukhjit)

Sukhjit forces attention towards the everyday classification processes in operation, and the painful intersection between race and class, just as she was forced to recognise these. While some distinctions are 'obvious' to Sukhjit, an outsider may miss the 'subtleties'. Differences of religion and ethnicity sometimes alienated women within their own class communities, for example, Cathy notes how her concept of 'community' and feeling of safety was ruptured by her parents' Irish identity. There was a similar sense of 'just knowing' she was marked, knowing where her place was. Working-class communities could act as a support mechanism or could impose further restrictions and judgements. They are not always safe or comfortable places to be: the working-class is not one big happy family and not everybody will be lent a cup of sugar. For Kelly, the tensions between her family and the neighbours results from class-based stereotypes around respectability and sexuality (Skeggs, 1997):

> I didn't live in a council house we lived in quite a nice house but when we moved in, I've got two older brothers, we had this clapped

out car and the neighbours were like 'Huh! That's edging on council house stuff', 'cause my mum had lots of children, that obviously means that you are fucking around ... Yeah, so when we moved in we got a few raised eyebrows. (Kelly)

Only a certain class of people 'fuck around' and you can bet they are not going to keep their garden tidy either.

All women spoke about the pressure of heterosexual expectations, although some experienced this more acutely than others. For example, the subtle, unspoken heterosexual expectation placed upon Faye was later modified to a (gendered) expectation that she would provide care for her mother – what else is there for a spinster to do? Lynn recognises the push towards heterosexuality while refusing to negate her hetero-sexual past (like Faye, Lynn has also been married); this was just what people did, it was simultaneously unspoken and effective. Kelly and Lisa had a long conversation about the ways in which their sexuality was affected by their working-class positions. There is a disagreement regarding the extent to which working-class culture emphasises heterosexuality more than middle-class culture. Relatedly, the different gendered expec-tations upon working-class and middle-class people are discussed with apparent negotiations and negations, reminiscence and reinterpretations, as class and sexuality are dis/connected.

K: Just that I actually think that it's harder, me coming out, it's harder from a working-class background than a middle-class background ... I feel like the expectation of me of my family, like job and career, is ... Well there's all the working-class expectations like you marry a man and bring up kids, you get pushed into it.

L: You're pushed into it no matter what class you're in. Everybody is pushed into heterosexuality.

...

K: Yeah, you get that in middle-class culture as well but what I'm saying is that I feel to me is they're more overt, maybe they're more subtle in middle-class culture.

L: I don't think they are.

K: I just felt, I mean where I grew up I didn't get encouraged to go and become a lawyer or a doctor or anything like that or go to uni. I got told to wait for the right man and don't lose your virginity.

L: I don't think that's to do with class.

K: Well it is! Because that's the expectations my parents had for me and why did they have such little expectations of me?

L: Working-class.

Lisa seems to be vocally resisting that which she too experiences, challenging the inevitability of constrained, heterosexist and classed pathways, while concluding that the path does dangerously twist between expectations, possibilities and refusals, all leading to and ending with class. On the other hand, Sonia is free from such pressure, within her family at least – instead her mum warns her of avoiding 'dirty men'. This still raises questions about the way sexuality is learned within families. As Grace indicates, there are connections between 'education' and sexuality:

> Whereas, I suppose, if we'd, if our parents had maybe been better educated, I use the term loosely 'cause I cannae think of another one but if they maybe had different life experiences, em, and had maybe met a different variety of people and had a better education themselves, it might have been more, it may have been more aware that there was other alternatives out there for me as well, as a kid, do you know what I mean other than heterosexuality or not. It was just never, it was never discussed, you know. (Grace)

The women's immediate social contexts highlighted the situated aspects of identity formation as divisions were drawn around gender, sexuality, religion and ethnicity, made visible and realisable within everyday encounters. These encounters were also mediated and regulated within formal and informal schooling settings.

The best days of their lives?

There has been much research on the significance of class in schools (Bettie, 2003;Hanafin and Lynch, 2002; Reay, 2004), as well as a vast body of research that highlights the inequalities of gender and sexuality operating within the school setting (Buston and Hart, 2001; Chambers et al., 2004; Nayak and Kehily, 1996). Rarely, has the intersection between class and sexuality, in the negotiation of identities, within and beyond the school setting, been considered (see Taylor, 2005d). A new body of research, operationalising more post-structuralist models of class and sexuality, as constituted and re/created in school settings, have arguably provided more up to date accounts of the complexity of such positionings and the 'moment to moment' resistances against these (Benjamin et al., 2003; Youdell, 2005). Nonetheless, despite such updated accounts, much of what was revealed by researchers in the 1980s and 1990s, still remains relevant, even given the supposed 'transformation' in intimacy and the implied shift in attitudes towards and ways of talking about sex: when exploring sexuality and class inequalities in school the vocabularies of 'oppression', 'silence' and 'exclusion' would still, I propose, not be out of place (Epstein, 1994; Mac an Ghaill, 1994; Skeggs, 1997). Although much has been said about the increased 'choice' of young people to be sexual, to claim – and reject – (sexual) differences (Roseneil, 2000), others point to the ways in which the neo-liberal framework of 'choice', serves to individualise structural inequalities, serving to problematise those who make the 'wrong' choice. Equally, not all sexualities are equally celebrated or valued and some may well be deployed to re-invoke a moralistic discourse of 'risk', particularly relevant in relation to younger women's sexualities (Buston and Hart, 2001; Kidger, 2005).

Nonetheless, times and debates have moved on, even as attention towards the intersection between class and sexuality (Skeggs, 1997), and specifically in relation to working-class lesbians, remains an enduring absence. The public debates about Section 2a/28 in the United Kingdom formed a significant context in which the fieldwork for this research occurred, perhaps representing a new climate in which sexuality in schools would no longer be silenced. Section 2a (Local Government Act, Scotland, 1986) also known as Section 28 (Local Government Act, 1988) stated that local authorities should not intentionally promote homosexuality, publish material with the intention of promoting homosexuality or promote the teaching in any maintained school of the acceptability of homosexuality as a 'pretended family' relationship. Section 2a was finally repealed by the Scottish Parliament on the 21 June 2000 while the UK parliament took another three years to repeal Section 28. This seemingly indicates a substantial improvement in discussing, if not tackling, homophobia in schools. Sexuality and sex education were the key sites of debate but the interaction between sexual identities and class positions received substantially less, if any, attention (Taylor, 2005b).

The classed, gendered and sexualised aspects of schooling have been investigated by many authors – but often these do not combine in such a way as to cast light upon the interconnecting inequalities faced by working-class lesbians, or the outcomes of these. The interaction of 'coming-out' about both a stigmatised sexual identity as well as a 'deviant' class position is rather new. Interviewees were positioned as 'failures', both in terms of their class positions and sexual identities, by teachers and fellow school pupils alike. Their tales of living with and through the lens of a 'double deviance', draw attention to the stark gap in theorising the intersection between class and sexuality, where consideration has been given to these two categories separately, rather than simultaneously.

While at school, interviewees encountered and made enduring classed and sexual recognitions and realisations and these recalled understandings were adeptly criticised, scathingly dismissed and still negotiated: these remembered experiences profoundly impacted upon their sense of self as well as their sense of what was possible and achievable, a sense forged from classed and sexual exclusions and discriminations. The experience of negotiating, naming and resisting classed and sexual inequalities would seem to combine to create a 'double jeopardy', demonstrating the unavoidable intersection of sexuality and class, manifest in feelings of 'failure' and in the related mis/recognition of their embodied, classed, gendered and sexual dispositions (Paechter, 2006).

All interviewees reported being very conscious of class as children, manifest by accent, lifestyle and money, made apparent in school settings (Bettie, 2003). Children, it would seem, quickly learn to reproduce wider social divisions and inequalities (Renold, 2000; Youdell, 2005). The sense of inequity, apparent throughout interview accounts, also featured in recalled childhood encounters between classed 'others'; middle-class children who were treated better, expected more and often got it – from better meals and clothes to better attention and better grades. Many women spoke of the emotional impact of feeling and being reminded of their 'difference' through the class signifiers of appearance and housing, which often formed the basis of negative judgements. This highlights the common circulation and awareness of class signifiers and the use of these, which may in fact be in operation even without the explanatory language of class: women often reflected back on their 'pasts' and spoke about 'knowing', 'realising', and being 'conscious' of class while also being unsure and uncertain about what (classed) judgements 'were about'.

Correspondingly, in a similar vein of confusion, uncertainty and merging articulation, sexuality was variously enacted, denied and 'achieved' in school settings. Dunne, in reflecting upon such processes, remarks that for those who questioned the giveness of heterosexuality during their schooling, the experience of being 'different' was consequential, supporting the 'mobilization of facilities which could facilitate the construction of a different life' (1997: 89). But such 'mobilization' seems to be profoundly classed, which is not to say that working-class lesbians fail to make realisations, reassessments and positive changes, but rather that they were rarely able to capitalise, emotionally or economically upon these, for they were often positioned as 'doubly deviant'. In contrast to such an optimistic portrayal of the facilitation of 'lesbian lifestyles' via engagement with education, it seems that the passage of a working-class student through the education system may be both problematic and painful constituting an attempted erasure, rather than affirmation, of identity. Not everyone capitalises upon their 'lesbian credentials' and being a working-class lesbian is rarely considered a credential in any school environment, whether that be formally or informally. For the women I interviewed, the 'best days of their lives' more often than not were not, and in recounting their schooling experiences the dominant narrative was often one of hostility and struggle as opposed to football stickers and school trips.

'Periods, poofs and pregnancy': sexuality in education

Instead of imparting knowledge and offering protection, many experienced varied invalidations, confusions and uncertainties within schools, as a result of who they were. For many, recalling schooling experiences brought back memories of playground taunts, laughable or non-existent sex education lessons, and a sense of being let down and left out. Many women reported a 'realisation' of their sexuality while at school, occurring through dis/identifications and mis/recognitions, which acted as barriers against positive identification. Experiences of poor or missing sex education lessons were recounted and, as a result, many interviewees had no language to express their feelings or to 'come out' as lesbians (Renold, 2000). At best sex education was taught in a brief and embarrassing one-off lesson, which emphasised heterosexual reproduction, with women across the age range reporting similar experiences, unfortunately suggesting a lack of improvement in this area. Thomson and Scott (1991) investigated the retrospective accounts of respondents' experiences of sex education and claimed that young women learn not about sex/uality but instead about the boundaries of femininity apparent through the enforced concern with protecting/damaging reputation. The power of sex education lies in what it excludes as well as includes, a point echoed time and time again in more contemporary studies (Buston and Hart, 2001; Kidger, 2005; Renold, 2000).

For all of the women in my study, learning about sex and sexuality was indeed experienced as paradoxical as they had to negotiate the in/visibility of heterosexuality as well as the formal silencing of lesbian and gay sexuality (Epstein, 1994). This silence contrasted with the very loud informal messages that many received in school playgrounds through homophobic taunts, indicating that children quickly learn and re-enact social norms, which have been both overtly and subtly conveyed to them, even if they do not fully understand them. Such 'policing' points to the powerful presence of an informal sexual 'subculture' within schools (Lees, 1986), suggesting that the women's realisations were mediated interpersonally as well as structurally. The negotiation of identity within in/formal 'moment to moment' inclusions and exclusions, still requires analysis of the structuring of such 'moments' and (material and subjective) 'movements' (Benjamin et al., 2003; Renold, 2000).

For many women an initial sense of difference was compounded by verbal and physical attacks, which went unnoticed and unpunished. In such circumstances, the 'correct', socially legitimised norm was quickly recognised. The 'right thing to do' is easy to recognise when there is little alternative. Lauren felt 'different' at school and this difference had to be managed: 'I just sort of said "Right I'm just going to have to, you know, grit my teeth and bear it." ' This strongly illustrates the uncertain and unconfident awareness of sexuality and the (temporary) inability to resist expectations, which features throughout interviewees' accounts of schooling. Despite having the responsibility as knowledge providers, many women spoke of teachers who refused to tell them what a lesbian was – yet knowledge was somehow confusingly received sometimes through the 'obligatory' (token) lesbian teacher. Speaking of her P.E teacher, Jo says 'She was also a lesbian, by the way. Do you know the story?' The story always seems to be the same and yet must always be different.

Informal knowledge was subject to pressure, homophobic bullying and name-calling. Rumours also circulated, based on ignorance, about the illegality of homosexuality producing fear, which served to generate conformity, as Rita remembers:

> I had a kiss with this girl in the school playground and they [school pupils] saw me and they told me it was wrong and that it was dirty and naughty and I would get locked up for it 'cause it was illegal. So I thought 'Shit!'

Apparently harmless questions about who had a boyfriend still caused many difficulties for interviewees in identifying their sexuality and claiming their difference. It is the playground catch 22 – 'Yes' makes you a liar in fear of being found out, 'No' makes you sad, stupid or highly suspect. Which is easier to live with?

In relating 'coming out' stories, it is necessary to avoid depictions of a straightforward transition from a presumed heterosexual state to lesbian existence, as the women's own 'contradictions' about this period in time show, but rather the purpose is to reveal the relevance this environment has for generating and perpetuating inequalities. A couple of women either gave up school ('dropped out') or changed school when their sexuality was 'discovered'. This had adverse effects on their self-esteem as well as having an immediate and future economic impact on their prospects, given the disruption to their education. The intersection between sexuality and class, in respect of attainment and achievement, adds to difficulties and drawbacks, conveyed in the sense of 'losing out' on both counts (Taylor, 2005a).

Many spoke of the negative consequences, such as isolation, of coming-out to themselves and to others while at school. Consequently, school was negatively experienced and many women excluded themselves or left at an early age.[4] Many 'opted' not to spend time in a place where they were often hated, ridiculed or despised. Jo moved school when her sexuality became known (why stay when nobody really wants you?), whereas Jeannette was asked to leave. Jeannette feels resentment towards the school system, which should have offered her protection. Her situation reveals the classed process of exclusion – her working-class mother, unwilling and unable to confront the middle-class authority of the school, did not challenge her exclusion (see Ball, 2003; Devine, 2004; Lareau, 2003). This is made more complicated by the fact that any protest would have required Jeannette to 'come out' to her mother. Jeannette's anger is recollected and, apparently, ongoing:

> I came out when I was still at school and I got kicked out of school, I didn't have much option. I was given an option to either leave or I had my parents come down, that was my mother, come down and discuss the situation. And things that were happening at home at the time … It didn't really feel like I had an option to get her to come down and discuss my acting out because I was feeling isolated and scared I suppose … So I chose to leave, which then made me really quite angry 'cause up until then, the system had really worked fairly well for me in terms of schooling and, you know, achieving and stuff. It had worked ok. It was only when I started to come out and my sexuality became an issue that the system stopped working. So that made me really, really angry. I still get really angry about it … I think that's where class left me being working-class left me much more vulnerable to, you know, slipping out the system.

The events and situations recounted in this paragraph are a lot to pile onto a teenager, especially one who is already confused and uncertain. No wonder getting out often seems a sensible option. Jeannette lacked support and affirmation from the school and her ability to challenge their views was constrained by her unwillingness to put more pressure on her mother, aware of the daily stresses which she already had to manage; she was then more vulnerable to authoritative judgements and devaluations, lacking the economic and social capital and time to contest this. The failure is not Jeannette's but she will have to bear the brunt of its impact. Leaving school at an early age has obvious implications for qualifications and subsequent employment opportunities (Taylor, 2005d); it can begin a cycle of disadvantage which can be very difficult to break and which must be heartbreaking if the reason behind it is the unfortunate interface of class and sexuality.

The interrelation between class and sexuality is graphically illustrated by Kelly who draws attention to the different expectations of working-class and middle-class pupils. In contesting and avoiding the linkage between ('hyper') heterosexuality and working-class femininity (Skeggs, 1997), Kelly is even more isolated, raising questions about the ability to refuse these positions – and the consequent dis/empowerment in doing so:

K: It's like at school middle-class girls could be more ... asexual because if you were a working-class girl, just in terms of your sexuality, I'm talking of heterosexuality here, em, was your kinda degree of power, girls would give blokes wanks under the table, it went on at 6th form. I just felt like ... I just thought, I'm not explaining it very well, but I didn't have to play that game, so that kinda alienated me from a lot of the working-class girls 'cause I wouldn't play along with trying to be popular with the boys. I didn't want to use my sexuality in order to be popular, I didn't want to wank some bloke off under the table.

L: I didn't even notice any of that going on.

K: It went on at my school a lot, you know, a couple of girls would always be the ones to do that.

L: Yeah, discussing sex, how far they'd gone.

K: But see the thing is, middle-class they were all seen as square 'cause they never kissed a boy, but they were alright. (Kelly and Lisa)

There is much research which suggests that common versions of acceptable teenage femininity are encapsulated in the labels 'slag', 'bad girls' and 'good girls', which construct identities and identifications against, instead of in common with, other boys and girls (Lees, 1986; McDowell, 2001). Skeggs (1997) argues that the central feature of women's educational experience involves developing tactics to deal with being positioned as sexual through intrusions and innuendos, classing this positioning. By resisting the official and middle-class ideology for girls in schools (neatness, diligence, appliance, passivity) and by replacing this with a more feminine even sexual one, working-class girls have been seen to display both a class instinct and an awareness of the nature of gender oppression within school (Bettie, 2003; Skeggs, 1997). In my study, working-class women were often 'marked' with (hetero-sexualised) meanings and expectations, as Kelly and Lisa suggest, and lacked the 'neutrality' available to their middle-class counterparts – although such neutrality is still gendered and disempowering.

Jude reports feeling different while at school not only in terms of sexuality but also in the ways that the story of 'the family', told at school, is a particularly heterosexual and middle-class version; alternative models are not validated because they are not spoken about or appear as pathological. For Jude, class is an *additional* problem, combining with her feelings about her sexual identity and causing greater uncertainty. To think you might be 'one of those' is difficult enough without the added burden of being from the wrong class in the first place. A hypothetical comparison is made with middle-class women and their struggles (or 'ease') in 'coming-out', although Jude notes the push towards heterosexuality across social class:

> What class does then in terms of sexual identity is that it, em, makes you feel even more insecure about thinking differently, because you don't have access to certain things that make you feel more normal ... So if you were middle-class and didn't have the same degrees of deprivation if you like, then of course you're going to feel a lot more comfortable with the challenges of exploring your sexual identity. It's going to be a hell of a lot easier to do that, than to deal with two, em, two more things that impinge upon your self-identity.

The interface in this case is one of two issues coming together to produce a weighty burden. If you are stuck in the maze of being working-class in a society that normalises the middle-class experience then it is going to be even harder to find the route to sexual acceptance within the hetero-normative context. If certain voices are silenced and certain experiences delegitimised then to be on the receiving end on both counts is quite something to deal with. It means that to come out, to tell the story of class and sexuality, you really are going to have to shout very loud to be heard and understood.

But many chose to avoid the issue of sexuality, which was easy to do in the context of formal silence. Identifications were mediated and constrained through these silences. Keeping your head down can become an art form, saying nothing to nobody about anything – ever. As Alice puts it 'As long as you kept it hidden you were alright. If you mentioned it out loud you'd get your head kicked in'. The silence on the issue does not mean it is not there. Instead silence generates confusion and fascination, which, although reflected on with amusement, can be very distressing:

> I remember being actually so confused in school as to which one's 'hetero' and 'homo', that I'd gone to the library and tried to find a book. And I can remember in a maths class, they were going 'Are you hetero or homo?' and I didn't want to answer first 'cause I didn't know what one it was and they all said 'hetero', 'hetero', 'hetero', so the answer you've got to say is hetero but as I said it I felt like I was betraying myself, you know, not to put a homosexual label on it but just say what if I fancy you? (Mandy)

Such processes are indicative of the enforced and acceptable identities apparent within schooling, creating confusion rather than clarity and generating feelings of shame and embarrassment. Positions, identities and confusions become structured through the educational curriculum, which operates with specific purposes and effects, apparent in the promotion of heterosexuality. Mandy spoke of the promotion of hetero-sexuality via sex education lessons: 'It was more like passing around condoms and how they fit and that.' The school sex education curriculum is thus not only about what is taught but how it is taught: this praxis in turn affords space for some possible identities and elides others (Buston and Hart, 2001; Thomson and Scott, 1991).

Many respondents felt that their class position, and the consequent standards of schooling and expectations placed upon them, also limited opportunities. For example, Sharon speaks of (university) education as providing a safe environment to discuss sexuality and possibly providing alternative options through this. She notes the contrast between this taken-for-granted aspect of middle-class existence compared to her own progression from working-class background to heterosexual marriage:

> Well I think there's more opportunity for you to come out and meet your own full potential if you have … have had the opportunity

to explore yourself, emotionally, it's usually doing it through education … I mean I was married at one point about a month before I was 18 but I knew I was gay but I thought 'Maybe every woman's attracted to women but you just get married anyway!' because it was never spoke about at school so if they said to me at school 'You can be attracted to women and that's ok' then I would have went 'Click'. Whereas I didn't want to ask. I think there is maybe a lot of women out there like me and then they get married and they don't particularly like it, don't like the sex of it but just put up with it for the sake of the kids. Then just get caught up with their everyday lives … Whereas if you're maybe in a middle-class background and a woman and you're encouraged to go out and do education, when you go to college or university you're able to have the discussions and the talks with other women and realise 'Hey, there's nothing wrong with me.' (Sharon)

Sharon highlights the gendered and classed messages and assumptions behind socially sanctioned expectations, which impacted upon many women's ideas of what was possible and achievable. Her account also implies resistance and empowerment – Sharon is now speaking from hindsight. Societal expectations shaped future possibilities and opportunities and many respondents were adept at recognising their manifestations, conscious of the classed channelling of themselves as children. They were in effect saying 'if you are not offered the options, how can you make the choices, how can you realise what you could be?'

Have you thought about factory work?

Working-class girls, negotiating their lesbian sexualities through school and other social locations are circumscribed by the classed and sexualised expectations of them, a material and subjective intersection and inequality, hidden in Dunne's (1997) assertion of the overwhelmingly positive effects of feeling, and living, 'difference' (Taylor, 2005a). Schools are attached to particular areas – the 'catchment' area is also a classed area. Often schools in middle-class areas are able to celebrate the 'success' of their pupils, while schools in working-class areas, and their pupils, are deemed 'failures' – the old school tie can close as many doors as it opens.

On reflection, many criticised the hidden curriculum operating in schools. Functioning subtly, often through unspoken mechanisms, schools make assumptions about the 'proper' place of their pupils based on class, race and gender, and school them accordingly (Mac an Ghaill, 1994; Skeggs, 1997). Many interviewees challenged classed expectations, making attempts to 'fight against the system'. But, lacking economic, social and cultural resources and capitals to entirely resist the authoritative devaluation of them, and facing a double depreciation via class and sexuality, they were often dismissed as angry, incompetent individuals; 'quiet at the back and less of your lip'.

As young children many got a sense of what their place was, noticing the differential treatments, expectations and resources bestowed upon middle-class children, where to have a better lunch box was to have a better chance of making it (Devine, 2004). This produced resentment at the schooling system and a deep sense of the unfairness of things, as Grace demonstrates:

> They concentrated their efforts on the kids that had come from the nicer houses whose parents probably would support applications to university and they knew that there was probably, in hindsight, they probably knew that it was the best way to expel their energy because there was probably less chance of any of us going to university or, in their eyes, maybe that's how it's seen at that time. (Grace)

Importantly, the structuring of these apparently individual judgements is revealed – teachers have targets to meet and working-class students may threaten 'standards' by their very presence. In such circumstances working-class students are seen to be of lower social worth, less valuable than their middle-class counterparts (Lareau, 2003; Reay, 2004).

As well as being restricted by pre-conceived ideas regarding their abilities and social positions (their 'places'), several women spoke of being able to challenge these negative associations: there is no success like failing to fail. For example, Kelly insisted that she do 'A' level Maths, despite being warned that she was incapable and would fail. She effectively subverted their expectations and judgements, although not without a degree of emotional cost (and benefit): 'They made me sit on my own for two years but I got a C in Maths. I felt like I'd beaten the system.' Several women sought to challenge the low expectations of them by excelling academically, although they still had to manage the low provisions and resources within working-class schools. Dawn, a 'high achiever' at school, speaks of her academic enjoyment of school, even though her school was 'rubbish'. Many women spoke of being 'let down' by the educational system, for example, Ali told how she was not allowed to do the re-sits offered to middle-class pupils because she got 'what she deserved', what was 'appropriate' for a working-class girl.

Some respondents were able to take advantage of patronising attitudes – but only if they were otherwise 'good girls'. Others suggested that, although they had made direct verbal challenges to teachers, this then served to reinforce existent low opinions of them, ultimately producing silence rather than debate: the 'gobby girl' in the corner is left to doodle in the margins. There was a careful path to negotiate, between the good/bad girl and the un/deserving poor but 'advantage' was sometimes accrued through accepting 'patronising' help. For example, Sukhjit spoke of taking advantage of the patronising attitudes of teachers but the 'advantages' were set against bitterness and anger, after all nobody likes to feel like an intellectual Oliver Twist:

> There was one woman she treated me like a *specimen* I think, like I was from a rough area and she was always very proud of me and I thought 'You twat' (laughs). But at the time I just thought she was being nice but it was really patronising some of the stuff. (Sukhjit)

There was also an awareness of a hidden curriculum operating within schools, in/validating certain experiences. The hidden curriculum may have more effect than the formal one in channelling children into social positions and in maintaining 'social cohesion', or social inequality. Subjects are, in theory, open to both girls and boys, yet girls are still channelled into certain subject areas, perhaps more so in working-class areas where there is an expectation that young girls will become (heterosexual) mothers with caring responsibilities (Mac an Ghaill, 1994; Skeggs, 1997). Teachers and career advisors can make powerful and enduring judgements and can restrict pupils' careers; the 'hidden' curriculum can in fact be very explicit. Rita, however, challenges the lack of worth associated with working-class women's typical career options. Despite what she was taught at school, she has learnt the value of her own skills:

> When I was in school I was told 'Oh, you'll never amount to anything,' 'cause I was always in the loos doing everybody's hair and I was being told off because in those days if you were clever with your hands that didn't mean anything, you had to be academic … They used to say to me in the high school 'You'll never amount to anything, there's no point you even bothering' … So I never learnt how to learn and I just wanted to leave school and work. I grew up thinking I was stupid and only fit for hairdressing. Not realising how clever you have to be and how artistic, I'm a bloody good hairdresser. (Rita)

Much of the women's class awareness was formed through such painful judgements, exclusions, and challenges, creating emotional and economic 'costs', which were daily experienced and moved through – and against. Such exclusion, pre-judgement and channelling made it difficult for many to positively claim their (classed and sexual) 'difference' (Dunne, 1997).

Attendance at middle-class schools, experienced by only three women, as 'placing requests', or as a result of being 'kicked out' of school because of sexuality, produced feelings of inferiority, owing to the judgements of both teachers and pupils. Some reported being told to speak 'properly', with the 'correct' accent. In Cathy's case this resulted in silence, a fear of opening her mouth as well as being 'closeted' about her sexuality, vividly demonstrating another embodied intersection of class and sexuality. Cathy demonstrates failure to protect at an emotional level, portraying her previous working-class school as more physically 'rough', yet more comfortable. The exclusions within middle-class schools can often operate at hidden and underhand levels:

> Cause with working-class kids if you've a problem with someone you go out into the playground and beat the crap out of them and you sort it all out. Whereas those middle-class girls they've got a completely different way of dealing with stuff. It's all to do with ostracism and bitching and if they'd just get together and have a fight and sort it all out, you know. So it was just really hard for me to deal with that, going to the school where you had to act like a lady and I've just got this memory of being about 11 years old … so you've gone through this working-class school where everybody is pretty rough, into this middle-class environment where everybody's wearing little white gloves and they were handing out books in English class and I got my book and I went 'Sir there's a dirty great hole in my book!' and he just looked at me and went 'Catherine, the whole is neither dirty nor is it great' (laughs). I didn't speak again for the next three years. I just thought 'Right, ok, I've got it now!' … All through my teens I was a closet case, 'cause I realised I was a lesbian when I was seven or eight or something, so that then affected it as well. I just thought, with all this other shit going on, I'm not going to announce it, I'm not going to draw attention to myself. (Cathy)

It is one thing to speak, it is quite another to speak and be accepted for that voice. Words mean different things depending on how they are pronounced and some women reported being told to speak 'properly', with the 'correct' accent. I speak therefore I am, but what happens when that speech, that being, is not quite right? The embodied aspects of class, such as accent and appearance, are clearly demonstrated, as are the enduring effects of these, which Cathy connects to (not) 'coming out'. It would seem that for Cathy the dominant recollection of her time at school is of not fitting in terms of class and so not even trying to broach the subject of sexuality. A double silence, a double discomfort.

Cathy's comments, like so many others, links the embodied and emotional aspects of class in school with the objective and material components, as charted throughout this chapter. A feature of all interviewees' comments were 'dealing with the consequences', managing and resisting the devaluations of them, their families, their areas – what they were, what they wore, where they came from, where they could go and who they could be, positionings to be negotiated, 'achieved' and resisted in terms of both sexuality and class. Such mediations affected realisations and identifications, moving between the 'obvious', the comparative 'other' and the socially il/legitimate.

A lot is learnt at school and not all of it is Maths, English and Chemistry. The experience of education sticks, after all it takes up at least 10 years, which is a long time to feel undervalued, sidelined and written off. As the women I spoke to have clearly illustrated the school system works on the common denominator, as long as it is not too common. (Working)class and (homo)sexuality are often perceived to be unwanted visitors at a middle-class heteronormative educational tea party. This was clearly illustrated in the women's attitudes to and recollections of education and schooling. Their narratives of education are often narratives of 'failure' and missed opportunities; their stories represent the intersection of class and sexuality even if the official literatures often do not. This chapter has shown the ways in which class circulates across social settings, from a young age, made 'obvious' in interviewees' interactions in their everyday family and school settings. The following chapter examines interviewees' work experiences.

4
What Now?

Here I will explore, mostly retrospective, accounts of immediate post-school transitions and continued experiences of un/employment, seeking to put class back in to the analysis of lesbian lives, albeit in a more nuanced manner, which takes into account individual agency, identification, dis-identification and classed embodiment: the signifiers and markers of classed struggles, resistances and responses (Lawler, 1999, 2002; Skeggs, 1997). In highlighting the dual operation of class and sexuality in the lives of working-class lesbians as they left school and home and entered the workplace (or did not), the lived interconnection between these two categories becomes apparent, not simply as an 'add on' but rather as a concrete, constantly negotiated material and subjective process, with real and felt consequences, reaching beyond and encompassing schools, workplaces, unemployment queues and classed and sexualised emotions.

The relationship between sexuality and economic status has been explored previously: Dunne (1997) claims that there is an inter-relationship between lesbianism and financial independence – being a lesbian calls for 'economic achievement' and requires career planning with a view to establishing financial independence; it entails a well thought through plan in developing a 'lesbian lifestyle'. But what then for working-class lesbians who may be excluded from such career strategies by virtue of their uneasy and unequal location in terms of both sexuality *and* class? For those who lack formal qualifications, Dunne (1997) suggests that manual work remains a popular path upon which to establish financial independence and career choices. Although some women I interviewed did work in male-dominated manual sectors, most did not and those who did rarely experienced this as comfortable or financially beneficial. Instead their choices and experiences, both immediately after school and beyond, were informed by continued tensions and constraints around class, gender and sexuality; less economic achievement and more of the same.

My findings concur with those of John and Patrick (1999) who document the extent of social exclusion among lesbians and note the ways that this group faces exclusion from the schooling system, and the real and devastating financial and emotional cost that often accompanies this. Most women in my study eventually, if not immediately after school, engaged in low-paid, 'feminised' and often insecure work, which contrasts markedly with Dunne's findings. The differing results, no doubt, are due to different studies, conducted in different times and locations, with different people – and for different and distinct purposes and so my point is not to discredit Dunne's (1997) findings, which do still point to the connections between sexuality and materiality. Rather, my purpose is to divulge and describe the 'difference' that class makes to lesbians' post-school transitions. While Valentine et al. (2003), in drawing attention to the vulnerability and marginalisation of lesbian and gay youth as they move from schools, homes and into scene spaces and workplace, suggest a deficiency in previous structuralist models of the 1970s and 1980s, which relied too heavily upon class positions as shaping youth transitions, I am suggesting the necessity of not removing, on a wholesale basis, the continued relevance of class in understanding routes into adulthood for young lesbians.

Feminist theorising has produced good analyses of the continued gendering of the workplace, although Adkins (1995) argues that most labour market theories, including work produced by feminists, either ignore sexuality or consider it unimportant for the gendered operations of the labour market. To extend this slightly, it is also necessary to think about those not in the workplace – or in certain forgotten sectors – to include their experiences in the account of interconnecting social inequalities. Prendergast et al. (2001), in exploring the experiences of leaving home among young lesbian, gay and bisexual people, do highlight the ways that for many, such transitions are rarely smooth, linear or unproblematic and in fact they suggest a widening gap between those 'getting somewhere' and those 'getting nowhere'. In rejecting the idea of a youth underclass, they still point to the devastating consequences of being a 'have not', being excluded from typical and normalised transitory pathways by virtue of being a member of a 'risky' (LBG) group. In looking at homelessness among young lesbian, gay and bisexual people in England, Dunne et al. (2002) primarily focus upon the impact of sexuality, rather than, for example, class and thus the possibilities of exploring two interconnected inequalities, operating in the lives of lesbians, are minimised.[1]

While some theories argue for the endurance of class in explaining continued inequality and social experiences (Devine, 1992; Marshall et al., 1988), others point to structural changes, inexplicable through and departing from class; subsequently they argue for the necessity of re-thinking the relevance of class (Beck, 1992; Beck, 2000a,b; Castells, 2000; Lash and Urry, 1987, 1994; Urry, 2000). Against such conceptualisations I situate my own work within those debates that do concede the continued relevance of class, as a factor informing economic and social experience (Devine, 1992; Marshall et al., 1988) and I also see the importance of enquiring into class identification, rather than denouncing its relevance without empirical evidence: for the women I interviewed class was clearly and regularly spoken about, in all its variety and complexity. Rather than there being a comfortable 'mixing' of employment 'opportunities', characterised by 'fluidity' and 'mobility' (Urry, 1995, 2000a,b), there seems to be a 'fixing' and a re-churning of the poor in low-paid sectors (MacDonald and Marsh, 2000). But try telling them that at the Job centre.

In analysing many aspects of working-class lesbians' lives and in seeking to situate my research in the broader literatures and debates on sexuality and class, I have constantly avoided a deficit model whereby working-class or lesbian identity is inevitably seen as problematic, while at the same time striving to represent potential problems in all their diversity and intricacy. Women gave me an account of their struggles with un/employment and the emotional and economic consequences suffered as a result, highlighting their own desires for something better – not many people put 'member of the underclass' on their CVs. Opportunities, such as voluntary work were occasionally seized upon as a 'way out', as something taken up in recognition of its best–worst status. Unfortunately such experiences could rarely be capitalised upon at an economic level. Voluntary work experiences, together with family networks of support do not form a bank of social capital to be drawn upon (Putnam, 1993); instead such strategies often indicate limitations upon employment 'opportunities', a case of getting what you can where you can.

Both class and sexuality were negotiated in – and out of – work, where structural and interpersonal positionings were daily experienced, performed (Adkins, 2000; Hoschild, 1983), recognised and misrecognised (Skeggs, 1999, 2001): there was an awareness amongst interviewees that what they did for a living, both in the past and in the present, positioned them in class terms while there was a simultaneous rejection of being told that what they did and who they were had no value. The women I interviewed had agency, opinions and choices and their powerful voices should alert us to this. Many women resisted prevailing opinions of them as 'failures' while in school, the labelling of which is widely recognised as a classed operation (Mac an Ghaill, 1994; Skeggs, 1997) but which also has relevance to the consideration of lesbian identities (Epstein, 1994; Renold, 2000). Here I look at the 'choices' of employment, or unemployment, faced by many women upon leaving school. Having already been deemed 'failures' in school, many women left with few qualifications and entered low-paid jobs, Youth Training Schemes or voluntary work – the choices they made were constrained by class, gender and sexuality. The women I spoke to made choices within constraining circumstances, actively deciding on their best move, or their 'way out'. Often this was as much about avoidance, evasion and escaping as it was about possibilities, progress and security. Evading the social security, avoiding the army, escaping the fish factory, never being 'under' class or part of an 'underclass'. It was also about being 'realistic' – knowing your place, knowing the problems in changing this. 'Vulnerability' characterised these movements, and indeed fixed the women in these positions, through stigma and poverty; a vicious 'Catch 22' with no clear get out clause – how then to move from 'working-class lesbian' to 'flexible', 'mobile' worker? Across the women's post-school transitions and continued employment experiences, both class and sexuality interrupted and channelled their job choices and their experiences of the workplace – it was often not a straightforward journey, or transition, from A to B.

And what would you like to be when you grow up?

Most women did not experience a straightforward transition from school to work or to university. Rather than a linear progression, their immediate post-school experiences were characterised by unemployment and low-paid, unskilled, feminised labour,[2] which supports – and classes – Glendinning and Miller's (1992) claim that women are more likely to be employed in 'pink-collar ghettos', doing poorly paid, part-time, insecure work. The vulnerability is evident through working-class lesbians' experience of unemployment and rapidly changing and unstable low-paid employment. Indeed, many women's transitions were characterised by uncertainties, fears, disruptions and limitations.

These limitations were re-produced through the women's school experiences and in the broader societal structuring and intersection of class, sexuality and gender inequalities. Many women were deemed 'failures' throughout their school careers, negatively impacting upon their choices; this judgement was reiterated in post-school experiences as structural inequalities and expectations devalued their abilities, ambitions and choices. In making a transition from school to often precarious locations women 'accepted', negotiated, and challenged social expectations of them, whilst also encountering economic barriers and physical limitations. They moved through insecure positions and without economic and cultural capitals, the resources of class (Bourdieu, 1984), which could offer protection from uncertainty.

Lack of formal qualifications and negative school experiences channelled women into already restricted options and career guidance became a matter of telling many interviewees which 'dead end' job was ideal for them. The economic imperative of having to work was negotiated alongside the lack of positive guidance and support, generating confusion and anxiety. Sharon's options were seemingly circumscribed by what she could not do – as well as knowing she would have to do *something*. Her rapid changes in the occupational direction are determined through avoidance and renegotiation:

> So I left school with the view of my mum that 'You've to get a job, nobody's going to keep you for nothing'. So when I went to school you could leave school when, I was 16 in November so I could leave at Christmas if I wisnae staying on for the exams. The teachers were quite glad to get rid of me, em, I left the school and got a job straight away in a bakery, so that was that, I had a job and it was an apprenticeship, 4 years, once you'd been onto the second year they sent you to food technology college, which then panicked me 'cause then I would have to start to *read and write*. So I worked in the bakery for 18 months and then went onto working on the buses. (Sharon)

Negative school experiences, where teachers are quite 'glad to get rid of you', especially, as in Sharon's case, in time for Christmas, affected post-school transitions, not just because of lack of qualifications but also because of the adverse emotional impact which 'failure' produces. Feelings of discontent and disillusionment were widespread. Jeannette illustrates this bitterness and disappointment, taking the form of an educational cliff-hanger with no easy answer:

> What was I gonna do? You know, was I gonna learn clerical work, you know, I just couldn't picture myself doing these things. But I was so

disillusioned as well with the education system, I don't think I could have gone back into it in any case, because I was just really angry and really bitter. I felt really, really let down. So I just kicked around on the dole for a long time about 7 or 8 years and spent a lot of it down here, getting trashed, you know, just running around. Not living here but running around here. Being angry. (laughs) (Jeannette)

Jeannette's expressed anger contrasts with some women's voiced satisfaction with their post-school experiences, although this was often talked about in the context of what could have gone wrong, where they could have 'ended up', walking a tightrope with a real chance of falling off. For others, unemployment was seen as the follow up to school, being precisely what happened to siblings, as Jill (28, Edinburgh) points out: 'All my brothers and sisters, the main thing was you left school, signed on, got a flat from the council'. This is therefore what Jill expected as it had proven to be realistic, a well-used route already outlined, tried and tested.

Yet, Jill's account also demonstrates the risk arising from occupying a disadvantaged labour position, where Jill for the first time, on a minimum and insecure wage, feels 'loaded', but still cannot pay her rent. She is unsure whether I really want to hear of her experiences, perhaps pointing to the expectation of such struggle; given that it is expected it seems unworthy of comment. Why point out the obvious?:

Do you really want to hear this? Well see when I was 18 I got a job straight after school, I was working in a bar, it was everything, the cook, the cleaner, the bar maid, everything. I worked all the time, I worked 9 shifts a week back to back and it was fine, I had loads of money 'cause I never paid my rent. I just got my wages in cash every month, I had no bank account or anything like that ... But then when I was about 7 months pregnant the restaurant burnt down, fucking burnt down, I was there when it happened and I was just working up until I couldn't work and then I would go onto maternity benefits but the restaurant burnt down and they let me go. (Jill)

Jill, who has few employment rights, demonstrates her anger, while Sharon speaks of her ability to manage possible options via her mother's employment position: 'The only reason I got that job was because my mum was an active trade unionist'. Informal assistance took the form of family members and friends advising of possible jobs. Here, several women spoke of being 'lucky' – which highlights their continued vulnerability and does not replicate the privilege of knowing the 'right' people. Sharon points to the 'favours' received through her mother's employment, as does Grace. However, instead of viewing this as an ability to capitalise on existing networks and generate social capital (Putnam, 1993; Weeks et al., 2001), I would suggest that a different analysis is required, given their entry into workplaces on a low, and still precarious, level:

> Then my friend got me a, I was unemployed, I got sacked actually from the last job that I was working in retail and, eh, my friend said, 'Look, I can get you on this YT scheme'[3] and I was 17 at the time. (Grace, 30, Edinburgh)

Little economic benefits are gained from this form of 'networking', which also fails to impact upon or prevent the regulatory constraints and punitive measures enforced in employment centres and other benefit agencies. These processes highlight the local manifestation and negotiation of structured, political decisions, increasingly targeting so called troublesome and de-motivated youth. Instead of receiving help from the expected sources (e.g., employment centres), these were negatively experienced, placing working-class people into working-class jobs, or at least trying to, as Elaine highlights: I thought 'Right, I've got to go' and plus the dole were pressurising me to go and get a job at the first factory. I thought 'I'm not going to get trapped in a job at the fish factory up here' (Elaine, 37, Highlands).

Youth Training Schemes were instigated as a way of dealing with youth unemployment, to little avail, as Michelle explains. Nonetheless, she is able to challenge her being positioned so and to 'escape', like Elaine, to get out before the going gets worse:

> I left school at 15 and I thought I would get the whole summer off and was told I would have to get a job, you have to pay your way. I was gob smacked that I had to pay my mum to live in the house. In those days it was YOP schemes, you know, Youth Opportunity Programmes and it was £16 or something ridiculous like that, it was really shit money and I had to hand over half of it to my mum. They were 6 month schemes and I did two then I decided I'd had enough of Fife so I just fucked off and packed a rucksack and went travelling, spent the next 20 years doing that (laughs). I guess I decided that there had to be more than this and I didn't want to work in shitty jobs for £1.19 an hour. (Michelle, 37, Edinburgh)

Despite constraints, such as choosing between £1.19 an hour or 'fucking off', opportunities, such as participation in voluntary work, were grasped. Voluntary work placements were sometimes seen to offer a chance to move away from their area, as well as potentially providing access to future careers paths. The choices which the women made, and make, should be placed within the context of the constraints upon them, while also acknowledging their ability to negotiate often difficult circumstances caused by the structural inequalities which they are subject to as working-class lesbians. For example, there are gendered and sexualised expectations placed upon these women that are class specific, operating with classed effects. Michelle's post-school transitions were regulated by 'the money' in so far as her options were driven by an economic imperative as well as economic constraint. Pam, Michelle and Fiona all got involved in voluntary work; they were motivated and did not need to undergo character reform via a 'Welfare to Work' scheme (Kefalas, 2003; MacDonald and Marsh, 2000; Reese, 2005; Zweig, 2000). Voluntary work was undertaken for political reasons and/or as a way of moving out of their immediate areas and circumstances, a chance to help others and themselves at the same time. Fiona moved into an anarchist co-operative, Pam went to work at a Catholic boarding school and Michelle chose Christian youth work over joining the army, exercising a preference for saving people rather than shooting them:

I left home at 16. I had two ways as far as I was concerned at that point, one was to join the army and the other was to get involved in the church. I had a vague interest in the church simply 'cause there was a kinda social aspect to it, they were a bit touchy feely and that was quite nice. So it was church or army and I thought 'Mmm kill people or save people?' and I decided I really couldn't do the army thing, I liked the whole idea of mud and guns and hey! But I thought 'not convinced'. So I fucked off to do kinda Christian youth work and I never ever threw my heart and soul into it, it was a way of getting out of ... a way of getting out of Fife, a way of fucking off, getting out of that kind of life that I just felt alien to. I thought 'I don't have to stay here, I don't have to do this'. I looked around me and I saw people getting into this spiral of ... . I don't know what, and not in a judgmental way *at all*, really, seriously, but just like 'That's ok but I can't do that, ever!' I didn't know how else to do it, I needed a safe way of doing it, I couldn't, I'd never do it on my own. (Michelle)

For Michelle, voluntary work is viewed as a safe and secure option, made in recognition of limited choices – less risk than joining the army, better than staying put. While laughing and making a joke of the decision-making process, Michelle is also very careful not to denigrate the decisions of others; her own movements occur in tension and conflict, rather than ease and comfort. Although Michelle speaks of voluntary work as a 'way out' she then notes the way working-class people are utilised in this service (later describing the disadvantages incurred through 'only' having (long-term) voluntary work experiences rather than formal qualifications):

> I got involved in youth work and got put in projects that involved drug work and because I was very, you know, one of the masses, I wasn't coming from a social work '*Oh, hello!*' [accent] perspective, you know, I knew it, heard it, seen it, done it. I suppose it's that thing, one of the masses so I was kinda popular. (Michelle)

Michelle is put in projects, being typecast as 'one of them'. Being 'one of the masses' in this context involves compromise and concession, not equal give and take; working-class experience is extracted and put to use, the price to pay for 'moving on'.

In looking at the ways young lesbian, gay and bisexual people move on, Dunne et al. (2002) note that parents can provide – or deny – crucial financial help in such transitions, and suggest this is particularly salient in the context of sexuality, where, given parental disapproval, support may be withheld (see Raffo, 1997). But this alone neglects the different classed abilities of parents to 'pay out' in such a manner – and the different abilities of young people, across sexuality and class, to 'move on'. Some women in my sample remained at home immediately after finishing school, although this was often problematic. Many had to share space (such as bedrooms) with younger siblings and contribute to household expenses; this period was not 'time-off' and comparisons with middle-class peers were made and resentments voiced. A year out in this context is a year out of work and in the top bunk, not the same as backpacking around Australia with a credit card and a return ticket (see Heath and Cleaver, 2003). Other women made conscious efforts to move away from home. Mavis highlights the importance of class factors in this transition: she attempts to hide her working-class self in order to generate a more positive (subjective and economic) result.[4] While trying to alter her classed embodiment, Mavis realises that she is ultimately misrecognised through it (Skeggs, 1999); the signs of class showed through and could be 'detected' by those in the know, those knowing where to place her:

> When I went to London I got a sense of relief that nobody would know that I was working-class anymore. They couldn't detect in my accent, but then what I began to understand was that middle-class people would absolutely, there was no fooling middle-class people they would *know* that I was working-class, no matter how politely I spoke. (Mavis)

Jude spoke of her desire to move away from home in terms of getting some space 'to live' as a basic need, rather than a creative or expressive desire.[5] Her choices are informed through sexuality and class, where the tensions of no/choice and moving/staying are lived out. Jude's language illustrates the imperative nature of her move, she is driven to leave:

> I hated my secondary school *so* much that, em, and not just the school in terms of sexual identity but I hated that my family life, em, in terms of having no money, in terms of sharing a room with my two sisters in a tiny council flat. I hated that *so* much that it, it wasn't even a choice. I mean there was a choice obviously in that I could have just stayed and put up with that but the choice was made for me in a way. (Jude)

Here Jude connects her 'choices' directly with her sexual identity and class position, noting the differential options which individuals have access to, an intersecting factor that is often absent in the analysis of lesbian lives. Maybe being a happy lesbian is easier if you don't have to share a bedroom with a younger sister and the accusing eyes of her Barbie dolls:

> I would maybe have been able to experience my sexual identity in terms of having a space in Glasgow, being in Glasgow, having my own space. Space wouldn't have been an issue 'cause I wouldn't have had to … it wouldn't have forced me to think about it, if I was middle-class. Em, I didn't want space to *express* my sexuality, I just wanted space to live … Perhaps other people, people that have their own rooms, didn't share with their brothers and sisters, people that money wasn't an issue, people that wondering where the next meal was going to come from wasn't an issue, you know. (Jude)

For Jude, the struggle isn't so much about expressing her sexuality but simply having a room, a space for possibility, be that sexual, classed or otherwise. This is a crucial departure from other studies on lesbian youth, which tend to prioritise sexuality as the most crucial issue of transition, with vulnerability and exclusion likely to arise from this alone – rather than as part of broader, interconnected locations. Broadening out the scope of a/typical routes into lesbian adulthood, other women I interviewed moved from home into heterosexual relationships[6] and marriage, which they themselves often explained as a consequence of the expectations placed upon them, as well as their own abilities in determining the best (classed) outcome:

> But when you worked in a factory and you were one of ten and you lived in the East End [of Glasgow], you knew your place, I knew my place. I knew the best I could hope for was a guy with a trade and that's what I got. I knew the best I could hope for was a job in Wilson's[7] 'cause they paid well. So I aspired and I got to that. You knew, it was all unwritten but I knew then that that was my little area and I wouldnae be allowed to step out of that, I knew that! (Lynn)

Lynn 'just knew' what was expected and made her choices through a realistic awareness of this, expressing a sense that when 'what you see is what you get' there is not much point flicking through the brochure. However, the limitations involved could be devastating – Kirsty (26, Manchester) was previously involved in an abusive heterosexual relationship, feeling compelled to be there through lack of alternatives, including a lack of employment which made her financially dependent.[8] Both these women have made substantial changes in their lives, but these transitions were and are not linear and often do not have an easily achievable outcome.

Class and sexuality interconnect in the lives of working-class lesbians as they move from school and/or home settings into – or out of – the workplace. On the whole, the empirical evidence presented describes remembered accounts, some more recently remembered than others. But they were all powerfully expressed, emotional and emotive accounts, with obvious enduring outcomes. I would therefore assert the need to further investigate the connections between materiality and sexuality, established by authors such as Dunne (1997), Valentine et al. (2003) and Dunne et al. (2002), with specific attention to the 'difference' that class can make in economically – and emotionally – 'achieving' a 'lesbian lifestyle'. There are continued classed differences between the 'haves' and the 'have nots'; attention to the classed voices and experiences of lesbians themselves, whether current or remembered, serves to demonstrate the importance still accorded to class and the agency, interpretations and resistances which individual actors can make as they move through social space and through the life course.

Jobs for the boys (and girls?)

Dunne (1997) demonstrates that for lesbians who lack formal qualifications a popular career path is male-dominated manual work, such as the Armed Forces, transportation and garage work, yet only a few women in my study worked in such occupations. Unfortunately, experience of such employment was still adversely affected by negative assessments and discriminations, often manifest in attacks against the 'unfeminine', 'masculine' appearance of the women who did these jobs, which influenced their enjoyment of their chosen occupation. Holliday notes that dress is intricately linked to queer employment patterns: 'the armed forces created opportunities and possibilities for queer men and women to earn money and leave home, to inhabit single-sex space, to engage in non-sex specific occupations, and to dress in a particularly codified way – in uniform' (1999: 477). While some women did speak about workplace uniforms, these were more often 'feminine', care-assistant dresses, rather than manual overalls – and it was an overwhelming discomfort and mis-fit with their identities, sexual or otherwise, which was reported in 'dressing up' to go to work (Holliday, 1999).

There was often a lack of investment in the 'professional', workplace identities. Many spoke of disliking and resenting their work – this was particularly true when considering the physical and emotional aspects of some work, deemed 'risky' or unhealthy. Many women were 'vulnerable' not only through their lack of choices but also through the type of jobs which most had 'chosen': the maze of employment is not always kind to those who get caught in it and their accounts often departed from the progressive career paths mapped out by Dunne (1997). There was an awareness of the constraints upon 'choosing' their desired job, such as formal qualifications and other knowledges and capitals, while still having ambition and drive to get what they wanted. Often these requirements were basic and necessary but 'nice' things were desired, 'material things', things which may be taken for granted. Sharon's account highlights the significance of class in her desire to construct an 'alternative' 'lifestyle', challenging the sole equation between sexuality and desired (and achieved) lifestyle:

> I always wanted to drive a bus, it was a bit of a sad ambition! ... You huv tae huv the driving power though. My jobs were all determined

because I wanted to buy a hoose, I wanted to go on holiday, I wanted to buy a car, I wanted material things. The job was determined by two factors: (1) How much money I could earn and (2) Did I have to read and write in it. So if I'd had the support when I was younger, being dyslexic, then I'd be pushing for another job. I couldnae dae it 'cause I couldnae read or write. (Sharon)

Like Sharon, only a couple of other women previously or currently, did manual work (Sally, 37, and Jo, 30, both worked as gardeners) and spoke of their experiences and the reactions towards them in male-defined employment. Sharon tells of her experiences of cleaning buses in the 'black squad'. She negotiated this male environment, taking opportunity of the things she could do in recognition that other jobs would be unavailable to her. The structural conditions of gendered labour markets, as emphasised by Hennessy (2000), are vividly highlighted in Sharon's embodied actions. Male colleagues offered a degree of paternalism and 'protection' and Sharon believes her lesbian status further protected her within the black squad, with the help of some wellies; 'performing' heterosexual femininity was undesired and unnecessary:

Went to the black squad where you wore overalls and wellies and you worked with men and the women, either cleaning out the buses or cleaning out the pits where the mechanics would take the buses over to … We were called the black squad 'cause we were dirty all the time, 'cause we were doing dirty jobs. They done the kind of office cleaning, they didnae wear the overalls and the wellies … You know, they were quite protective and because I was young, usually you didn't have such a young person on the black squad and I went to it because the wages were good. So I found it ok working with guys but I think being a lesbian helped as well 'cause I was quite happy to be mucking in there and I don't think if you wanted to wear make-up and put nail varnish on you would have fitted in too well! (Sharon)

Sharon is able to 'fit in' to this male-dominated environment precisely because she does not conform to 'feminine' appearance or wear feminine attire; she then goes on to partly explain the absence of women from this 'dirty work', given the compulsory requirement of wellies and overalls and lack of nail varnish, which codes this work as 'masculine'. Bodies, appearances and economics intersect in this example, as illustrated by Sharon's previous statement about her pragmatic desire to get 'nice', material goods. Working in the black squad makes financial, and aesthetic sense, although it is unclear how well Sharon entirely fits in, with her lesbian identity being a protection as well as a secret.

Often women were judged incapable of manual work, as experienced daily by Sally (37, Manchester), a self-employed gardener. For Sally, gardening offers her the ability to work independently and with pride, resonating with Dunne's (1997) account – she is proud of the fact that she can carry out these tasks, despite the stares. While both Sharon and Sally may be 'unfeminine' in their work, for Sharon this fits with the task whereas Sally is seen as a 'misfit': make-up, nail varnish or even wellies – you don't stand a chance. The disjuncture between aesthetics and economics in this example combines to produce a weighty burden, rather than a subversive capitalisation.

There are many commonalities between my research and existing feminist research on gender and the workplace. For example, most women I interviewed experienced some occupational disadvantage whether this was low pay, gender divisions and discriminations, or poor and stressful working conditions. There is a lack of 'investment' in low-paid work because of the lack of reward. It seems it is difficult to get stuck in when you get nothing out:

> I got jobs in shops but it was all very not very well paid jobs. And then, I quite liked working at … the jewelers. I just used to give people things free, you know shoplifters – 'Yeah, just take it, it's crap anyway'. (Kirsty)

The necessity of working was often emphasised over work as choice or enjoyment as many women disliked their jobs but just 'got on with it'. Kirsty had previously engaged in sex work, while several others mentioned this as an option that they had considered: being a lesbian did not open up alternative work paths in this respect, sharply contrasting with the positive relation between lesbian sexuality and economics offered by Dunne (1997). Kirsty reflects back on her experiences, and the financial imperative in her decision. Notably Kirsty, like many working-class women, is managing and handling additional loads; her 'choices' are based on needs and involve risk assessment, a choice between one thing or the other, captured in her statement that 'sometimes if you need things, you have to do things that you wouldn't want to do'. Fiona also states that she has seriously considered sex work as an 'option'. Is this a proactive choice or simply the result of nowhere else left to go?:

> If you are poor you're more pushed towards considering entering sex work. I do think about it, one of my best friends was saying to me 'I'm

going to have to do a drastic job this year', she's probably going to
have to work as a pole dancer, there you don't actually take off you
clothes you just ride around a pole for quite a lot of money and I'm
sort of thinking 'Mmm' ... it still presents itself to me as an option on
quite a regular basis. (Fiona)

The 'choice' was often between working in an unsafe environment, or
not working. Some workplaces are more 'healthy' than others, contributing to emotional and physical well-being, other environments
must be negotiated despite the lack of these provisions. Often illness is
accepted and endured as part of the work itself, in manual and non-
manual work, a factor which Diane, 37, Michelle, 37, and Tracey, 23,
who had worked as care assistants/carers, all mentioned. Rita's narrative
has a timeless quality to it, this tale of work and illness and struggle
feels like it has been repeated a million times and yet is as moving
as ever:

But the struggle for me is I'm a hairdresser, I'm 53 years old, been
doing it since I was 15 'cause you left school when you were 15 in
those days. I've now developed osteoarthritis all through my body,
it's everywhere, it's in my hands, it's getting worse and I struggle ... So
to stand hairdressing well first of all this is gone [hand] and that's
worse 'cause I'm right handed and I've stood hairdressing all my life,
my back's bad. I can be at work sometimes and have to go in the back
and cry 'cause I'm in agony and I have to get the clients to go further
down in their chairs because I can't move my hands up. It's painful so
it's hard working. (Rita)

What happens to hairdressers who can't cut hair any more? For Rita, the
risks of not working are greater than those involved in working and she
manages this strain through lack of alternative options. The job 'choices'
and experiences open to the interviewees were highly gendered, even for
those who worked in male dominated spheres. In addition, their class
positions affected employment experiences, an aspect that has been
overlooked in the research on lesbians and employment (Dunne, 1997),
often leaving many with little real occupational choice.

Sign on and fall out

Many women spoke of the isolation and poverty suffered as a result of
unemployment, detailing the small sums with which they were

expected to live on and, sometimes, bring up a child. Often extensive knowledge of the benefits system was acquired and 'scams' made to allay the effects of poverty. Reference is made to the changing political climate, which increasingly seeks to punish those on benefits, emphasising the need for individual character, rather than structural reform – 'pull your socks up and get a job'. Those who, in re-starting work, are worse off than what they were on benefits highlight the ineffectiveness of governmental policy; the vicious cycle of poverty perpetuated by low wages and continued vulnerability. Despite these adverse experiences, many women were able to describe them with some humour and an ironic awareness of the impossibility of reconciling the 'Catch 22' situation of unemployment and poverty (Kefalas, 2003; MacDonald and Marsh, 2000; Reese, 2005; Zweig, 2000).

For some, the experience of unemployment was revealing and shocking – low-income employment was still seen as advantageous and a desired option, when faced with this prospect. However, for Kirsty, like many of the women (younger and older) the negative effects of long-term unemployment are, unfortunately, all too obvious: It's totally, it's really, really awful and people think that when you're on benefits, it's easier. It's not. It's a nightmare. It's a very depressing time.'

Jill speaks of her experiences as a single-mother living on benefits, making clear that her income only allows for the satisfaction of one of their needs, more so as her child grows up. Extensive knowledge and effort is required to negotiate the benefits system, which hides entitlement, making it difficult to recognise what is yours and pursue claims. In a bureaucratic 'Catch 22' it would seem that you need to know what to claim before you can claim it and if you were confused at the beginning, you will be more so by the end. It is to her credit that Jill is able to manage this, while doing so becomes a matter of 'survival':

> I knew what benefits I was entitled to, what I could get 'cause I was pregnant as well it entitled me to anything. So for the last 2 months of my pregnancy I got cheques from the dole coming in every week, maternity grant, this and that. So it was fine to begin wi'! (laughs) ... Being on the dole was fine for me 'cause I had a wee girl so when you've got kids you're entitled to full housing benefit and you're entitled to however much a week and if you're in any debt they can take it off your benefits, so you don't even have to think about shit like that. I got loans and grants every 26 weeks, I knew how to fill them in so I kinda went through the entire benefits system.

Whatever they had I just grabbed, I never saved a penny of it but you couldn't, being on the dole is a survival thing, you don't live on the dole you just survive. (Jill)

Despite being aware of her entitlements, Jill was still in poverty and had to make harsh choices. These choices render Jill vulnerable to criticism from outside authority (as so often happens with single-mothers); her desired wants (such as cigarettes and alcohol) may not be seen as 'necessary', yet they are basic items which many take for granted, without fear of judgement and without making any sacrifices. Jill details this 'balancing act', the constant and never-ending negotiation of every day life:

It was fine where I was living and all that but the thing about just having no money and being in the house wi' the bairn, maybe going down to the shops and gettin' a carry oot, 6 bottles of beer or 3 bottles depending on how much money I had that week ... I mean 'cause it was literally a choice between 'Do I buy a packet of fags or does Katie need the money?' You know, she got her dinner money free but it's like trips all those wee things that's when it got really difficult. (Jill)

Re-starting work after a period of unemployment can be very difficult and is often not financially rewarding; benefits are withdrawn and rent and living expenses become unaffordable until the first pay cheque, which can often be a bridge too far. Previous debts are also recalled, and demand notices issued. Jill humorously speaks of the continued economic hardship faced when entering the workforce as previous debts had to be repaid and housing benefit and hardship loans were suddenly stopped:

I ended up with a grand and a half on my switch wi' nae job, the bank were going nuts but I was saying to them 'I'm on the dole, what are you going to do? I don't own anything.' They were really pissed off but once I got my job they were like 'Start giving us the money now or we'll arrest your wages.' ... So I worked out all my incomings and outgoings and rent and she [lone parent adviser] said 'Right, so you should have £40 a week.' I was like 'What? Is it worth getting a job?' Then I had to pay for school dinners, I had to pay for all that stuff and school uniforms. I had to start paying for prescriptions for me and things like that, £40 a week, I must've had this look on my face, I'll never forget she was like 'Look honey this is life.' I was like 'Do I get a grant at Christmas?' (laughs) (Jill)

As well as having adverse economic effects, a somewhat ironic outcome, entry into employment produces subjective discomforts. Jeannette speaks of her difficulty in getting used to a workplace environment, feeling that she was 'seven years behind everybody else in terms of their development and how they related to society and the workplace and all of that kind of stuff'. Jeannette's account reveals the emotional and social effects of long-term unemployment; the individual is made to feel that their experiences do not count – lacking a CV they lack a self and are 'under-developed'. What counts are qualifications and a nice neat employment history, none of your dubious 'jobseeking'.

Despite this, many women were also able to resist and challenge these same processes. For example, in contrast to the isolation experienced by Jill, Jeannette reflects on the support received by those in similar circumstances, notably under a different political climate – a feeling of all being in the same boat, even if that boat has a big hole in the side:

> Well, there was a lot of people in the same situation. I mean, you can't like, obviously you couldn't go out for meals and stuff like that. But, you know, it was also an age thing. At that age, you're just kind of dossing around, a total lack of existence. Like just crashing on each others floors and sharing stuff, you know. It wasn't, I mean, it was bad in terms of not being able to afford clothes, not being able to afford food, having to do loads of scams, you know. We had to do scams constantly to get a bit of extra money. I used to go out some nights shoplifting all the time. Those kind of things, you know, just a lot of scamming. (Jeannette)

Jeannette's unemployment occurred in what she described as a more politicised, critical and supportive environment during the 1980s' 'Jobs Not Bombs' and 'Coal Not Dole' UK campaigns. There was a rejection of the 'system' that had rejected her (i.e. the schooling system which made her leave when she 'came out'), an opting out and acting up:

> Well, I was constantly poor. At that time, there was a certain kind of dignity about it as well because politics you know, there was lots of stuff around. There was all the unemployed workers centres, you know, the trade union movement, there was all these campaigns, you know, Jobs not Bombs, you know. There was a certain amount of kind of romance I think to it. It wasn't romantic when you were having to move out your, you know, fifth flat in four years because once again

you had blown the housing benefit or you couldn't pay the electricity, do you know, and none of that was particularly romantic ... there was a certain thing around about, you know, being pure, you know, not colluding in the whole capitalist patriarchal empire ... I had felt I'd been so let down, I just refused, I think, to kind of compromise. It was a case of 'Well, what the fuck have you done for me? Why should I?' You know, and the notion about authority and stuff that was very much, you know 'I've been let down, so fuck you all.' (Jeannette)

But at the same time Jeannette positions herself as an individual 'failure', lacking confidence and motivation and relying on misplaced working-class 'romanticism', when in fact she had 'no skills, no idea how to go about doing things'. However, other 'creative' responses to unemployment, and the possible stigma of this, were generated, though not without fear of being found out. Nobody wants to put 'idle looser' on their CV, not when 'career re-evaluation' covers a multitude of sins: 'I spent eight months unemployed, doing "freelance work" as I put on my CV (laughs)' (Sukhjit).

Some women became unemployed when employers found out about their sexuality. With little workplace protection or safeguards, employers could choose to discriminate – and did. This highlights the ways in which class and sexuality mediated the women's 'choices'. Amy is quick to laugh these judgements and discriminations off, ridiculing such ignorance and pretension, while still suffering from them:

I was just talking to somebody in the shop and stupidly mentioned it, so the father found out. Oh my! (laughs) he started going aff his heid 'We can't have people like you', 'cause it was quite an upmarket butchers it wisnae like Lawson's round the corner, people came there to buy minced up steak for their dogs! It was a really good butchers. Hill Top is quite an upmarket place, it's a retirement town and there's a lot of money in it and they just couldn't have someone like me working there, how terrible, how dare I be a lesbian! How dare I seduce his daughter, he was like that. So I got two weeks notice, he paid me two weeks notice and I'd two weeks to get out the flat, so that was it. (Amy)

The unspoken and implicit reactions are just as effective in causing unemployment – women were alert to both overt and 'subtle' homophobia. Getting and keeping a job is not easy at the best of times and not many employers list being a working-class lesbian in their must have criteria.

Water cooler sexuality

Various workplaces were often viewed as restrictive environments, especially apparent in the required workplace performance, which often involved presenting a specifically heterosexual (and classed) image (Holliday, 1999; McDowell, 1997; Skeggs, 1997). This was particularly true of office, shop and care work where many women worked. Many women sought to manage their workplace presentations, seeking to modify and adapt the embodied signifiers of lesbian status, which could identify and 'out' them at work (Holliday, 1999). In contrast, other women deliberately signified their sexuality through their appearance; clothes were invested with meanings and had positive as well as negative associations (Adkins, 2000; Holliday, 1999). Nevertheless, the ability to manage appearances was mediated by subjective and material factors – the desire to feel comfortable, included and to 'fit in' was also an economic imperative. Just as the women's sexuality was read through appearance, it could also be misread and although this challenges any simple equation between sexuality and appearance (Adkins, 2000), the women's challenges to heterosexual workplaces, through the display of lesbian signifiers, were effectively erased by such misreadings. There is a contrast between being 'obvious' – and others being oblivious to this 'obviousness', while at the same time being too 'overt' could mark women out for homophobic discrimination.

Accounts of the regulation of workers' words, looks and attitudes imply that there is insufficient attention to workers subjectivities and the consequences of passivity and insincerity for self-image (Adkins, 2000; Hochschild, 1983; Leidner, 1993). This can be extended to the women in my study who often had to manage mis/recognitions and feelings of self-deception in their workplaces. Far from the 'transgressive' possibilities noted by McDowell (1997) many women in my study spoke about the negative economic and emotional effects of being read as a lesbian in the workplace. Knowing that you have the wrong look – as well as the wrong qualifications and experiences – adds to the sense of exclusion, demonstrating the regulation of 'workers' even before they enter the workplace.

For example, Alice speaks of her awareness of being read as a lesbian, signified through her dress and overall appearance. This is also discussed in class terms; her working-class embodiment also generates a sense of discomfort, of not being able to fit in. There is a contradiction between 'being' herself by dressing in her 'own' way and fitting in with the 'proper' presentations required, a contradiction which generates embarrassment and shame (Adkins, 2000; Holliday, 1999). The economic effects compound these emotional consequences: Alice believes her appearance signifies both her lesbian and working-class status and explains her current unemployment. In order to 'achieve' you have got to get a job and lesbians in ill-fitting jackets are not the most sought after employees, perhaps pointing to another aspect of the 'commodification aesthetic' highlighted by Adkins (2000):

> Eh, I think it is quite difficult for me to go to interviews 'cause I don't know what to wear, I don't have a wardrobe that's really suitable for interviews ... I do behave in a certain way and there's certain meanings with that, em, which I'm quite aware of and which probably do count against me ... I look quite gay I think, which is a good thing but I think interviewers are aware of that, that I don't wear a nice short skirt and tights and high heels, that all I do is wear Doc Martens and a pair of trousers, which is smart enough for me ... There's enough known about my way of presenting myself and common stereotypes about gay women. That they've got short hair, they wear white shirts, which is a stereotype I have myself, you know, flat shoes ... I don't know how to work within these rules of what to wear and where to wear it and some people do ... I'm constantly pulling at my shirt or playing with my jacket, so I look even more uncomfortable and even more stupid ... I've never had reason to wear those kinds of clothes ... I don't go into an interview thinking 'This is so obvious', it's something that's more subtle, it's something I think of later on.
> Y: When?
> A: When I don't get the job! Sometimes you go to an interview and you don't feel comfortable, you don't feel like you like the people or they don't like you. You do go 'Well why don't they like me?' it could be that they don't like my accent or they don't like my school shirt or they don't like the fact that I could be gay, which I think is, you can *read* that. Someone who doesn't know the signs might not think that at all, they'll just think 'She's just wearing a school uniform' but I'm aware of the signs and read them in other people so I assume people read them in me. Of course I try to think of reasons why I'm objectionable or why I didn't get the job, that's something that occurs to me. (Alice)

From Alice's account the determining of 'who can wear what and thus who can be what' is strongly demonstrated (Holliday, 1999). Alice makes conscious efforts to avoid being too 'obvious'; her avoidance is, however, very different from dis-identification. Alice herself says that looking gay is 'a good thing'; it is the consequences of this that Alice seeks to avoid. Gay is good but, in her view, at certain times getting a job is better. Sharon speaks of combining the practical requirements of her current job, as a health promotion officer, with the desire to signify sexuality – these items of clothes have been invested with meanings, and Sharon is literally able to capitalise on them. Her (classed) appearance is vastly different from that conveyed in Alice's 'school uniform' ensemble; this is a look, 'M&S blouses with cuff links', rather than Sunday best, a truly 'dykey style'.

Workplaces present themselves as 'neutral' environments where the presence of lesbians is often viewed as polluting and threatening to the 'natural' order of things, illustrating the pervasiveness of 'compulsory heterosexuality' (Rich, 1980). Many women's struggles for identification and recognition within the workplace were mediated by both 'subtle' and 'overt' homophobia. A subtle but powerful form of homophobia occurred in the silencing of experiences and many women were often 'complicit' in this silence, producing contradictory feelings around self-deceit and dishonesty. However, even vocal and explicit challenges, as well as open 'outness' could easily be incorporated and ignored in het-erosexual environments, through failure to take this seriously. Accordingly, many women's identifications were rejected and dismissed as a joke, which further highlights the position of lesbians in the workplace – as a source of amusement (Adkins, 2000).

Alternatively, Cathy makes deliberate and unhidden attempts to signify her sexuality in her workplace, she is aware of the meanings of the signs (dress, hairstyle) she deploys but her colleagues, in contrast, remain oblivious:

> It makes you wonder doesn't it? I mean I'm walking around now in essentially men's clothes, I get a crew cut every few weeks and no-one's realised I just think 'Come on guys, work with me!' (laughs). They've got no fucking idea, you know. There's somebody new started just the other week and they went 'Are you married?' I look at them like 'Ha! *No*' I mean what can you do, you don't want to spring it upon people, you like them to kinda work it out themselves and then they think they're dead clever! (laughs). They wont even come half way – you can try to come that far with them but if you come out to them it's just going to frighten them 'cause they'll have no idea. (Cathy)

The fact that appearance can be misread, or not even read, challenges any straightforward association between dress and sexuality (Adkins, 2000).

Effective performances are mediated through economic resources as well as 'sympathetic' audiences. There may also be mis-readings between class position and appearance (Skeggs, 1999, 2001); middle-class people may also 'dress down', although this is less likely to occur in a workplace setting. It is more likely that working-class people will have fewer resources to play with and 'perform' classed identities. The aestheticisation of work does not, it seems, 'afford these workers possibilities for cultural invention' (Adkins, 2000: 209) – or at least not ones which will be recognised and validated.

Cathy's 'overt' 'outness' is easily incorporated and accommodated within the heterosexualised work environment, while Michelle is aware that the humour she uses to disrupt heterosexism can be re-worked to re-produce more conservative meanings (Hawkes, 1996):

> I'm very happy to say things but nobody picks up on it when I say 'or girlfriend'. People are just going 'Oh ha ha! Michelle's so funny!' There's just no concept, people are just thinking 'Oh she's just being political', or a feminist, or a numpty. (Michelle)

The workplace is often thought to be 'neutral' and apolitical until the entry of the polluting, or political, 'other'. Tracey decided to challenge the homophobic climate of her workplace but in doing so it was she who was labelled as too political and 'too much', she was 'flaunting' her sexuality. Even if attempts at 'subverting' workplace norms are made these can be quickly accommodated and normalised:

> When I first started at the Club there was a few people that came over, then I had an argument with this guy. It was something in the paper about gays in the army and he was like that 'They shouldnae be allowed in', so we were arguing about it. So I had only been working there about two weeks and know those models in the index catalogue? I cut one out and stuck it on a bit of paper and wrote 'Guess who's coming out of the closet?' and I put my name under a wee bit of paper that you had to lift up. So I went into work the next day and the supervisor went like that 'There was a poster put up about you', I said 'I know, I put it up'. But this woman she still won't even look at me, she really didn't like it and she tore it off the wall and ripped it up and put it in the bin. I was called into the managers office and then, she was trying to give me a bollocking about it. But there's posters up, I don't know if you've seen them ... how folk have aids, as in hearing aids and stuff like that. I says 'You've got all of them

hanging up and I've got that poster hanging up myself, it's not that someone's done it for malice', and she was pure arguing with me. We spent ages arguing about the fact that it was no different to another poster and then she just gave in and said 'We'll just have to agree to disagree', so I just went out. (Tracey)

Agreeing to differ is not agreeing at all. It would seem that Tracey was being just a bit too out and her attempted subversions, while stirring things up somewhat, are reduced to individual disagreements. This in/visibility is also reflected in Jill's discomfort when a bisexual woman entered her workplace. The heightened discussion of sexuality meant that Jill could no longer blend in; what is challenging and empowering for one woman is disempowering for Jill, unwilling to be too 'obvious'. She may not want to get pushed into another's limelight, illuminated and perhaps shown up. This highlights the necessity of personal disclosure and outness in asserting difference, as well as the comfort of silence and invisibility:

It wisnae made noticeable until somebody else was there who was quite focused on it all the time. It was kinda like 'Can you not bring it down to sexuality all the time, can you just say that my bird's really pissing me off and your boyfriend's really pissing you off and that's it'. (Jill)

Often silence, is experienced as powerfully as outright condemnation. For example, Fiona speaks of the classed response, vocal or otherwise, of her work colleagues and notes the classed differences in being 'subtle' or 'overt'. Fiona's account demonstrates the interpersonal and embodied 'othering' between workers and the overlapping and intersecting sexual and classed dimensions to this:

When Agnes was saying 'Do you have a boyfriend' and I sort of said 'No' and I explained that I'm in a relationship with a woman and it prompted this big long story, she always brings in stories of her relatives at any given opportunity, she's like 'Oh Deirdrie ... ' and tells me a big long story about Deirdrie's struggle in coming out, one of her cousins, and how 'I always knew she was a bit different' (laughs) ... The other Agnes walked away, she sort of walked, physically walked away which is quite interesting and the other Agnes was saying 'You're not saying much Agnes!' (laughs) and she still didn't say anything. Certain things do register in my mind as being like working-class patters of conversation behaviour, like that kind of thing where something's a bit kind of, it was obvious that there was some sort of discomfort on her part there and I think it's quite a working-class thing just to make things really obvious like 'You're not saying anything', we can't just ignore that! We really now notice that Agnes has not said anything! (laughs) and she's still not saying anything. (Fiona)

Lisa actively 'announces' her sexuality and puts work colleagues in a humorously awkward position; the joke is on society and they can all have a laugh, while Kelly feels that such a challenge would not be possible within the middle-class climate of her work. She could make the joke but would not get the laughs. These processes point to the classed aspects of homophobia (Taylor, 2004b, 2005b); dis/comforts are mediated by classed notions of 'subtle' or 'overt' in/decency:

> L: We laugh and joke about it in the staff room, the conversation gets quite bad sometimes. Matt, the science teacher offered a KitKat to Joy the music teacher and he said 'Do you want a finger Joy?', he said 'Do you want one Lisa?'. I said 'I'm not taking one off you mate, sorry I'm gay didn't you know?' (laughs). Then Joy said 'Do you want one?', I said 'Oh yeah Joy, I'll take a finger off you any day but not him, he's a bloke!'. It's great fun.
>
> K: Yeah, I couldn't make it like that, they're much more stuffy and boring. They're very Mary Poppins. I get really annoyed, 'One will only drink filter coffee only', just irritate me 'cause all these pretensions. (Lisa and Kelly)

Often lesbians have to cope with more explicit and overt displays of homophobia as well as ignorant silence. In rejecting the advances of a male colleague, Jude's (31, Yorkshire) lesbian status became known, adversely affecting her employment status, while May (23, Yorkshire) was free, for a while, from homophobic harassment, as she did not conform to stereotypical notions of what a lesbian should 'be', 'appear', 'act' like. Like Jude, it was only when she rejected a male colleague that her workplace became difficult and uncomfortable. These numerous incidents point to the overtly (hetero)sexualised atmosphere within workplaces, which simultaneously sexualises and de-sexualises women by objectifying them and diminishing their choices. For May this results in a separation of work and home, as she seeks to establish her identity and 'who she really is' (Holliday, 1999). But 35 hours a week is a long time to feel not quite yourself.

Sexuality, like class position informs access to future and current jobs but, for Jane, her sexuality is experienced as more of a constraint:

> That's the first conscious decision I've made about hiding my sexuality, it's not hiding it, I'm just making a conscious decision not to exploit it. I wouldn't worry about going for a job and telling them I was working-class. I came from a working-class background but I would worry about going and telling them I was a lesbian. (Jane)

Some revelations are more shocking, more problematic, than others. Many highlighted the notions of threat and danger, applicable to specific jobs, which 'the lesbian' represents. Desire to work in these environments, especially in child-care settings, are constrained by recognition of the silences this would compel; yet as working-class women, caring often provided one of the more viable career choices (Skeggs, 1997). Economic rewards and employment choices are again mediated by and interact with emotional dis/comforts. Faye explicitly highlights emotive class processes, feeling the impact of class discrimination to be of more importance than sexuality: 'I think I've had more discrimination about where I live rather than on sexuality.' For Faye it is classed location and association which engenders misrecognitions but such judgements often combine both class and sexuality – swings and roundabouts with no soft landing.

The experiences of working-class lesbians at work highlighted the worth in combining materialist and performative perspectives on sexuality, and indeed class, given that class and sexuality intersect emotionally, aesthetically and economically in the workplace. The combination of materialism with a sense of the economics of performativity best explains working-class lesbians' subjective and material journeys through classed and sexualised environments. The performativity of identity was clearly demonstrated when discussing the appearance and embodiment of sexuality, utilising the work of Adkins (2000) and Holliday (1999): it was extended by classing workplace aesthetics, giving attention to the ways that bodies and identities are rendered un/entitled to occupy workspace through in/adequate 'performances'. Capitalising on the self, 'performing' at work, can be difficult when the performance is not that good, is self-deceptive and not economically rewarding. To be recognised as something is often also to be in receipt of material resources; systems of evaluation are deployed and these have real effects on material movements through space – and for individual movers (Bourdieu, 1984; Skeggs, 1999). There are material, embodied and subjective consequences of occupying both working-class and lesbian identities, affecting journeys through and within social space, as class and sexuality combine and collide in workplace settings, benefit agencies and in everyday settings. The next two chapters explore interviewees' sense of not/belonging in working-class 'home' space and lesbian 'scene' space, revealing an often uneasy occupation of these spaces, as insiders and outsiders.

5
Negotiation and Navigation: Emotional Maps

This chapter focuses on respondents' sense of place and their relations to the often undervalued territories that they inhabit, suggesting that space is constitutive of identity in terms of where it places people, both materially and emotionally (Reay and Lucey, 2000; Sibley, 1995; Thrift, 1997). 'Movements' through space are fractured by homophobia, as Valentine (1995) points out, but they are also mediated by classed dis/comforts. By re-claiming working-class territories as positive sites of self-identification the women I interviewed challenge the authoritative devaluations of their communities; their struggles for recognition and esteem both within and outwith their localities mirrors, yet differs from, other analysis on the importance of space and place in the reproduction of class (Charlesworth, 2000; Howarth, 2002; Nayak, 2003b). For interviewees, it was the spatialised intersection between class and sexuality which made their occupations in and exclusions from space both painful and pleasurable.

Rarely do analyses of sexuality and class, and their spatial manifestations, combine in such a way as to highlight interconnections and interactions. Binnie (2000) compares the management of particular classed spaces with the regulation of places of public sex, arguing that both the sex industry and the manufacturing industry are seen as polluting and unsightly, but this gives no indication of the effects this has upon the individuals who daily experience, use and live in these places. More generally, there is a lack of attention to the ways in which classed space is sexualised or sexual space is classed, yet discusses the spatialisation of class, situated in terms of geographical location; a location which simultaneously interconnects class and sexuality, apparent in Lawler's example of 'Essex girls' and 'Scousers', and in US terms 'white trash', 'hillbillies', 'rednecks', and so on (Wray and Newitz, 1997).

New technologies arguably intensify such demarcations, with websites on where to buy and where to avoid, and working-class areas represented in metaphors of drowning ('sink' estates) and defecation ('bog standards') (Burrows and Ellison, 2004; Reay, 2004). Such research pays attention to the ways in which classed space is sexualised (as sexual space is classed). For the working-class boys in Nayak's (2003b) research, location acutely featured in their positive self-positionings as 'Real Geordies', a spatially distinct 'sub-culture', yet there is a comparative absence on working-class women's spatial occupation and classed resistances, other than those studies that demonstrate avoidance, escape and dis-identification.

Research into lesbian and gay space has typically focused on scene space, and although there have been proposals for a re-conceptualisation of where lesbians are, and therefore who and what they can be, these still ignore class as an important component of everyday space (Bell and Valentine, 1995; Binnie, 2004; Valentine, 1995). The experiences of working-class lesbians, their relations to space and identities constructed therein, are all but disappeared.

I aim to rectify this erasure by exploring the means of navigation and negotiation interviewees deploy to find their way through everyday life. Everybody, by default of having lived, has a personal map of where they are, where they were, and the time in between. For some this map is more real, more enduring, than for others. Working-class areas are not only spatially marginalised but also increasingly depicted as 'sink' estates, symbolic of decay and degradation, and synonymous with an 'underclass' status (Murray, 1990). Ideas of an 'underclass' feature in both academic and political discourses (Bradley and Hebson, 1999; Campbell, 1993; Haylett, 2000; Haylett, 2001), perpetuating class inequalities as individuals become responsible for remedying their own situations (MacDonald and Marsh, 2000). This emphasis on individual character traits leaves structured disadvantage situated within working-class areas unchallenged. If it's a case of you are where you live, what happens when where you live is 'a bit rough'?

Places 'form an important source of meaning for individuals which they can rely upon to tell stories and thereby come to understand themselves and their place within wider society' (Thrift, 1997: 160). However, little consideration has been given to the possible challenges, limitations and negotiations in identifying with stigmatised spaces or communities (although see Howarth, 2002). Charlesworth (2000) deals with the consequences of poverty and class and the effects of growing up as part of a poor and stigmatised group, focusing on a particular town – Rotherham – in South Yorkshire, England. A 'thick description' of working-class life emphasises that the 'brute reality' of working-class life leads to the articulation of a culture of necessity, and to a passivity that can only be responded to by embracing the hard realities of the everyday life. However, Charlesworth does not pay substantial attention to gender, or indeed to sexuality, and his engagement with feminist interventions is minimal, mirroring a criticism made of Bourdieu's work: the 'habitus' of class, whereby class is instilled, entrenched, recreated and embodied, is also gendered and sexualised, generating a series of dispositions, attitudes and tastes (Adkins and Skeggs, 2004). The concept of 'habitus' allows a consideration of the lived, and often emotive, aspects of class, alongside the ownership of classed capitals (Lawler, 2004). My interviewees, far from having a 'culture of necessity', managed to invest 'working-class' (and 'lesbian') with positive value, while not understating the economic hardships faced. This positive, insightful and often humorous expression of class, and strong identification, provides a comparison with studies which show 'dis-identification' away from working-classness (Lawler, 1999; Skeggs, 1997). Furthermore, the idea of a more 'fluid' social structure fails to address the constraints upon individual mobility as well as continued working-class identification with, and location within, working-class communities.

Most, if not all women in my study challenged critical judgements by positively identifying with (marked) working-class spaces, revealing a re-assessment on their own terms, rather than subscribing to a 'middle-class'[1] estimation. This is not to evade the very real problems women experience in living within economically marginalised communities. Rather, I suggest that most women do not inevitably seek to 'escape' them – not everybody actually wants to live in Hebden Bridge.[2] Weeks et al. (2001) highlight strategies of networking and community building and the generation of self-consciously created communities whereby locally embedded constructions of capital compound familial resources. The ability to relocate to 'friendly' spaces with 'sympathetic' schools and supportive social networks is nonetheless affected by material inequalities. The overt optimism of the account of Weeks et al. glosses over potential exclusion. The concept of 'social capital' is deployed to speak of the ways 'non-heterosexuals' seek to resource themselves and their families, actively creating and embedding themselves in solid support networks. However, such a concept is devoid of the economic, which Bourdieu (1984) highlights through his conceptualisation of interconnecting social, cultural and economic classed capitals. Yet, where Weeks et al. (2001) lack a class analysis, Bourdieu (1984) fails to appreciate the significance of gender and sexuality.

Thus, it is not simply a matter of packing up and moving on, of imagining a new map and getting on with it. And without something or someone to show us around, friends, family, memories, knowledge, it can be very easy to become lost, to lose the skills of navigation. Here, class, sexuality and geography combine to produce secure feelings of belonging as well as tensions and resentments, compounded and augmented by intersecting capitals, played out in the context of everyday movements and (im)mobilities.

Sexuality, class and geography

The degree of 'comfort' in classed space can be mapped onto the level of comfort, safety and belonging within heterosexual space. Here multiple inequalities co-exist and regulate who 'fits in'. Working-class lesbians manage 'outness' within space, at times feeling unsafe, whilst many also explicitly and impressively challenge homophobic attacks, thereby attempting to change their social landscapes. For example, Rita humorously ridicules the accusations against her, whilst also highlighting a serious point about the 'kind of person' she is:

> We do get very, very drunk and we do shout a lot when we get out the taxi! And the neighbours don't like it, they've decided, because we go out a lot and because I allow my kids to have parties, we have actually proved that we are gay (laughs). That's what the nice Catholic lady across the road said! Her son's football kept hitting my window and I went out and said 'If that happens again I will put a knife through your ball', he said 'I'll tell my mum on you.' He did it again and I slashed his football. His mother came storming over, she said 'I suppose that's what you kind of people do!' I said 'What's my kind of people, I'm a mother, I have windows and doors, that's the kind of person I am – I don't want them smashed!' I don't see them anymore. (Rita)

Most women's views of their various locations were informed by their own and others' feelings towards their sexuality. Operating along a continuum, homophobic acts can be as 'subtle' as verbal abuse or as overt as physical attack (Corteen, 2002; Namaste, 1996; Munt, 2000). Silence can also be experienced as homophobic, as a refusal to enter into conversation with the 'other'. Several women were 'closeted' in their current locations but 'outness' should be thought of as a process, rather than a state of being ('out'), which is negotiated daily. To this extent all women had to negotiate and manage the straight places in which they lived, producing complex feelings around (self)deception.

There are dangers and difficulties, both practical and emotional, in navigating through different localities (John and Patrick, 1999). Sometimes the private sphere can offer a degree of protection against the outside: as Valentine (1995), Twigg (2000) and Gabb (2005) suggest, the home can take on a vital role as a lesbian social venue in particular areas. But middle-class lesbians may have more resources to protect themselves against discrimination – they can choose to re-locate to a more 'liberal', 'trendy' area, choose to enact their sexuality in a space they know is going to be more 'tolerant' (Weeks et al., 2001; Weston, 1995). This is not open to those who, like Lynn, lack the financial means to choose a different location and her anger and resentment at this 'easy option' is very clear. She is not staying put because of any notion of duty or pride, she is keeping her head down because there is nothing else to do:

> It depends where you live as well, if you're in the West End [of Glasgow] and you're trendy it's fine. If you're in Cranhill it's no fine, you'll get your windies put in ... I'm very working-class and I know that probably in working-class there's hellish prejudices, people are intolerant, attitudes that stink, racist, sexist, you name it, homophobic. It's very strong and there's a very thin veneer of civilised behaviour down there. Even in the middle-classes there can be a thin veneer. Ideally as well if I was going to move I would like to live in the West End with Mary 'cause it would be fine. But I'm not going to be able to do that 'cause I don't have the money to go and live in the West End, get a trendy wee flat. There's a bit of, you can hear it, resentment and upset about that. I'm going to have to live somewhere where it's not cosmopolitan, you're not able to be open because of consequences, because of fear of prejudice. (Lynn)

Lynn teases out the classed characteristics of homophobia; while working-class people are seen to be more blatant about discriminating, middle-class people are believed to be more 'subtle'. Participants in Moran's (2000) focus group research perceived the working-class to be key perpetuators of violence, leading him to warn against 'producing problematic correlations between the lower class and violence, in the context of a new underclass' (214). While I endorse this statement, my data suggests a more complex and conflicting perception of homophobia.

Amongst the women I interviewed there is a frequent desire to protect even working-class voices that would condemn them because of their sexuality. The middle-classes are perceived as displaying a liberal pretension; they may not voice their homophobia but it nevertheless remains evident and felt (Kadi, 1997). For those living in proximity to middle-class people, the classed and heterosexual judgments are more overt, challenging the equation of middle-classness with 'tolerance' and decency. Still, it is working-class lesbians who are labelled as 'indecent', overt and imposing on heterosexual and (middle)classed space.

Jill compares the respective attitudes towards her in two differently classed areas and claims that it is in the middle-class location where she suffered the most. Verbal abuse, jokes and stares were everyday experiences in this 'nice' space, culminating in the physical presence of a large group of youths camped outside her house, who were simultaneously doing nothing and everything; making their presence and opinions felt through numbers alone:

> It's funny, see where I live now, when I lived down in Morningdale it was £275,000 houses, all private, everybody else there apart from us owned their houses, we just rented and when I was down there I got all the kids giving me hassle on the promenade every fucking day, at one point there were fifteen of them camped outside my house and I was ready to go out with golf clubs and smack them on their heads but my sister stopped me ... So I got that down there and then I moved to the schemie-ist place I've lived in for a long time ... and that was fucking cool, nobody says a word ... I think it's 'cause in schemie areas they just chuck lots of people together so there's loads of gay people up my bit. You see people during the day and you're just like 'Oh my God!', there's me and Max going 'She's gay!', it's quite funny. It's mad that thing, that exposure thing, you know, nice people live in nice houses with a nice promenade, they're exposed to fuck all, they're exposed to nothing, they don't know any other part of life apart from mummy and daddy's parties, the people they meet there, they're quite extravagant. And then you go to schemie bam land where they couldn't give a shit as long as you dinnae steal their car. (Jill)

The 'differences' in the respective areas mean different things and it is in the middle-class area where Jill's sexuality symbolises a lack of 'standards' and 'decency', leading to homophobic attack, via spitting, shouting and scandal. Jill does not portray working-class areas as free from homophobia – but notes the multiple inequalities, tensions and hardships experienced there. These produce a more stressful, but also perhaps paradoxically, less introverted and less judgemental environment.

Homophobia does exist within working-class areas, but rather than being confined within certain areas, it seems to have multiple expressions, with differing effects and purposes. Like Jill, many respondents had to move from one area to another to get away from homophobia. Amy re-located, having been labelled as 'the lesbian' of the town. Interestingly, in this example, homophobia is equated with 'small town (working-class?) mentality' and 'naiveté' – this resonates with Binnie's (2000) claims about the distinction between 'queer cosmopolitanism' and 'provincial', 'unsophisticated' working-class sexualities. But where does this leave Amy? She inhabits neither a 'sophisticated' nor an 'unsophisticated' location, working-class, working to get away, working to stay put.

Most women lived in urban areas, only a minority of women came from rural areas and some remained there.[3] For Fliss and Elaine the rural climate of the Highlands generated a more insular, homophobic atmosphere, explained through the religious influence within the area. The respective differences between urban and rural locations were also discussed by the Manchester focus group, where the city was seen to offer greater diversity and exposure to 'differences', more anonymity and consequently more safety (Brekhaus, 2003; Weston, 1995). But Lauren, a member of the young person's group, notes that the feelings of comfort are not immediately achievable, as she has to negotiate the difference between rural and urban living:

> I don't know, I've just been brought up in like the countryside and I mean being out and doing things on my own. I mean my family's all out in the country, my mum doesn't come to Edinburgh all that often. There's none of my family or personal friends that live in Edinburgh so I've sort of had to find my own way about Edinburgh and stuff. I feel more comfortable here but I've not been brought up to feel comfortable here. I've just had to find it myself, you know. It's been a bit hard for me. (Lauren)

Feelings of belonging can be displaced through sexuality, class and geography but when moving from the Western Isles to Edinburgh, Shona felt 'protected' by her local community, who offered to defend her against city dangers. But Shona recognises such 'protection' may not always be extended:

> But no direct bullying or certainly coming out in [Island] didn't create any problems, if anything I had locals coming up to me in the pub

going 'Shona if you have any problems let me know', even when I moved down to Edinburgh I had a few people saying 'Any problems we'll be down to sort it', I've not taken them up on it, I've not had any hassle (laughs). But I don't know if that's people, I don't necessarily look like, whatever a lesbian looks like, I don't go out of my way to look butch and wear dungarees 'cause that isn't what I'm about anyway. I'm probably quite femme if I'm going to identify as any kind of lesbian it's probably quite femme. (Shona)

Others felt distanced from their own working-class communities as a result of re-locating. For example, although Kelly is currently living in a working-class area, it is not her area and she describes the sense of displacement that can be produced through movement, revealing that geographical mobility and class mobility are not necessarily the same thing:

But see you're a lot different Lisa 'cause you're still in your home environment, you come from Hull, you still hang around with your mum you know. I've, sexuality has moved me, I belonged in that group em, and what my class identity means as a woman, and as a straight woman it would have been assumptions that I would have got married, live close to my mum and have some babies, live in each other's pockets. But I'm alienated from that because I've felt myself actually moving further and further away and I don't really fit in this area, that's obvious on some levels to me. (Kelly)

Kelly feels she has been 'moved' and became removed, physically and emotionally, from her family as a result of her sexuality. Kelly is an active 'chooser' in this process but this does not mean it is an easy transition. The tension is spatialised, affecting feelings of not/belonging in both places. Just as sexuality is 'felt' (Valentine, 1993a), class can also produce feelings of being 'out of place', informing experiences and perceptions.

Valentine (1995) claims that heterosexism influences which urban areas lesbians choose to live in, avoiding areas where they think they will stand out, preferring areas where they can 'blend in'. She argues that spatial concentrations of lesbians are products of individuals coincidentally making similar housing and 'lifestyle' choices (Weeks et al., 2001). But not all lesbians can 'choose' this option. Valentine speaks of her inter-viewees as being able to avoid 'rough' and 'dangerous' estates but what one avoids is another's home. Crucially, social relations of class are embodied in housing 'choices': 'Housing exists not simply as a means to satisfy a need, it embodies a set of social relations' (Bell, 1991: 323). This continues even when there is movement between locations.

Negotiating the ladder

'Movement' often tends to be conceptualised in a straightforward manner – as up, down or across – and as something which is becoming increasingly easy to do (Urry, 1995, 2000a,b). Yet, in my study, movements were not easily, if ever 'achieved' due to the strong retention of class locality amongst interviewees. The ways that some women 'moved' again challenge current notions of 'upward mobility' – does swapping council houses constitute an upward 'escape' or is it in fact possible to carry on moving and yet never 'arrive'? The difficulties, but also the pleasures, in existing in working-class space suggest that the women should not be thought of as potential, or actual 'escapees': there is no need to go on the run when your home is not your cell.

Many women felt more at ease in working-class locations, being 'out of place' in middle-class space, and accordingly did not want to move. Others were unable to move even if they wanted to because of their financial circumstances. Lisa expressed a desire to move away, aware of this as a class judgment – the joke she shares is based on Kelly's suggestion that she is displaying pretensions (her refusal to watch TV is seen by Kelly as a 'pretentious' class judgement, while her desire to move is seen as realistic) and points to the idea that some of our needs are seen as more defensible, more valid than others:

> I would never move into a place like Brandon or anything like it again because I wouldn't want to live in that kind of environment in that kinda area. In our little street of 10 houses there's a drug dealer, there's this bloke who gets sectioned every few weeks 'cause he goes mad and throws things around, three out of ten houses are empty and the others have got massive families and they're alright. But that's kinda the worst area I'd put myself in … I don't know if that's a class attitude or what, 'cause you were saying that to me earlier weren't you? About what type of area that I'd live in, 'cause I don't want to live in a bad area, I don't want to move onto Brandon Road. [Kelly agrees]. You've got a problem with me not watching TV but you haven't got a problem with me wanting to live in another area? (laughs). (Lisa)

Moving away, or the desire to move away, can be seen as a 'pretentious' attempt to move somewhere you don't belong; 'habitus' is ruptured by these articulated and disputed tensions, where there is a desire to move but a feeling that something, some reality and sense of belonging, would be left behind (see Figures 5.1 and 5.2). Comfort, within location, is desired but not always attained. These desires may also be subject to (self)ridicule (and laughter), as the classed significance is recognised, something which has not been captured in either the account of mobilities and spatialised 'creativities' by Weeks et al. (2001), nor in Bourdieu's (1984) or Charlesworth's (2000) accounts of the spaces of 'necessity' or 'deficiency'. It is, however, important to remember the objective constraints against movement and the boundaries between and within areas, as affected by class and sexuality.

The means and the motivation

Physical and emotional investments made in areas can themselves be mirrored back onto resources or claims for resources. The ability to control and enact change in turn relies on economic and cultural capital, such as knowledge and confidence supported by economic security. More recent discussions of social capital depart from Bourdieu's (1984) framework: for Putnam (1993) social capital is seen as a resource generated through voluntary associations, which enhance civic engagements and support norms of reciprocity, as a resource to make claims upon space. Such usage individualises the structural causes of poverty; the poor are depicted as disadvantaged as a result of their failure to generate 'empowering' social capital. Instead, financial means inform and restrict abilities to capitalise on resources within areas, thus informing 'movement' and belonging.

The inequalities and tensions within shared spaces are apparent in judgements about 'standards' and 'investments', produced in comparison to the 'dirty' other. For example, Sharon makes explicit her investment in the area and is keen to present herself as a 'decent' member of the working-class, concerned with presentational standards, as against the indecent, lazy and incompetent 'other' (Skeggs, 1997). Living in Port Glasgow, Sharon invests in the locality but her investments are compared with those who 'sell out':

> But usually what you find is that, see people who've bought their houses, ex-council houses so they've bought them at a reasonable price and then they'll sell them, make a good profit and move on to a better area. Whereas if we all start to do that the area will just go down, it will be the people that are on low incomes, that are maybe

125

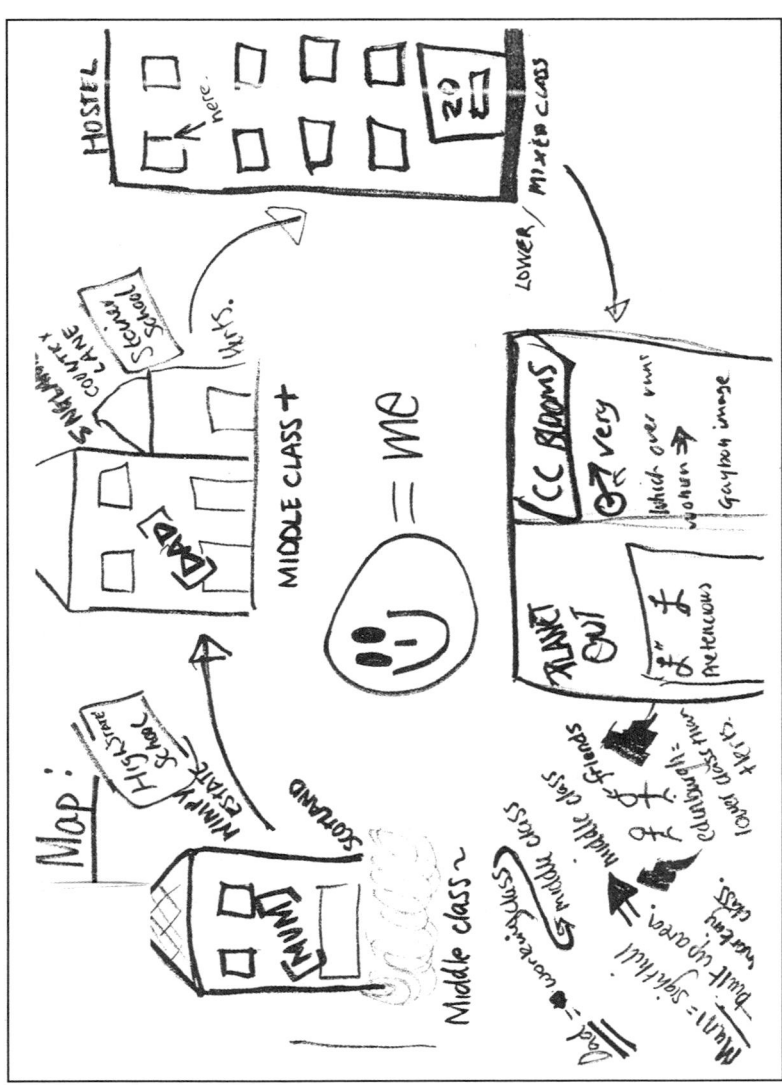

Figure 5.1 Vanessa's map.

126

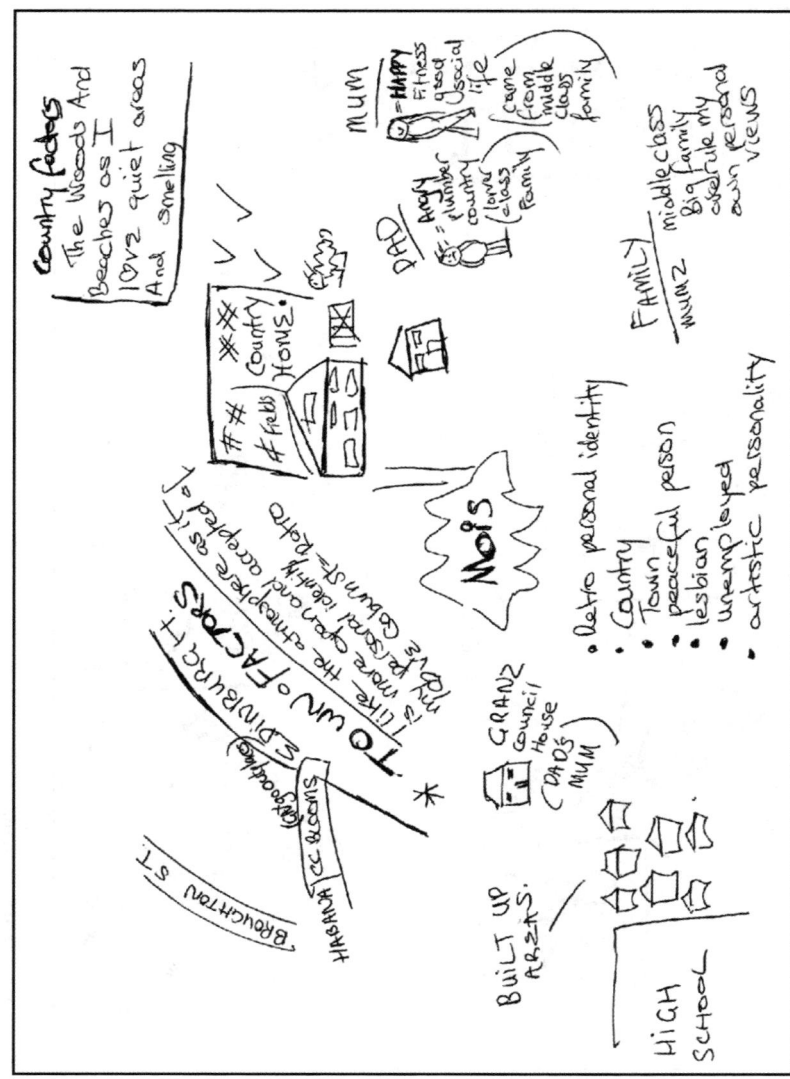

Figure 5.2 Lawren's map.

struggling to maintain a good area, it'll be people who won't lift up the phone to the council and say 'Hey, come and sweep this street', things like that. I think we should try and stay in a working-class area to try and bring, to keep the standards up, you know. (Sharon)

Hers is the language of duty, of keeping up the standards that the 'others' may not be capable of maintaining.

There has been long-standing criticism of working-class council tenants who 'sell out'.[4] This is significant in itself but can be contrasted with the 'fixing' of others who are unable to move and remain geographically and economically marginalised, as many reported.[5] Kirsty's sense of frustration and despair is reproduced throughout in the women's discussions about their homes and areas:

So I had no transport and when you're on £90 a week, you can't afford to get the bus but people don't understand these things, these problems, you know. Therefore me and my daughter, you know, are stuck in the house all the time or you just go to the local shops, which are like about 15, 20 minutes walk away. But, yeah, I mean, there is a big town ... which is like a bus ride away. But like I say, it costs money to go there. I mean, some weeks I would have enough money at the end of the week for a loaf of bread. (Kirsty)

Kirsty is quite literally stuck, geographically and economically, and going nowhere fast. Regardless of motivation the means are just not there.

The homing instinct?

More attention has been given to public spaces, such as city spaces and street spaces, as opposed to the limited focus on the spaces of home (Leslie and Reimer, 2003). Homes are more private and intimate locations but they are still subject to the same economic inequalities and cultural judgements applicable to working-class areas (Howarth, 2002). They can signify worth, or lack of it, since housing standards and tastes are recognised as worthy and valuable based on image and location. 'Tastes' are all too often seen as innate but, as Bourdieu (1984) reveals, these dispositions fulfil a social function of legitimating social inequality, where those in powerful positions get to define what is 'tasteful' (Lawler, 2004; McRobbie, 2004; Skeggs, 2004). This theorisation is useful in outlining the women's economic and subjective negotiation of housing 'standards' – it can be extended by a consideration of women's own understandings of these processes.

Many women in my study were conscious of the practice of symbolic investments and presentations, offering insightful critiques into the classed processes regulating 'tasteful' standards (Skeggs, 2004). Their insights derived from being marked as 'distasteful', unwilling to display the 'proper' standards. This was apparent on an interpersonal level, through contact with housing agencies and middle-class others (Skeggs, 1997). However, such awareness did not exempt women from expressing unease about their (housing) presentations as judgements could not easily be deflected ('When you were coming over I thought "God she's going to look at my home interior!" ' (laughs) Kelly). First impressions count and nobody wants to be cast in the role of the tasteless other.

The type of housing occupied is often taken as an indicator of economic status, a bricks and mortar version of bank accounts. Likewise, housing can symbolise investments in cultural ideals; both the house itself and its contents can function as a form of cultural and economic capital. A 'dirty' house is one that does not conform to presentational standards, but this is not just a matter of taste when the visible and objective 'evidence' of poverty is clear. Sharon re-calls *seeing* poverty as a child:

> Eh, as a kid the notable things for me were the clutter and untidiness of other people's houses. Not to have a lot of things, for it to be dirty as well, we were never brought up like that, the housework had to be done, it was clean. You went into other people's houses and their wallpaper was off the wall and the carpets were bogin and you kinda, you could *see* the poverty in some of it. (Sharon)

Poverty, disorder and 'dirt' were 'obvious' in Sharon's landscape; the visual markers of poverty and class were also discussed in relation to housing 'standards'. Sukhjit describes her family's desire to present an impressive image of themselves, to their extended family, via managing and manipulating the exterior and interior household. Working-class people also have investments in presenting a positive image of themselves, as when 'what you see is what you get', tidying the front garden can be quite important.

'Standards' are also displayed through recognition and acquisition of 'tasteful' household objects; working-class homes can be viewed as not only dirty, but also tacky, failing to demonstrate cultural 'taste' (McRobbie, 2004). Are car boot sale finds only 'cool' when they have been re-christened as kitsch? Although not expressed in this language,

Kelly and Lisa have an insightful awareness of this process. Notably, it is their sexuality that offers contact and familiarity with the middle-class area discussed (and ridiculed):

K: Well there's a hippy thing going on in Hebden.[6] There's this big class thing going on with people's home decorations and mini-malism and things like that. The hippy stuff, there's a certain way you have to have your house, have it cluttered and ...

L: I have my house however I want to have it.

K: You can actually tell from these houses, working-class, as well. It's stuck in the '80s' with borders around it. You know, they just don't have the 'taste'! (Laughs). Middle-class try to be kitsch as well, I've got a few friends who are kitsch and that's very middle-class 'cause the irony of it would just be wasted on somebody who didn't, the thing is you have to have the knowledge to know it's irony. They've got Princess Diana plates and they think it's funny but somebody who's working-class may see that as, em, serious. I'm getting delirious now. (Kelly and Lisa)

Kelly has an awareness of what constitutes dis/tasteful items and her knowledge of this may in itself form an element of cultural capital. On the other hand, it is not an entirely confident assertion and she continues to express apprehension about her own household presentations. These concerns may seem less important when considering the financial hardship experienced, apparent in several women's struggles over housing necessities. But presentations and perceptions remain important factors in the women's views of themselves and their positions. That said, many interviewees lived in inadequate housing and/or experienced periods of homelessness, which replaced a concern with 'decorations'. After all there is little point worrying about the kitsch value of plates if you haven't got a wall to hang them on.

Financial difficulty is experienced and debt incurred when renting accommodation. Many women rented privately while remaining on the Council housing list as they had done for years. The ability to take up council and indeed private tenancies was also circumscribed by sexuality (Blumenfeld and Raymond, 2001; Dunne et al., 2002; John and Patrick, 1999). Most experienced numerous housing shifts, as a result of poor living conditions. Fiona, for example, speaks of the negative effect poor accommodation had on her whilst growing up, affecting performance at school as well as her health and well-being. She experienced episodes of homelessness throughout her childhood – both Fiona and her mother had to rely on help from relatives and were then constructed as unwanted dependents. Given these factors it is not surprising that Fiona's mother expressed such anger at the Council for failing to adequately accommodate her, or that Fiona was upset in recalling the following incident:

> She hated them so much and that emotional like *bitterness*, do you know what I mean, my mum was bitter with the Council. The woman who run it was a real bitch to us, I remember when I was nine her son got cancer and we read about it in the local paper and my mum was like 'Good, that woman deserves all the shit in the world', and at the age of nine I was like 'mmm' 'cause my mum's not normally like that, I remember thinking 'Oh, is that right to feel that about her and her son?' (Fiona)

It would be easy to mis-understand the anger conveyed, instead presenting such emotion as evidence of pathology, as often occurs. This is life on the bottom rung of the ladder, hanging on by the fingertips, where home is an aspiration rather than a given and 'fighting' becomes second nature. The concern with 'culture' and 'taste' becomes less 'real', but Fiona and her mother, like other women in my sample, still had to present an acceptable image of themselves to become eligible for 'decent' housing, a factor informed by class position as well as sexuality. Most women were well aware of, and angry about, the bureaucratic and inefficient systems operated by Councils. For Jeannette, Shona and Amy 'movement' through social space occurred through swapping council houses, quite literally going round the houses.

Defence and demarcation

The spatial, material and emotional boundaries erected between classed individuals ('us' and 'them') living in close proximity are highlighted by Southerton (2002), who argues that the process of becoming included, or belonging within classed 'communities' requires 'boundary work'. In my research, boundaries are enforced and identities regulated from within as well as outwith working-class areas and this is clear in the accounts of 'differences' and inequalities in operation here. Internal classification hierarchies reveal that it is no easy matter to locate the cause of class discrimination and judgements to a middle-class outsider, as these continue to be played out in close interaction with working-class peers and in working-class communities, affecting a sense of comfort and belonging. However, I would suggest that the ways in which classifications operate between as well as within classed space serve different classed functions. For example, working-class areas are often denigrated in their entirety, without awareness of how different areas, streets and houses within such space are differently 'classed' by working-class occupants (Howarth, 2002). Insider classifications point to the tensions in drawing boundaries around the self and the 'others' and the dis/identifications involved in this process.

In general, women in my study were aware of the classifications operating within and between areas (Howarth, 2002; Nayak, 2003b). The feeling of pride and solidarity in the area could be produced from a feeling that everyone was in a similar position: 'everybody was in the same sort of boat' (Angela), which can be quite a comforting thought. These feelings of 'sameness' were emphasised through shared communal decline and vulnerability; there were structural reminders of shared class positions and a feeling of together we stand, divided we fall. In contrast, differentiations were produced on the basis of who lived where, down to a particular street, and who displayed what, the visual signifiers of class. Although many women generally ridiculed such differentiations as 'pretentious', distinctions were occasionally made on the basis of in/decency.

'Differences' were highlighted in their shared social space. For example, Kelly shows how her family were judged as deviant when entering what initially seemed to be normalised middle-class space – this occurred through a classed reading of her mother's 'hyper' sexuality. Kelly believes that her mum was judged as having had too many children, an accusation often thrown at working-class mothers (Lawler, 2002). However, what is interesting here is that the 'accusers' are also working-class, a fact realised on reflection. Their distinctions are generated through fear and wanting to be 'something different' (other than working-class?), wanting to prove that they are 'not one of those':

> They tried daily to differentiate themselves and they all turned into snobs. When we moved into the area my mum refused to do that, you know, it was ridiculous, I look back now and think 'God, they thought they were better than everybody else!' They were all working-class! (Kelly)

These are the daily divisions which individuals make clear in their occupation of space, whatever the real differences.

Despite this, many women spoke of positive feelings and experiences within working-class communities, for example, playing on the street in 'gangs', leaving doors open and relying on neighbours for help, which produced feelings of security and belonging. Sharon describes, with great detail, the spatial aspect of communal belonging in her childhood. Within her emotional map this space is still real and as such her description seems to come alive:

> A housing schemie kid! Em, I came from an area in Glasgow called Possil Park, commonly known as Possil and em, the drug capital of Glasgow I think, housing scheme. It was a tenement with a sort of back and front door and we stayed in the top flat. I think everybody, where we stayed you came into the street like this [picture] and the houses were all around there and there was a wee road there then there was another square so we stayed in a house there. That was called the first square, so everybody in the first square had rivalry with everybody in the second square, all the kids, right, with this street dividing us. We had a big grass area in the middle so all the kids used to play, me included, on the grass bit, football or kick the can or ropes or whatever. But out of this close here my mum was the only person who worked in this close and there was Mr. Sharp, he worked and Mr. Walker worked then I don't think anybody else worked, unless they worked casual. My mum she worked on the buses and she used to work shifts so my gran and my granda used to watch us a lot. Then when my sister was old enough to watch us without my mum getting into trouble with the police for having us on our own we went and stayed with my mum permanently. (Sharon)

Sharon charts the positive and negative aspects of working-class space. The area is 'commonly known' (suggestive of an outsider judgement) to be a container of social problems, she fears being 'caught out' and getting 'into trouble' – but the threat comes from outside the area rather than from within. Sharon remembers and draws her map while she talks, which indicates that it is still pervasive, as is the location of those without work. Her mother is one of few in her close who works but Sharon's description is not one of contrast and differentiation but instead seems to demonstrate an, albeit unequally, shared vulnerability.

Similarly, Becky was, to a degree, brought up by neighbours and friends in a place where everyone knew each others' business and where the offer of help was made accordingly. Her account is self-consciously nostalgic and seems to hark back to a time and a sense of community that has since fallen into decay:

> It was very kinda, something like the Broons,[7] kinda very family orientated, everybody knew each other, everybody used to sit in their

verandas, bellow to people, you know, it was really good, kinda protective. I suppose there was a very kinda old style working-class, everybody would look out for each other, everybody knew each other and helped each other out in times of trouble. I probably had about 50 grans and grandas as well 'cause I was this wee lost child! Everybody took to me. (Becky)

Unfortunately community decline caused by unemployment can easily rupture such protection, such old-style values. Becky's opinions are grounded in her experience of growing up there and appreciation of the past does not have to mean whole scale denigration of the present. 'Defence' was often produced in response to the stereotypes applicable to their areas and to themselves as inhabitants of those places; prejudice was often challenged through a sense of pride in their areas but more 'mixed' feelings also existed.

Pride and prejudice

Where we come from says something about our (classed) selves. Many women often spoke of being stigmatised or stereotyped when they 'revealed' where they came from. There is a concern to reject these stereotypes, sometimes at the cost of fully identifying with their communities and homes, made clear through the occasional desire, voiced by several women, to prove themselves as different, as members of the respectable working-class, as opposed to the less desirable 'others'. There is an overwhelming awareness of the lack of value attached to their communities, but also a corresponding feeling that those outside the area hold a 'superficial' understanding, based solely in terms of poverty and degradation (Howarth, 2002). The overall feeling is one of anger and rejection of middle-class standards while remaining honest and pragmatic about the lack of resources, and lack of space, within the places to which they belong. The prevalent feeling is that what is ours is ours and while we can knock it, you definitely cannot.

Here, Kelly and Lisa describe the negative associations surrounding Lisa's home, which is also known as a 'sink area', and the feelings this has produced; a secrecy and silence on the matter, even if Lisa resists these classifications ('probably'):

L: It's 100 per cent council housing estate, it's the biggest one in Europe, so it's like a sink area basically. Not just people who were working-class, people who were unemployed, one parent families, there were a lot of young parent families. It was only built about

20 years ago but it's gone right downhill because you get drug abuse, fighting, gangs. It does get a lot of bad publicity, probably more than it deserves and there's a school on there which accommodates the whole catchment area, the whole of Brandon, so it's 100 per cent working-class intake, 100 per cent council housing ... I went there and no-one ever expects anything of you as well.

K: When I met Lisa, about a year and a half ago, didn't I? You kept that really quite a *secret*. (Kelly and Lisa)

As can be seen in many of the women's comments on the areas they come from, the language Lisa uses is very definite ('100 per cent'). With this there is an almost apologetic feeling to the latter part of her description, that on one hand she is attempting to convey the sense of deprivation while at the same time feeling that she must stand up for where she came from. Alongside this narration of geography and meaning is also the revelation that she kept silent about her background within her friendship, and although it may only be a figure of speech, her 'admission' of where she grew up is described in terms of 'coming out', of revealing something important.

Lisa's description encompasses the material signifiers of working-class space, as well as (stereo)typical working-class inhabitants. There are many visual signifiers of classed space, and of poverty, as places and people looked 'rough' and 'poor'. For instance, Grace recognises the 'look' of poverty while at the same time qualifying her assertions. An acknowledgement of the possibility of misrecognition, the likelihood of visual markers being read as indicative of entire personhood, appears in her account:

Everywhere you look, there's still extreme poverty, do you know what I mean ... even where I stay, even in the council schemes now and you can tell street by street who doesn't have money and who isn't in employment, do you know what I mean? Just by the conditions of the gardens, do you know what I mean, and I'm not running people down because their gardens aren't nice 'cause they're unemployed. But it's just that whole kind of – that look of poverty. (Grace)

The geographic descriptions given by many women I interviewed were often vivid and insightful and it was clear that their maps emphasised not only the physical aspects of their environments but also the feelings and experiences contained therein (Howarth, 2002; Reay and Lucey, 2000;

Weeks et al., 2001; Wray and Newitz, 1997). Several women noted the contradiction between the 'image' of the area and the 'reality'; appearances and perceptions can be deceptive. There are hidden levels of poverty, unapparent through surface appearances, particularly when inhabitants are complicit in this 'covering up' ('It's what I call a fur coat and no drawers town', Ali). This suggests a degree of shame in poverty or a necessity to 'pretend' to be otherwise, revealing the deep and conflicting meanings contained within space, recognised by 'insiders'. Surface images of places can be later contrasted with real-ness based on increasing familiarity, conveying ideas of the visible and invisible aspects of poverty. The negotiation of 'outsider' and 'insider' meanings also forms patterns of identifications, affecting a 'coming-out' about where you belong.

Many women were conscious of the value (or lack of) attached to their particular locations, they knew they were immediately recognisable and would be 'placed' as unworthy. Cathy and other members of the Manchester focus group show how *even* 'educated' people make judgements. Cathy's account is very revealing of the way in which positions are denied and authority achieved and legitimated. As Cathy does not match the classed expectations of coming from a specific area, she is told she cannot and does not belong – it is a middle-class woman who refuses Cathy's working-class identifications. Cathy enacts the office scenario, exclaiming with disbelief about such misreading/erasure:

> C: She was a *fully trained psychologist*, someone who's supposedly aware of people's prejudices anyway she says 'Oh, where are you from? I said 'I'm from Manchester' she said 'Oh, I know Manchester really well, what part of Manchester are you from?' I said 'I'm from Mosside' and then she said, know what she said? 'No you're not.' Honest to God she said 'No you're not.' I said 'Yes I am,' she said 'No you're not, where are you from?' I said 'I'm from Mosside' she went, 'No you're not, you're joking.'
> E: Yes it's that idea that everyone has their proper place ... The ways that you just know that you're nobody at all, again it's where you come from. (Cathy and Emma)

This exchange also illustrates the pride and identifications that many women felt towards their areas; the fact that nobody has the right to take that away from them, that no matter how bad it may be, it is still theirs and that to deny is to devalue. Others were conscious of the more 'subtle' ways this operated through 'postcode discrimination', an example that clearly shows how whole areas and the individuals within them, are condemned by a few letters and numbers at the end of an address (Furlong et al., 1996; Webster et al., 2004). These judgements are perhaps more enduring and less easy to resist: it is almost impossible to escape from or deny a postcode and for a simple collection of characters its influence can be immense. Several women explained their long-term unemployment by having specific, devalued, 'crap' postcodes.[8] However, there are powerful vocal challenges to the automatic connection between location and assumed character, a digging in of the geographic heels:

> I think it's because people look down on it *so much a*nd there's an automatic assumption that people who live in the area and people who come out of the area are going to be a particular type of person, they're going to have low academic attainment, they're going to have no job prospects and it's like 'Up yours!' Yeah, that's the sort of feeling I've got 'I'm from Drumchapel, so what?' ... I don't know if it's a kinda pride thing, you know to say 'There's nothing wrong with coming from Drumchapel' ... it's like if I felt embarrassed about that then I would feel embarrassed about particular members of my family, that's *not* how I feel. (Becky)

Becky refuses (expected) shame and embarrassment, her language is combative and her feelings clear. She recognises the negative associations from negotiating these in everyday encounters and confidently challenges the automatic denigrations through positive assertions. At the same time, many women expressed mixed feelings towards the places they came from precisely because they symbolised contradictory things, were seen as problematic by wider society and because these places were also where they lived out and experienced inequality. Their 'communities' remained vulnerable to structural decline producing feelings of bitterness and grief.

For example, Jeannette speaks of Clydebank as being a 'heartbroken' area, through the disappearance of shipbuilding and other heavy industries, which the area was once renowned for. Similarly, whilst identifying strongly with Liverpool and the surrounding areas, Jo regrettably asserts that it is 'the saddest place':

> Liverpool was just horrendous. It's just the saddest place. I mean, it's totally run down and it's horrible, it's really horrible. Even when we were there, it was getting more and more run down and there was less

and less jobs, more and more people moving out of the city. But now, like where she [Jo's mother] was living recently like, you're not safe in the street and it's just derelict buildings and it's really sad to see. (Jo)

The language Jo uses is remarkable, illustrating perhaps better than anything else the depth and strength of geographic emotion. To claim that an area is 'heartbroken' is to imbue it with an almost human dimension; by doing so an area transcends mere bricks and mortar and becomes the mirror of its occupants, the personification of their sadness and lost hope. Such emotional descriptions and reactions rarely feature in research on social space but here they constitute a powerful 'structure of feeling' (Howarth, 2002; Sennett and Cobb, 1977; Steedman, 1986). The emotion and grief is easy to see in these accounts, whereby happiness is often simultaneously expressed alongside pain and anger. Such moving realities are disrespected by 'underclass' conceptualisations, which denigrate these spaces and fail to consider them as places of worth and (emotional) value. Many women often experienced harsh realities in the areas where they lived, but this sense of reality, no matter how harsh, was often valued, measured against a more 'middle-class' 'pretension' and unreality (Skeggs, 2004). Dis/comforts were formed through moving about in, rather than moving away from, classed and sexualised spaces and sometimes points of 'intersections' were more collisions rather than comfortable combinations.

Bourdieu's (1984) concept of classed 'habitus' conveys the women's entrenched identifications with classed space, challenging straightforward conceptualisations of 'movement' and 'mobility', although gender and sexuality were also clearly relevant to their feelings about and material journeys through community and home spaces. It would seem evident that for many of the women I interviewed, past geographical identifications are not something that can be neatly packed away in a box and put in the back of the wardrobe. Their current identities and identifications are profoundly bound up with where they came from and what that meant. This geographical past could be imagined, remembered and researched. Narratives of experience are narratives of personal perception and identification; they create a version of the self which may be rooted in the past but which both impacts on and involves the personality of the present. In the following chapter I explore the women's occupations of and exclusions from scene space and the various dis/identifications then produced.

6
Scene Spaces – Inclusions and Exclusions

Here I consider interviewees' experiences of scene spaces, defined as the range of city venues in Glasgow, Edinburgh, Manchester and Yorkshire, such as cafes, pubs and clubs, frequented and recognised by lesbians as the typical and commercialised lesbian and gay space on offer in their towns and cities. All too often research into scene space has concentrated upon London (Binnie, 1995; McDowell, 1997) Manchester (Moran et al., 2004; Skeggs, 1999, 2001) and Brighton, in the United Kingdom, San Francisco, in the United States of America and other emerging urban 'gay ghettos' in Sydney and beyond (Binnie, 2000; Brekhaus, 2003). Scene spaces are leisure spaces, where people go to meet others, consume and spend time in a 'friendly' space, but such leisure space is also formed and fractured by material and interpersonal inequalities, with consequences for the enactment of sexual – and classed – identities. I argue for the necessity of including the experiences of classed individuals, in order to understand the socio-economic inequalities operating in scene space, which have been given attention in terms of the structuring of scene space, via commercialism, regeneration and 'sophistication', serving to produce upmarket and 'classy' scene space (Chasin, 2000; Hennessy, 2000; Warner, 1993). While the general 'structural' forces defining the trend of commodification have been well commented upon, there have been few attempts to understand it from the perspective of the meaning that individual lesbians find in commercialised scene spaces.

Skeggs (1999, 2001) and Casey (2004) show that scene spaces are increasingly becoming leisurely spaces of consumption, where the claiming of a lesbian or gay identity is no longer necessary to 'consume' such leisure space, but where the 'intrusion' of a straight presence into scene space is still far from unproblematic. Skeggs suggests that hetero-sexual working-class women enter scene space in order to be 'safe from the constant male gaze in heterosexual space. ... It is a space to be invisible, to not be forced to partake in the heterosexual market' (1999: 225). However, the broad inattention to working-class lesbians, either in or out of commercialised scene space, consequently makes invisible and unrecognised their spatialised struggles and the processes of identification and dis-identification operating on 'their' territory. Although Skeggs notes the 'consequences for others' that a straight presence creates, 'hetero-women destabilize the claim just by reiterating the practices of normalized hetero-femininity', working-class lesbians' physical, material and subjective 'entitlement' to scene space may be more momentary and tenuous than that of a middle-class lesbian (1999: 227). The lesbians in Skeggs's study remain un-identified in terms of class, suggesting that sexuality became the primary classifying device for the lesbians. Indeed the contrast with the identified working-class women suggests that the lesbians' class positions were neutral or unmarked, which implies a middle-class status, again highlighting the need to more thoroughly 'class' scene space, the bodies within it, and the occupation of it.

Straight intrusion, like the commercial scene space itself, appears to be gendered (heterosexual women seeking 'safety' in gay men's space), but are working-class lesbians also intruders in 'their own' space, priced out, marginalised and excluded? Casey (2004) notes that the presence of straight women in scene space adversely affects the comfort of lesbians as well as *some* gay men – I am hoping to highlight the intersection of sexuality, class and gender in order to demonstrate exactly who can feel dis/comfort. Considering the classed experience of working-class lesbians and their struggles for recognition, entitlement and identification can extend the complexity and understanding of the power relations operating in scene spaces. Most women described how lesbian and gay venues were located in 'trendy' areas with the result that particular classed displays, images and performances were required to enable entry, and this applied across the varied locations where respondents came from.

My attention to scene space is based on working-class lesbians' desires to 'fit-in' and achieve identification through becoming part of this (commercialised) 'community', by literally appearing to be part of it – as well as the limitations upon and impossibilities of doing so, the frustrations of never quite getting it right. The overwhelming lack of entitlement to such space, of uneasily, awkwardly and even agitatedly occupying it, amongst the women in my study, produced an acute consciousness of the boundaries of inclusion and exclusion, shaping criticism around notions of 'pretentious' scene space, as opposed to 'real' working-class space (Taylor, 2004b) and the various classed and gendered fracturing of scene space. As the previous chapter has shown, it is not the case that 'real' working-class space existed autonomously, or was seamlessly occupied as some kind of alternative utopia, but rather that the repeated contrast between the 'real' and the 'pretentious' served to highlight the tensions and distances, both physically and emotionally, between these two, often separated territories.

Within scene spaces bodily appearance can legitimise presence, demonstrating the relevant claims and entitlements upon that space – a kind of communal affirmation of sexual identity can follow as signs, labels and embodied characteristics are read and understood. But such readings are reliant upon suggested, projected and even rejected physicality, dependent as they are upon the encoding and deciphering of bodily capitals. Importantly, within such processes of display and affirmation, devaluation and denigrations can also occur: entry to scene spaces often involved learning 'gay' signs and dressing accordingly. Unfortunately, for many working-class lesbians, these 'designer', gendered and classed presentations were often over-expensive and unachievable (Chasin, 2000; Hennessy, 2000). Signifying sexuality thus becomes a pleasure and a danger – getting it right can be affirming; getting it wrong often means you can't, won't and don't fit in.

The various restrictions, regulations, dominations and even emulations operating in scene space, and forming entitlements, work to exclude working-class lesbians, and this functions on an embodied level. Having the money buys you in – having the 'right' clothes, the right style and taste can indicate that you 'deserve' to be there but 'looking like a lesbian' in these settings often requires unaffordable presentations, classy, and not working-class, ones. While many women spoke of learning and trying to adhere to these 'codes' there was much criticism of scene space as 'pretentious', 'middle-class' and male, perhaps representing another aspect of what Casey (2004) calls the 'de-dyking' of queer space. All of the above processes mean that it is difficult to get desired affirmations in these spaces – it is not their space but many working-class lesbians still make claims upon it, albeit often through a resigned sense that something is 'better than nothing'.

The reading, naming and assignment of bodies to positions involves power relationships and has material and subjective effects, applicable to working-class lesbians' experiences of commercialised scene spaces, with their entry, and thus entitlement, being dependent upon certain visual displays. The restrictions to entry came in the classed component of such displays, the unease in being 'super trendy', and in the increasing trend towards looking like gay men, which nevertheless ensured some access to scene spaces. Their critique of these processes as 'pretentious' shows that many were highly aware of the 'unreality' of these spaces, the pretence being in the assumed correlation between appearance and identity; yet to criticise was not to overthrow and in accessing lesbian and gay venues the women I interviewed were implicated in, and responded to, such processes of mis/recognition.

In her *Formations* research, Skeggs (1997) shows how working-class women invested in heterosexual femininity as a way of 'putting a floor on their economic circumstances', affecting their self-presentations, but also their negotiations and resistances. In this case, attention to appearance was invested in as a kind of physical, bodily capital, a creative solution to 'blocked chances'. But what are working-class lesbians' solutions to 'blocked chances'? How do they establish themselves as 'entitled' to occupy scene space, and is the difficult, desired and un/achievable equation between looking and being ever fully legitimised in a space which is fraught with divisive gendered, sexualised and classed exclusions? Are they similarly devalued for excessive femininity, for 'getting it wrong', where getting it right would involve a smooth movement between looking, being and being 'in place'? While Skeggs (1997) notes that working-class femininity is associated with excess, Corteen (2002) suggests that lesbianism is signified through absence or lack – for working-class lesbians devaluations can occur from both judgements: too much or not enough, as class and sexuality were written on, and thus read from, their bodies. This also applied to the performance of 'butch' and 'femme' identities/appearances; there was a sense that middle-class women could display 'femme' and still be recognised as a lesbian, whereas working-class lesbians would more likely be misrecognised as straight, as displaying the 'wrong type' of (heterosexual) femininity – a judgement also attached to the women of Skeggs' research.

Class differences formed a powerful barrier against entry and equal participation, as is exemplified by the following accounts: Jeannette reports a polarisation of middle-class and 'neddy' (working-class) space, neither of which is felt to be adequate, whereas Alice reports outright exclusion from the middle-class nature of scene space:

> But I always get the feeling that there's a kind of – it's very polarised. There's women doing quite middle-class stuff, like Glasgay and then there's the clubs that are quite neddy, you know, what's that place? Sapho's, you know. (Jeannette)
>
> You are usually identified before you go into a pub or club, why you're going into that pub. Gay pubs tends to be exclusive, more middle-class,

yeah. Very middle-class. And in it's outward appearance ... Unless you feel comfortable in middle-class surroundings then you're not going to go in there. It's like a barrier, unless you can operate in this nice middle-class space. But it's the same in straight bars, you don't go into those spaces unless you think you can operate within the criteria. (Alice)

Alice feels identified before she goes into scene spaces; she 'just knows' that they are not 'for the likes of us' and is then also pre-defining the venues as middle-class, before even entering these locations: she feels she does not know the rules and cannot fully operate in the 'nice middle-class space' and so does not venture beyond the door, beyond the flashy exterior which emits certain welcoming signals to those 'in the know'. Both these accounts testify to the obvious and unspoken class differences operating in scene space which impact upon identifications and a sense of belonging. Alice also relates this to the boundaries of inclusion and exclusion operating in 'straight' space, which generate dis/comforts. The language used is that of the outsider, the implication that in order to make your face fit you might have to rearrange it somewhat.

Read my label

Several women in my study felt inadequate and negatively judged in scene space, particularly through physical appearance (Holliday, 1999), whereby identities were subject to regulations and constraints, mediated by other bodies and by the appropriateness of dress codes for particular spaces. The scene was felt to be an intimidating and pressurised place, where they had to learn the 'codes' of behaviour or risk being outsiders. These codes included dress and appearance as well as an ability to spend and consume, as realised and recognised via economic inequalities. Legitimate appearances were produced and regulated within as well as outwith scene space, serving symbolic as well as functional purposes (Holliday, 1999). For example, lesbians also rely on these signs themselves, charting the difference in appearance between lesbian and straight women, a visual dimension of 'gaydar'; lesbian appearance and signifiers had to be managed to attract the 'right sort' of attention while in other contexts these same things could 'attract' unwanted attention and even violence.

Many described their lack of connection with the scene and attributed this to prevailing stereotypical notions of what a lesbian should look like, suggesting that stereotypes are produced outwith and within scene space, regulating the respective boundaries of inclusion and exclusion.

Like May, many interviewees reported discomfort as well as a degree of cynicism about these practices, feeling a glare upon them as they entered the scene, a glare that is both critical and unforgiving:

> It's like you've got to wear designer clothes to get in there. If you don't then people, they do, they just look down on you, definitely … It's people being so nasty just because of what you look like … If you go over and you're dressed quite casual you go 'Oh I'm not going in there! Because I'm not dressed like I should be'. So I think there are underlying rules, if you like but then again that's down to restrictions and obviously they want a certain kind of person in the club or pub just to make it look good. There's just loads of attractive people in fancy clothes and therefore they reflect the status of the pub as well. I think it's more about appearance and image, an image thing. (May)

Appearance, and the management of it, could function as a means of gaining access to scene space, of being the 'right kind of person' who has grasped the 'underlying rules' – or as a mechanism of exclusion, experienced by looking 'straight' or 'sub-standard'. Within such a context, 'you are what you wear' takes on a whole new significance.

Appearance could indicate sexuality and class status, made apparent through certain signs, and many spoke of learning these signs as a way of gaining entry, recognition and acceptance within gay and lesbian spaces. They are read and understood by those 'in the know', those who know what to look for, as Angela states, 'When I was 17 and, you know, you're thinking there's a secret handshake, do I have to wear my hair a certain way, do you have to look a certain way?' Perhaps contrasting with the 'big hair' displayed by the straight working-class women in Skeggs' study, Adkins (2000) still points to the ways in which such a commodification aesthetic can be seen as constituting sexual subjects, her example of this being the display of 'lesbian hair' – this, of course, says much more about lesbian presence than hair styles alone, and the relevance of it is in the negotiation, display and reading of both class and sexuality through appearance. Sukhjit also illustrated this process, as well as her discomfort at the thought of adopting these signs and styles. Her 'failure' to do so meant that she risks being misrecognised as straight, of lacking clear visibility. It would seem that being a plain-clothed operative is just not enough:

> The whole uniform thing because people don't talk anymore and you have to have an appearance that lets people know that you're gay.

If you want to be recognised. So apart from the really tacky T-shirts I don't know what to do (laughs). (Sukhjit)

If you want to be recognised, it would seem that the T-shirt has to fit, tacky or not. Kirsty makes deliberate attempts to modify her appearance and present these signs to others in an attempt to attract attention; this requires a process of reading and managing presentations, sometimes unsuccessfully:

I saw this woman in this café yesterday and I sat there and I thought, she's really, really nice ... So I sat there looking at her and I thought, now what do I do? Right, OK, show the thumb rings ... that's not worked. Ok, show badges on bag, you know, I hung my bag around the place. No, no, it hasn't worked. So she just walked off and I thought, she doesn't know, oh no, and I can't say anything to her. (Kirsty)

The signs Kirsty offers are so small, so easy to overlook that the lack of response could very easily have been a case of forgetting ones reading glasses, rather than misreading the signs. While important as a way of identifying and affirming sexuality, appearance could be regulated through these same signs; failure to display them, or 'inappropriate' appearance could produce exclusions. This was experienced physically by women who were refused access to scene spaces and also on a more subjective level in feeling that they did not belong or couldn't match the visual displays of identity in, for example, designer clothing or particular hairstyles. There was a pressure to conform to notions of what a lesbian should look like, perpetuating the assumed correspondence between image and identity.

But as well as feeling pressurised into these displays, many women took pleasure from signifying their sexuality through their appearance. The signs can be played up or down and they can also be a way of demonstrating pride and solidarity, a nod in the right direction, as Lisa (23, Yorkshire) conveys when stating that 'I never want to hide it, now I've got it tattooed on my arm. I wear that [women sign necklace] all the time'. Rita (52, Manchester) speaks of a change of dress ('I'm wearing all the clothes that I like to wear, leather, rubber, chains, mad clothes, mad make-up') as indicating a change of self, one compatible with lesbian and gay space and which would enable access into it. Similarly, Sharon describes her initial reaction to the different dress codes adopted in scene space, thereafter adopting these (modified) patterns – finding out the uniform then going to the outfitters. An apparent movement from conventional feminine appearance, to something a bit more 'tom-boyish' then ensues, as Sharon 'dresses up' to be read as a lesbian:

> Now you've got to remember at this time I was quite girly and I think the scene changes you a bit em, so I turns up in a pair of jeans and a blazer and really flat shoes and a wee bit of make up on ... I said to them 'Those 4 guys keep looking at me' and they said 'No, they're lassies'. Very androgynous and I thought they were very masculine looking. So that was a complete shock to me, my perceptions of lesbians was kinda tom-boyish, as I would perceive myself but these women were so more men looking. So the scene was a bit scary at first.

And then:

> I went out and bought a denim jacket and I'd wear trousers and blah, blah, blah. And my sister kept saying ... 'Are you no goin' oot?' and I'd be like that, 'Aye', 'Well where are ye goin', you've no got dressed?', I'd be like that 'I'm goin' to play ten pin bowling' or 'I'm goin' to the pictures' 'cause it was ok to go to the pictures in my jeans and a T-shirt but if I was going oot to a dance or clubbing it my sister wondered 'Why the hell are you no gettin' dressed?'. So my sister was like 'You're goin' tae the pictures a hell of a lot!' So yeah, my dress sort of changed from getting dressed tae go oot tae gettin' dressed as in jeans and a T-shirt to go to the scene. (Sharon)

Sharon's appearance does not fit with her sister's expectation, unaware that Sharon is attempting to signify something other than heterosexual femininity. Both Rita and Sharon, among others, speak of gradually learning 'proper' displays and the codes of dress and identity, the re-arrangement of which fits with lesbian and gay spaces and eases access into them. A display of the proper signs enabled entry – failure to do so could result in being questioned as to why they were there. However, many women made challenges to mis-readings, as Jill shows in her forceful response to the questioning of her role within scene space:

> I remember this wee poof talking to me one night for ages and he said 'It's nice that you come down here wi' yi' being straight and all' and I was like 'Who said I was fucking straight?', 'Well you've got long hair and you've no got a big leather jacket on'. (Jill)

Another faulty hair style (Adkins, 2000; Skeggs, 1999), as pointed out by a gay man, yet this example also illustrates the in/visibility of different 'types'/styles of lesbians – and the corresponding entitlements on spaces which can be made. Ainley (1995) illustrates the historically class-specific images of lesbians, and the in/visibility of butch/femme lesbians (Browne, 2004; Munt, 1998). There may be a blurring of these styles but there are still pressures to conform within this, mediated through class, gender and race, which produce a 'tasteful', or otherwise, self-presentation. Several interviewees also commented on the classed aspects of butch/femme appearances and the simple fact that to present a butch appearance requires less of a financial outlay. It could be said that by being butch you get more gay for your money:

> I still think it's more acceptable to be butch than to be femme. I think that's the thing. If you get dressed up and you've got less of a budget to do it on and stuff then I think people think you look a bit more like a hooker. (Fiona)

Fiona hints at the ways that it may be easier, with middle-class capitals and privileges, to have a feminine appearance and still be recognised as a lesbian. Here, Fiona speaks of the discrimination and exclusion experienced through failure to 'look like a lesbian'. She herself then becomes the embodiment of danger, a contaminating 'other' and a possible infiltrator, plain clothed or otherwise; her 'excessive' femininity is read as being 'out of place', her identity denied:

> I've got long hair and am I suppose in some ways em, it's all quite hard to tell 'cause these things do lie in the eye of the beholder but I think I do appear quite feminine to people and when I go out as well I like to get dressed up ... I'd went to this party and we were in this car park and this woman was quite drunk and she was sort of chatting me up and she was sort of just being drunk and friendly as well and one of her mates ... she said 'Oh you can't trust her' ... think there was something there connected with my appearance like, like if I demonstrated more visibly 'No I'm renouncing men forever, I'm going to cut my hair off!' then that would have been more acceptable, I don't know. (Fiona)

Sharon's presentation of a 'butch' appearance can be related to class and 'taste' as evident in her testimony about 'quality' and designer clothes:

> I think I went through a stage, if I wanted to be really butch I'd be wearing my Ben Sherman shirts ... I've got loads of shirts that I'll

wear with cuff links and you know, they're men's shirts. Or with women's blouses that you can get out of M&S [Marks&Spencer] and they have cuff links. (Sharon)

Both Fiona's and Sharon's comments highlight the ways that working-class lesbians negotiate ideas of both feminine 'excess' and lesbian 'lack' (Corteen, 2002; Skeggs, 1997). Many women spoke of a fear of 'getting it wrong', of feeling the need to learn specific codes and/or feeling pressurised to conform and 'buy' support. There was much criticism of the necessity to wear designer clothes and the latest fashions within the scene: many felt worried by their inability to match designer styles given their low incomes and feared being misrecognised as unworthy and unentitled to be there. When the rules are strict to the point of specificity, what happens when the specifics are simply out of reach?

There are achievable presentations and unachievable ones and 'designer identity' may only be accessible to those materially poised to occupy the position, those with the ability and opportunities to engage in 'lesbian chic' (Hennessy, 2000). Becky describes the pressure to wear designer clothes and doubts the standard of her own wardrobe:

'Fuck I've worn this so many times before, can I wear this?' Kinda keeping up with what other people are looking like I suppose and the expectation, em, it's very difficult. (Becky)

The idea of having a 'starting wardrobe' to 'come out' may seem slightly strange, but appearance does affect access into certain places and can provide opportunities to meet people. Within an appearance obsessed environment, having the right wardrobe can mean the difference between getting in or staying out. However, there were critical responses to this, perhaps representing different solutions to 'blocked chances' (Skeggs, 1997). Cathy and Emma discuss the possibilities of working-class lesbians 'investing' in designer styles; where there is a will, there is often a way, even if it is not quite legal:

C: Yeah I was going to say you can always obtain it without buying it, can't you?
E: And it's a question of resisting temptation, isn't it? How desperately you want it.
C: There's always stuff that falls off the back of lorries and stuff down the market and stuff like that, so people always manage to get hold of it. (Cathy and Emma)

Adopting a different strategy, Amy challenges the idea that designer clothes are inherently better than high street brands, commenting on the similarity and availability of styles. Again, there is a critique of the 'pretentious' nature of designer labels and a challenge to worth of 'designer identities'. Liz contrasts her preferred location (Preston) with the Manchester area, where she currently lives and notes the differences in the scene within these two areas – differences which manifest themselves in people's incomes and clothing. Liz is critical of the 'bitchiness' and 'pretentiousness' of the Manchester scene, instead preferring the more 'real' working-class space, which is signified through working-class bodies who wear working-class clothes:

> People here seem to be flashing their pink pound, showing that 'We've got the money, we can go out every night', they can wear bloody DKNY clothes and French Connection. In Preston it wasn't like that, everybody was wearing bloody TK MAXX clothes, couldn't afford to go out every night. (Liz)

In highlighting her preference for the 'real' Preston scene space, as opposed to the 'unreal' commercialised Manchester scene space, Liz demonstrates that it is not all about 'resisting temptation'; sometimes working-class lesbians do not want to achieve a designer lesbian identity or appearance, but this preference may be hard to exercise in spaces which demand such, varied, displays. Tracey expresses a degree of confusion over new appearances and new possibilities for indicating sexuality, which suggests that these signs are subject to a degree of change and may be unrecognised by 'insiders':

> I think in some cases you can just tell, like my friend he's got a skinhead and everything, this wee tank top and he prances up the road, it's obvious. With lassies it's like short hair or dress sense, but even then, see I was reading this article in *Diva* about 'Lipstick Lesbians' and I couldnae tell them a mile away, no chance, I cannae spot them. (Tracey, 23, Glasgow)

Sexual expression, through appearance, may be becoming more varied but this still functions within certain constraints. Even new ways of being bring pressures and can reinforce inequalities, rather than representing more fluidity in styles and appearances. Jill speaks of one style replacing another rather than co-existing:

> Then the fucking trendy dyke thing hit and it was like 'Hurray!' So it was like you could go and have a laugh and not sit in a corner and be

all fucking moody and staring! … Even though the trendy dyke scene hit that backfired on itself 'cause everyone had to be trendy and if you didnae have, if you wirnae super trendy and if you didnae hang about with trendy people then still nobody spoke to you, it was like 'Here we go again back to square one'. But a horrible scene and I feel sorry for young lassies that have to go out on that now because if you aren't super trendy then they don't really stand a chance. (Jill, 29, Edinburgh)

Some groups can spatialise their claims for visibility and recognition while others, like Jill, are misrecognised via appearance, as being unentitled and 'out of place', and the classing as well as gendering of space is fundamental to this.

Have you got the balls?

Those who do not share a sense of 'entitlement' and are not able to articulate their interests do not occupy space in the same way as the more affluent, who are able to spatialise their interests. Inequalities were perpetuated here as occupants of the various scene spaces, across the different localities, guarded their 'turf' – but 'women's space', especially in Manchester, was increasingly felt to 'emulate' gay men's space in its commercial focus and consuming clientele. The predominance of men was not just a symbolic issue – it was not only their numerical dominance which defined the space as male; rather it was more a substantive issue of gendered resources and entitlements. Owing to persistent gender inequalities in incomes men have more power to enter into and enjoy these, often expensive, pubs and clubs (Binnie, 2004).

Experience of sexism within scene spaces affected feelings of comfort and belonging, challenging notions of lesbian and gay 'community' space as lesbians often felt 'out of place'. Like heterosexual women in clubs and pubs, women felt their presence to be de-legitimised by the behaviour and actions of others, as they made claims on 'their' space. Gay men were repeatedly depicted as 'misogynistic', 'over sexualised', 'bitchy bastards', suggesting that being in the same space, or indeed the 'same boat', is not a comfortable experience, especially when some occupants are rocking it more than others.

Many women were highly critical of the 'pretentiousness' within the scene, made visible through self-indulgent and extravagant 'performances', namely those enacted by gay men. As well as restrictions and regulations, many women believed that processes of domination as well as emulation were in operation. Some believed that other lesbians were imitating gay male culture in order to make entitlement claims and access space, viewed in terms of increased individualism, exhibitionism and sexism. Liz spoke of the sexism directed against her at a Pride meeting, where she was making the case for 'women's space' in a 'gay space' – interestingly her claims are delegitimised through reference to her physical appearance:

> I went down to the floor to ask a question, I hate public speaking but I was really wound up, eventually the really polite chair said 'Let this lady speak', at which point I had people behind me going 'Well she's not much of a lady, she's not very bloody feminine!' and then as soon as I started to speak all the men started to jeer at which point I just completely lost it and shouted out 'Please respect me when I'm speaking'. (Liz)

'Women's space' was de-legitimised and criticised as an 'intrusion' on 'gay space', and entitlements were denied; further marginalisation occurred through the inability to compete with the business approaches increasingly utilised to gain and mark out territory. Women from Manchester spoke at length about the lack and inadequacy of women's space at recent events, which fractured their sense of belonging and identification with the lesbian and gay 'community'. Many felt that the climate and tone of the events had already been pre-defined in the interests of gay men: lesbians were presented as 'intruders' on 'their' space, making unfair and biased demands – an ironic parallel to the assumed neutrality of straight space.

Similarly, it was often gay men who were thought to be most visible in meetings and in parades, in a position of advantage, it becomes clear that men are more able to 'perform' or 'subvert' gendered identities – they are able to 'play' at being camp in a way that lesbians aren't or aren't meant to. However, some women noted a similar trend in the 'performance' of lesbians and described this as attempted assimilation:

> Em, I guess maybe I'm making judgements, working on stereotypes but a lot of gay women now seem to be acting like gay men, they seem to be wearing the same clothes, getting the same hairstyles, doing the same things and not following their own path. (Liz, 23, Manchester)

Skeggs (1999) suggests that heterosexual women may claim spatial entitlement via gay men, rather than, for example, using scene space to socialise with lesbian friends, as highlighted in the disparaging term 'faghag' (Casey, 2004). It would seem that the option of 'emulating' gay men might also be a choice for lesbians in seeking spatial entitlement. A concern with appearance, materialism and a general 'excess' of both of these are seen as reproducing scene spaces as male; thus the only option may be to integrate into or emulate these patterns:

> We're in materialistic times where nothing matters apart from money. Money and what you can do with it and, you know, 'We lesbians are just as liberated as gay men. We can go cruising', you know. What's it gonna be next? Are there gonna be lesbian cottages? (Sonia, 32, Yorkshire)

If there were lesbian cottages what would people wear to them?

Turf wars

A common 'problem' expressed was the 'intrusion' of straight people into gay and lesbian space – this was seen as a further infringement upon their own desired sense of belonging (even though this was rarely achieved). The growth of cultural variety or 'cultural omnivorousness', in leisure and consumption can be seen as aspects of a 'tolerant pluralism' cutting across straight and gay spaces, producing a 'mixing' of both. However, the struggle over 'entitlements', which reinforces inequalities, provides a barrier against this (Warde et al., 1999), constantly re-drawing the boundaries of inclusion into or exclusion from scene spaces, as a rather different and painful kind of 'queer tendency' (Roseneil, 2000).

Moran and Skeggs (2001) claim that fear of the heterosexual 'other' functions to enable certain proprietal claims to be made on (scene) space, which includes recourse to purity, where gay identity matches gay space, and where those 'out of place' or those 'invading' the space are seen as a threatening imposition – heterosexual women, especially when grouped together in 'hen parties' – become particularly contaminating upon gendered and sexualised scene space. This relation is apparent in Sonia's desires for her ('my') space, but notions of 'purity' and 'respectability' are harder to apply to working-class lesbians when, as Sonia notes, the (desired?) space does not actually have anything for her:

> I kind of think 'Well, I want my space, you can sod off, you've got enough space'. Then again, you think it's good if you've, you can

bring members of your family there. But then again, it's just like a big bloody goldfish bowl, you know, when you have all these people ... And you're gonna get your hen parties going to it and whatever and it's like, what the hell would I do? The kind of person who wants to go out to be surrounded by hen parties ... That's what it's turning, that's when the gay scene's turning out to be, isn't it? We're a form of entertainment now. Or you can go because they're smart glitzy bars where people can dress well. There's loads of brass and it's trendy. So nothing for me. Sorry. (Sonia)

There are contradictions and tensions within Sonia's statement – her desire for equal space and equal participation contrasts with her current knowledge of the inequalities operating there. On a theoretical level she is demanding her right to a space, which on a practical level, she cannot afford and does not want. These emotions, while seemingly contradictory, represent a strand running through many of the narratives of space, a feeling that 'this is our space, even if we don't like it'. As Tracey reveals 'straight' presence in 'gay space' can generate discomfort on both sides, and a battle over entitlement occurs:

There's more straight people in those places too, aye ... so there was three straight couples and we were sitting, I was sitting kissing my girlfriend and they said 'Can I ask you to stop it?' I was like that 'Wait a minute, if I was in a straight pub I might consider it but you are coming into a gay pub and asking me to stop it!' and I was like that 'If you don't like it then leave!' They just looked at me. I didnae care. If I was in a straight club I might consider it, but in a gay club! (laughs), you know, it was just a bit of cheek ... I think they find gay pubs more friendly ... For lassies, the straight lassies that come in 'cause they all think all the gay guys are absolutely amazing. (Tracey)

Tracey's account also highlights the gendered aspects of 'intrusion'; it is gay men who are seen as 'fascinating' and 'exciting', and straight women are portrayed as potential 'contaminators' who are not entitled to be there, as also indicated in Sonia's account of 'hen' parties (see also Skeggs, 1999, 2001). The 'fascination' and corresponding de-sexualisation of gay men is rightly pointed to by Casey (2004) (a de/sexualisation also happens to lesbians) but there's room to move in that, room to claim space and resources. Neither lesbians nor straight women fully occupy 'gay' social space; their occupation is always precarious as well as challenging. Spatial occupations were often marked by misrecognitions, refusals, disappointments, tensions and avoidance.

There are various processes at play within scene spaces, which work to create material, subjective and embodied discomforts and constraints; there are re-assessments and reclamations of worth despite the mis-recognitions, exclusions and devaluations enforced within. Scene space, as leisure space, mixes consumption and leisure with identifications and subjectivities (being 'gay' in gay space): with this, though, is the potential for exclusion as 'leisure' is not the only thing happening in such space. The right to space is not pre-given but must be negotiated across different territories, which have different rules of entry and multiple checks upon continued 'entitlement' to be there – swapping your 'TK MAXX' outfit for a 'DKNY' one involves more than re-arranging the letters, and the fit will depend upon and vary according to gender, class and sexuality. When intersecting scene space 'performances', and the embodiment of identity, with a reading of material inequalities and circumstances, it is difficult to fully utilise and appropriate the fundamentally theoretical Butleresque readings of queer. Although Butler (1990) usefully illuminates aspects of the operation of queer identity, the 'higher' reading of performance and performativity may mean little to working-class lesbians inside and outside scene spaces. A material 'reality'-based reading of performance and portrayal is more suitable, offering a useful illumination of the performative, embodied and spatialised aspects of classed, gendered and sexualised interactions and the ways these can – and cannot – be capitalised upon (Bourdieu, 1984). The next chapter explores the ways in which these interactions, distinctions and materialities are re/produced in intimate life.

7
Ties That Bind

There has been increasing recognition of same-sex relationships across Western Europe.[1] with the introduction of the Civil Partnership Act in the United Kingdom (December 2005) effectively mainstreaming same-sex rights, some would say, to marry in all but name. With this Act has come the proliferation of new sexual stories, taking up much coverage in the lesbian and gay press and in the international media. Commentaries and controversies then run from the celebration of (monogamous) coupledom which has been extended to same-sex partners, in a thoroughly 'tolerable' way, to partial mockery and ironic humour, to outright condemnation, where the featuring of 'homosexuality' as a 'sin' is endlessly repeated. While some evangelical Christian groups have disapproved of civil partnerships, given that they supposedly parody and make a mockery of traditional heterosexual marriage, others question why lesbians and gays would want to adopt the conservative values of marriage in the first place, given that it places sexuality in its 'proper' place: within the private, monogamous, (tax-paying, dual-income) household (Richardson, 2004). For many working-class lesbians and gays, civil partnerships may mean little at best, given that extension of pension rights are less likely to apply, but the implications and consequences of civil partnerships may actually be restrictive and penalising.

Viewing sexuality as interconnecting and intersecting with other social inequalities offers an understanding of who can and cannot occupy the category of sexual citizenship – or indeed citizenship more generally (Taylor, 2005b, 2005c). While lesbian and gay activist groups have been, and continue, to demand equal rights, prominent in both the repeal of Section 28/2a and the introduction of the Civil Partnership Act in the United Kingdom, they have often done so, for pragmatic reasons perhaps, on a platform of essentialising, homogenising discourses

(Rahman, 2000, 2004). In prioritising sexuality as the focal point of resistance, other social inequalities affecting lesbians and gays are often sidelined. Elsewhere, I have explored working-class lesbians' political awareness and activism, within a changing political climate that promotes notions of 'classless', yet in which classed conflict remains apparent (Taylor, 2005b, 2005c). In emphasising the daily politicisation of their lives, inequalities of class and sexuality in the sphere of citizenship are interconnected.

Yet lesbian relationships are widely depicted as examples of 'pure relationships' (Giddens, 1992), shaped by 'equality' and 'sameness' (Dunne, 1997). Such qualities are seen to reform patterns of intimacy, structured through a 'family of friends' rather than through couple relationships alone (Weston, 1997; Weeks et al., 2001). Much has been said about ever increasing 'families of choice' who are free from hetero-sexual family formations and traditional familial obligations (Giddens, 1992; Roseneil, 2000), yet this again fails to consider class as an important component in generating resources and opportunities to live 'differently', in well-protected and resourced 'communities' (Weeks et al., 2001). In privileging accounts of 'reciprocity' and 'accountability' in lesbian rela-tionships, inequalities and challenges within lesbian relationships are smoothed over. 'Sameness' is highlighted with reference to shared gender but there is little attention to the 'differences' of class within this. While I argue that class can effect, enhance, disrupt and fracture the relationships of working-class lesbians, the dominant academic position tends to emphasise individual agency, creativity, autonomy, choice and mutual responsibility; on establishing 'pick and mix' relationships, rather than being confined to traditional family ties. However, other factors such as poverty and unemployment have an impact on 'picking and choosing'.

In my research, some relationships are avoided altogether and although some commentators would point to the element of democratic 'choice' involved here, the ways these are realised and experienced point to the continuation of class inequalities. This runs contrary to notions of 'democratization', a process that is seen to undermine and even erase inequalities in intimate relationships (Giddens, 1992). In pointing out the continuing inequalities at play in inter-personal working-class lesbian relationships, it is not my purpose to pathologise respondents' relation-ships (to idealise anyone's relationship is also flawed) but instead to explore the ways that class manifests itself in relationships.

Giddens (1992) talks of sharing thoughts and feelings, of talking and listening within intimate relationships, all pointing to an emphasis on 'mutual disclosure'. Giddens's (1992) 'self-reflexive' state conjures up ideas of positive choices and reflections, as individuals self-consciously consider what kind of relationships they want (Skolnick, 1992). But as Jamieson claims, intimacy can only take on this character if participants can remove social barriers and transcend structural inequalities; while noting that stories of equality and 'disclosing intimacy' may be popular, she suggests that these are 'easily matched by more conventional tales predicated on gender inequality and conventional heterosexual practices' (1998:134). Yet, while continued divisions are often theorised in relation to gender, the influence of class on relationships is under-researched.

All respondents in my study did indeed make choices within their relationships but these were informed by fear of exposure of classed and sexual selves, access to and dis/comfort within social and leisure spaces, and the in/compatibilities generated through different class positions and experiences. Boundaries around class identifications, experiences and empathies can produce dis-identifications, disassociations and mis-understandings (Johnson and Lawler, 2005). There are continued tensions and withholding of important identifications, as well as classed resent-ments. To be a lesbian is not, alas, to belong to one open and equal happy family. Different things and different experiences have different meanings, even in bed. In this chapter I examine the combined cultural, economic and emotional capitals in operation within personal relation-ships (Bell, 1990; Reay, 2002, 2004) in order to argue that class 'remains a structuring force in terms of how people experience and enact their "personal" relationships' (Johnson and Lawler, 2005: 3). While love may be thought of as authentically personal, once again the social organi-sation of who we love or feel 'at home' with is again revealed.

Intimate relationships can be sites for intense hostilities and battles, with mis/understandings about what and how the women identified occurring. Class inequalities and differences produced emotional, physical and material distance between potential and actual partners (Johnson and Lawler, 2005). For instance, several women spoke of the problems they had when having relationships with middle-class women – feeling 'inadequate' and unable to compete with middle-class capitals and entitlements. These 'inadequacies' produced intense discomforts and insecurities within intimate relationships. Unequal economic resources and capitals created dependence and fostered feelings of resentment and jealousy. Insecurities and 'threats' to identity also appeared in relationships, as challenges were voiced over the entitlement to properly identify as working-class – potential commonalities were ruptured through hostile refusals.

The women in my study had a variety of different relationships, currently and in the past, which calls into question the homogeneous picture portrayed in some studies. My sample included women who were single, women who were seeking partners, women in long- and short-term couple relationships, and women in non-monogamous relationships. Fifteen women in my study had children, and ten of those women were single parents, which had an added effect upon not/meeting women and (not) 'coming out'. The 'pure (adult, couple) relationship' immediately becomes more complicated (Gabb, 2001). Broader family and friendship networks also feature in the construction of intimacy, where class could act either as a bridge or as a gaping distance between intimates and between respective families. Not all relationships were happy and/or healthy. Several women reported isolation, dependence and even abuse. Jeannette, Elaine and Becky previously experienced abusive lesbian relationships, while Kirsty previously had an abusive relationship with a man. Sukhjit, Kirsty, Mavis, Sally and Becky experienced abusive family relationships while growing up and all left home at a young age. Many of my respondents were, or had been previously, isolated from other lesbians. Support systems were frequently lacking, further fractured by silence, non-disclosure and a fear of exposure.

The dark end of the street

Lacking a legitimate space where meetings could occur, and lacking social and economic capital to 'buy into' available (gay) space, meant that meetings were often 'accidental', temporary and 'unsafe', thus they were often limited in 'mobilising facilities which could facilitate the construction of a different life' (Dunne, 1997: 89). All women had to negotiate a degree of 'outness' when meeting other women, causing a fear of exposure as well as anxiety and apprehension about the safety of 'coming out'. Potential intimacy required personal disclosure at the out-set, rather than as a gradual process. In a world that tends to assume one thing, heterosexuality, lesbians have to show that they are 'the other', to mark themselves out as it were. This kind of personal disclosure is not always comfortable. Angela, for example, spoke of the 'terrifying' process of 'coming-out' into often 'unsafe' space, while Sally talks about her lack of knowledge about social places, and potential support mechanisms, as putting a strain on her relationship:

> We didn't know about Manchester. We just went into pubs and went over into Leeds and Newcastle. The relationship was strong but I think we was naïve, you know. We didn't have many places to go. We didn't know of these gay pubs. (Sally)

Non-participation and exclusion from scene space meant that meetings and relationships often occurred in 'unusual' settings. Unfortunately, these locations were often temporary and unstable, producing a high degree of vulnerability and potential exposure. Nevertheless, several enjoyed and laughed at such 'accidental' encounters, as can be seen in Pam's tale. The ridiculous nature of the encounters are acknowledged, as is the make do and mend attitude, the idea of 'getting it on and getting on with it':

> Em, in a car park (laughs). Outside a pub, in Riverton. We were both drunk and waiting for lifts home from respective parents … Then I moved and worked as a fruit picker and lived in a tent for three months and met someone from Poland. This was a much freer relationship 'cause I was living in a tent (laughs). So I had my own space, in my tent. And she had her own tent. (Pam)

Often these locations contained an element of risk, requiring a high degree of self-exposure. For instance, a lot of women spoke of 'accidentally' or co-incidentally meeting partners. This involved guess-work regarding the sexuality of potential partners and if this was mis-read the consequences could be severe – embarrassment or bruising. As such, many women had to manage a balancing act between being out and being out there. Isolation (both geographically and emotionally) was a common feature of working-class lesbians' accounts and many were prevented from meeting other women, either accidentally or through structured support mechanisms. To overcome isolation several women placed advertisements in newspapers, magazines or on teletext, as Amy explains:

> I met Steph through teletext adverts on the telly, how cool is that! (laughs) … We were on the teletext one night and I said I'm going to send one in so I did, I got some pure dodgy replies I'm not joking! (Amy)

As Amy suggests, this approach is not without problems, although on this occasion the response is one of amusement rather than being upset.

However, meeting other lesbians was sometimes strange, out of the ordinary and even upsetting. On meeting Amy, Steph's apparent furtiveness was a consequence of feeling unsafe and awkward in public space and had the effect of reproducing this sentiment:

> I hated her on first sight. Oh aye, I hated her I thought she was so ignorant. But that again comes doon tae carryin' yerself off and

because she's no oot, I was supposed to meet her somewhere and she walked round the corner and just went like that 'c'mon then', I was like 'What?' (laughs). Pure big scary person dragging me doon the road. (Amy)

Although 'safety' is theorised in relation to sexuality (Corteen, 2002) notions of 'safe space' are complex, compounded by class and gender (Haylett, 2001; Moran, 2000; Quilley, 1997). Working-class lesbians had to manage their sexual and class identities and positions, which informed perceptions of safety and danger about meeting places and the individuals within those places. For example, when meeting other women, interviewees often had to deal with and manage 'first (classed) impressions', coping with secrecy and fear of exposure. As Amy illustrates, her discomfort was heightened by the danger of 'outing' her classed self, and the potential judgements which this would incur:

I had to be home 'cause my wee sister was watching David [son] and she was like 'Oh well I'll just come hame wi ye' and I was like 'Oh naw! (laughs) my hoose is a shit hole!' (laughs) (Amy)

Many women were at risk in the public sphere and these risks were often carried over into private spheres. Rather than a disclosure of lesbian identity it would seem that there are often repeated silences, self-censoring and negation.

In 'coming out' to their families, none of the women in my study spoke of 'queering' them, instead there was often a fracturing of intimacy – disclosures were not affirmations and acceptance not celebration. Academic references to 'coming out' rarely include references to 'coming-out' about class position, yet this was evidently significant for many of the women in my study. Valentine et al. (2003) explore the familial outcomes of 'coming out' and highlight the ways in which this process can contribute to the reproduction of existing social and economic inequalities: they argue that in middle-class households young people were motivated to compensate against awareness of their sexuality with educational and employment success, in order to fulfil at least some parental expectations, while this was not the case for working-class youth. Further, they assert that working-class families were more likely to respond in terms of violence and rejection, a rather problematic conceptualisation which dangerously positions working-class families and individuals as more homophobic, without attention to the range of homophobias present, silenced and vividly vocalised in a range of familial contexts. I examine the classed manifestations of 'coming-out' across different settings and relationships, charting family relationships, family reactions, parental roles and responses, and the problems in managing sexuality across these sites.

Coming-out – a class act?

The lack of support and affirmation of lesbian relationships, both by their immediate families and friends and by wider society, meant that many women often experienced isolation. There were a variety of negative, positive, mixed and delayed reactions by families when they 'came out' to them. Kelly states that her mother went through a 'grieving process' when she told her mother she was a lesbian:

> K: My mum went through a grieving process when I came out to her.
> L: Did she? That's awful!
> K: She went through a grieving process because, and also a lot of mother-daughter relationships are kinda based on this mutual heterosexuality about our families, it's all what we do with the babies and all that kind of stuff, it's like connections and relationships and what you do when you come out, you shatter that, that kind of relationship. (Kelly and Lisa)

Being a lesbian spoiled Kelly's mother's (classed and gendered) expectations of her, the effect of which is powerfully described as 'shattering'.

Differences between respective families were highlighted in relationships. Discourses and practices constructing family intimacy can be seen as classed discourses – with class effects. The preferred self-disclosing emotional intimacy that has been associated with middle-class families (Jamieson, 1998) can serve to pathologise other family types, yet, as several women realised, 'openness' is not necessarily positive (Reay, 2004). There are also practical time constraints that prevent a disclosing, emotional intimacy, and there are risks in staying silent as well as being open. Although Sonia notes that, in contrast to her mother, Joan's [girlfriend] family are more open and talkative about their emotions, she demonstrates that openness and expressiveness are not conflict free. Inequalities are still produced here in terms of what can be disclosed and who gets to say what. Sonia is 'out' but her family are not out about it, while Joan's 'touchy, feely' family don't want to discuss this particular issue:

> We're very close but we just don't talk about it and it's strange. I mean, Joan's accepted into the family. There's no problems. Where

I am, Joan's there ... But we just don't ever talk about it, which some people find really strange. It is in a way but it's kind of like that stereotype, you don't speak about your emotions, your feelings, you know ... Their family – totally different. But when we first got together, it was crap with her family. Now, my family's never had a problem with Joan, which is weird, but her family, which is why we don't talk about emotions or whatever, hers are a very huggy, feely family – oh God, it was hell. Absolute hell ... my family who don't talk about our feelings and we never discuss it, but yet Joan's never had a problem with my family, you know. But yet touchy feely middle-class family had a big problem with it and it took them ages to acknowledge our relationship. (Sonia)

Class differences affected relationships; they also affected the ways that families responded to partners. For Jo's mum, the ability to 'have a laugh' with Jo's current partner and relate through shared class experiences, meant that sexuality was less of an 'issue'. Class was a connecting experience whereas sexuality could have been disconnecting. Lynn experiences class difficulties through her child's relationship with a middle-class man. Lynn's statement reveals a lot about class processes and the emotional impact of class, her anger is apparent even though she has to bite her lip:

There's a bit in me that thinks his mum doesnae think Rosie is good enough or that she should be grateful, you know 'cause he's a 'good catch', that really fucks me off! I just can't stand it. She's brighter than him, he's had the education but he's a bit dim, he wouldnae be where he is if he didnae have the background. Makes me angry! He's no got a clue about life, 'people who are drug addicts and unemployed *choose* to be', oh, I've got to watch what I say when he's in ... Do you know what I mean, oh I'm probably quite angry still int I? I think there's probably quite a lot in my background that makes me feel these people don't have a dammed clue, because they have more *things* and money and they think they're superior. (Lynn)

Lynn also criticises the way in which gender inequalities construct her daughter as a 'lucky' dependent and her own anger is made against the continuation of such norms. Her unwillingness to meet the parents of her daughter's boyfriend is affected by her sexuality; she is both proud and ashamed of her distance from the norm. Lynn's account can been seen to both challenge and critique the condescending 'interest' in her, as some fascinating 'other'. Paradoxically, she remains frightened of and 'dreads' this judgement:

> I dread meeting that woman and that man, I don't want to meet them and I don't know if it's fear, I just have this awful, I don't want to get into that! Again, me and Mary not only are we working-class but *lesbian* as well! (laughs). There's a bit of me that thinks '*Good*, I don't want to be like *that*'. (Lynn)

Many of the women who were also mothers spoke of protecting children against possible stigma, becoming more secretive and less visible. Gabb (2005) focuses on lesbian mothers' management of their maternal-sexual identities, typically uncharted and absent from studies into lesbian/queer spaces, occluding other facets of lesbians' lives and experiences. The home, in Gabb's study, was found to be crucial in lesbians' consolidation of their (whole) selves, wherein lesbian and maternal identities could be reconciled (Twigg, 2000), rather disrupted by the heterosexual gaze upon them in normative everyday spaces from the school to the supermarket. Yet, for some, home may be neither sweet nor safe, failing to provide such a reconciliation of identity. Most mothers commented on the difficulty of occupying the categories of 'lesbian' and 'mother'. For example, Kirsty said that she found it difficult to meet or sustain relationships with other women because she has a child, making her a 'less attractive option'. In contrast, Jeannette claims that having children gives her a certain degree of 'respectability', moving her closer towards heterosexual family norms and the respected, although precarious, position of 'mother'. Studies of 'alternative' lesbian families often fail to address the issue of sexuality in families with children (Dunne, 1998) while Gabb's study of lesbian mothers offers a challenge to the taken-for-grantedness of Giddens's theorisation: 'It [lesbian parent families] is no longer the "pure (adult) relationship" ... but one where others' needs take precedence' (2001: 336–337). Taking account of their children's needs often meant not 'coming-out', not being open and maybe not even having a relationship at all.

Relationships were not always comfortable or safe. Several women reported being isolated within relationships, which were often affected by mutual pressure and stress, as each partner negotiated 'outness' in everyday contexts. To be in a lesbian relationship is often, on a very practical level, to exist within a stressful and fraught environment and this cannot help but impact on the relationship itself, especially if there is nowhere else visible to turn. In fact, a couple of women spoke of previous abusive relationships, which were often explained through lack of 'alternatives' and isolation. Abuse within lesbian relationships is an under-researched area (Lobel, 1986; Ohms, 2002; Renzetti, 1998), the existence of which compromises the conceptualisation of lesbian relationships as alternative sites of equality (Dunne, 1997; Giddens, 1992; Weeks et al., 2001).

Jeannette felt that she could not confide in her family about her abusive relationship and felt disappointed by the lack of support when she eventually did so, as they offered no practical or emotional support but instead elected to ignore the matter. If the whole relationship is denied, then so too are the individual components within it, bad or good:

> So she [Jeannette's mother] kind of confronted me and I said, yeah, it was true. Then, as they often do, they just ignored it then for a few years and hoped it would go away and then I broke up with my first girlfriend and it was really nasty. She had been quite abusive and I told my mum because I was too upset all of the time really to hide it and she pretended that she thought we were just friends and I was like 'How could you?' (Jeannette)

While wanting to avoid the portrayal of working-class and lesbian identity as inherently problematic and/or abusive, it is necessary to highlight the factors that the women themselves viewed as *causal* in abusive relationships, as demonstrated by Elaine's account:

> She was really screwed up, I was quite screwed up. When things went wrong for her to take my mind off things I'd go out and flirt. I kinda felt I was in the middle of this tornado, there was quite a lot of things happening round me. I got money stolen from me, my Giro got stolen right at the end. Things got stolen from me by that lassie I got involved with, she stole money from me. Another lassie stole cash from me and she actually beat me up at one point. I got her done for that, I went to the police about that and about the money. She got done for assault. There was another lassie who attacked me as well, somebody that I'd been flirting with ... We just didn't get on as lovers, you know, she was 18 and she was cutting her wrists. (Elaine)

Kirsty also speaks of the isolation and lack of alternatives available to her when she was in an abusive relationship with a male partner, narrating the desperate hopelessness of having nowhere else to turn and nothing else to do:

> I stayed with him because I thought, well, what do I do when I leave him? I've got no family to go to. I haven't got any money. I'm not educated. What sort of job could I get? What am I gonna do? I'm gonna be stuck in the house on my own. I've been isolated from other people. Do you know what I mean? What do you do?
> (Kirsty)

Abusive relationships cut across all classes and sexualities, fracturing intimate encounters. It would not be right to idealise personal relationships as conflict-free zones, or as areas of personal sanctuary; barriers erected can be impassable, harmful and even dangerous. Heterosexuality has been theorised as an unequal site of gender, with potential abuses of power likely, while in lesbian relationships other imbalances, for example, class and/or other social/personal circumstances can provide the context for abuse (Jamieson, 1998). The potential for, and actuality of, abuse is present in lesbian relationships, perhaps heightened by the compelling grounds for silence, secrecy and non-disclosure.[2]

'Coming-out' is experienced differently across different contexts and receives different responses. While not wanting to attribute non/acceptance and support, or lack of it, to any particular social class, I would suggest that these can be classed processes, in terms of opportunities, responses and interpretations. As was seen, shared working-class experience can sometimes bridge potential problems amongst and between some of the women's families. Class processes, tensions and inequalities also featured in intimate relationships and friendships, where 'pick and mix' didn't really 'mix' very well.

Friends like these

Dunne (1998) outlines the 'rules' of friendship and suggests that they are based around equality, support, reciprocity and balance, factors which may be particularly relevant to lesbians and gays given their institutionalised rejection from (heterosexual) society. The notion of 'friends as family', friends becoming a modified, extended family, is widespread in the literature on lesbian and gay relationships (Weeks et al., 2001). However, friendship is much more problematic than this – friendships formed by a shared marginal identity may fulfil the need to belong, but for many women in my study not/belonging occurred in terms of sexuality as well as class. In both cases there was rarely a voluntary disclosure of the self, instead class and sexual boundaries were created around friendships and around intimacy. This supports the claim that friendships are a much more 'mixed bag' than the ideal 'pure relationship' depicts (Jamieson, 1998: 89). Jamieson also raises the question of whether working-class friendships may be viewed in terms of necessity, versus middle-class 'pure intimacy', where disclosing intimacy becomes a luxury. Although she suggests that there is little evidence to support such theorisation, this does begin to point to possible classed differences within friendships.

Friendships are shaped through a sense of shared experiences and shared 'lifestyles' (Heath and Cleaver, 2003; Weeks et al., 2001) – but they are also lived through economic and cultural inequalities. Interestingly, many of the same women who asserted their greater commonalities with working-class women and the importance of this in intimate relationships, also claimed to be able to 'mix' with all classes and form friendships across class groups. However, this could be interpreted more as aspiration towards egalitarian *ideals* as the financial restrictions in different social contexts did not always allow them to mix *equally* with middle-class people. Many lesbians spoke of the difficult friendship encounters they had with middle-class friends. Problems were caused by the different and unequal conditions of the friendship, such as ability to go out, spend money and 'know about' certain ('worthwhile') things – finding common ground was often difficult.

Others spoke of having 'understanding' middle-class friends; often this meant that friends would understand their inability to socialise due to lack of finances, but the inequality was still in place. This 'understanding' also contrasts with empathetic understandings, in that it is based on sympathy from a distance. Interactions highlighted differences, divisions, and privileges, which often worked against potential commonalities. Although Mandy emphasises her ability to mix, she is still conscious of her 'difference', even if friendships with middle-class children had certain material advantages:

'I felt kinda like, em, a little bit upset, but it was good too 'cause I got good things off people. So even though they had more money than me I don't feel they used it against me in any way.' In Mandy's account class is presented as 'not an issue'. Mandy notes that some middle-class people are not 'snobs', although to state that is to acknowledge the unspoken hierarchy between classes, otherwise what reasons would they have for basing 'snobbery' on in the first place? Shona also speaks about 'mixing' in social settings and, in describing her working-class friends' reactions towards this, she is conscious of their 'defensiveness' and of the varied abilities to 'match' certain 'standards':

> I know a lot of people who go 'How come you mix with such and such?' To me it's not an issue to go out with someone that other friends consider very posh or outwith their social scene, whatever … I certainly don't feel that I'm worthless or for want of a better word, I think some of my friends just would refuse to go out with my other friends. As I said I've got a very mixed group of acquaintances and good friends that I've got and I do slip in quite well. They just, I don't think they can see themselves, I think they would just feel that they don't have the right clothes, or the right accent, or the right attitude or em … It's not about money, for me it's not about money, for them I think possibly it is about money, yeah. I'm always skint! (laughs). My friends know that but I think I always give something back whether it's financial or somebody to chat to or whatever. (Shona)

Even though Shona obviously perceives her role within her social group as being a rewarding and positive one, she still positions herself as 'the other', 'slipping in' and giving something back in return for membership. Emotional capital is secured by 'paying back', though not in financial terms.

Many spoke of their disappointment in 'finding out' about the 'real' (middle)class position of friends. The resulting devaluations reveal that friendships can be discredited and rendered unworthy on the basis of middle-classness, as well as through working-class status.[3] Others reported being let down and feeling, sometimes inexplicably, disappointed when finding out about their friends' 'true' class position. Here Pam describes how previous commonalities were ruptured by a classed discovery:

> I think I probably am friends with Sophie … She considers herself not well off and I went to her house. I was really, really good friends with her actually and so I went to her house and there's like seven bedrooms and studies and bathrooms and I just felt this, all of a sudden, I just, it's changed the relationship. I don't know why. It shouldn't change the relationship, should it? … her dad was stood there doing her ironing for her. Do you know what I mean? I just, I just knew that we were very, very different, you know. (Pam)

Pam's tone is one of betrayal, of being told one thing and then finding out the other.

An overarching theme in many women's accounts was that working-class people were often viewed as more expressive, direct and honest, in contrast to the dishonest 'pretence' displayed by middle-class people. Many women were fully aware of their own stereotypes – but their perceptions were backed up by their own experiences. Even so, Grace 'admits' to her position as 'anti middle-class', suggestive of the discomfort felt when realising that you can't or won't 'mix' or 'fit in', as well as highlighting processes of defiance and challenge.

In her social circle, Dawn has to challenge stereotypical views about working-class women, as 'dole scroungers' and 'deviant' single-mothers, while Liz talks about a previous group of middle-class friends from whom she gradually became more distanced due to the increasing pressures and expectations placed upon her. In/compatibilities were generated through a combination of economic inequalities, which could support a certain 'lifestyle', and 'arrogant', 'pretentious' attitudes: 'The friends I lived with were very opinionated, very image conscious, it was always about having the right clothes and looking the right way and going out and taking drugs' (Liz). Generally speaking, many women in my study suggested that, as well as being more 'real', working-class friends have more 'real', consequential and significant conversations; they talk about things that matter, as Fiona does: 'So they just seemed more, oh I don't know, just more the sort of people I would want to socialise with, more sort of *real things* were being talked about.'

While at school, Mandy's friendships were predominantly with 'tolerant' middle-class girls and, on reflection, she speaks of having less in common with a working-class girl. Here Mandy invokes notions of 'decency' (Skeggs, 1997), positioning herself with the 'decent' middle-class girls, and tends to individualise class concerns as personality issues, a position which she is sceptical of elsewhere. A 'real' (working-class) position can sometimes be too real or basic and dis-identifications were evident here, as working-class friends were marked as 'a bit gobby' and 'quite rough'. Notions of in/decency, apparent in sexual relationships, also fractured compatibilities with working-class friends.

Interviewees made 'investments' in knowing certain individuals but were also restricted in this process through economic, social and cultural barriers. For example, many spoke of the difficulties in meeting lesbian and gay friends and in finding commonalities when they did not 'fit in'.[4] Women spoke of the difficulties in meeting lesbian friends, especially when their current friendship groups were heterosexual – this meant that they were more likely to continue mixing in these circles, which was sometimes experienced as isolating and restrictive. Inequalities were played out in friendships themselves as different members had different investments, in meeting 'different' people. As both Dawn and Grace suggest, interpersonal and structural inequalities work in tandem and restrict friendship choices and possibilities:

> I don't really have many gay friends which kinda cuts down my options for going out really 'cause my friends don't want to go to a place where there are no men and I don't want to go to a place where there are no women. People tend to know that gay men are gay a lot easier than they know that lesbians are lesbians, so you're not likely to get introduced by friends of friends so it's difficult. (Dawn)

> Em, my friends that I drink with most of the time are all heterosexual women, so we're normally not out in the scene unless one of them's being nosey, do you know what I mean? (Grace)

If you are 'one of them', then meeting similar women can be difficult. When gauging affinities and differences between friends and partners, many women in my study were similarly 'nosey' about their partner's class position. Clearly, intersections between class and sexuality affected the boundaries of in/compatibilities, re/making hierarchies through a series of distinctions, dis/identifications and material im/possibilities (Bourdieu, 2000; Illouz, 1997; Johnson and Lawler, 2005). Jamieson notes that personal relationships 'are not typically shaped in whatever way gives pleasure without the taint of practical, economic and other material circumstances' (1999: 482); Johnson and Lawler (2005) agree that 'taint' is a particularly good word, conveying how class is reproduced interpersonally in the ways individuals feel about each other. The 'taint' goes against working-class individuals, while here working-classness is imbued with positive, worthy associations, to be denied to those who don't quite meet this required standard.

Call yourself working-class?

The continued salience of class identities is apparent in intimate relationships, where class identification, class experience and class 'defence' lead to denials of others' entitlement to claim a working-class self. This 'defensiveness' appears in other research accounts where the unwillingness of respondents to align themselves with class is explained through the moral connotations which class contains (Savage et al., 2001); you do not call yourself that which you do not want to be. Savage et al. explain class defensiveness as a classed process: a group of self-confident, 'reflexive' individuals are described as those who have the cultural capital to play reflexively with the ideas of class, in contrast to those who 'lack these resources and feel threatened by the implications of relating class to their own personal identities' (2001: 875). In contrast, the strong identifications, anger and resentments within relationships, evident in my study, can be viewed as a result of the strong effect of class, and a consequent 'inability' to be 'ambivalent' about it. If something hurts it hurts actually and reflexivity goes out of the metaphorical window.

Class contributed to ideas and feelings about 'attraction' and 'worth'. This was the case in relationships with self-identified working-class women as many women sought to 'check out' their partner's class, highlighting its continued importance. Class was a significant factor in shaping their sense of self and many women wanted this affirmed and taken seriously by partners, or prospective partners. Several women were themselves engaged in complex processes of de/valuations as they estimated other women's class positions and challenged partners' identifications. Here, anger surfaced through 'unjustified' class identifications made by partners – those who 'pretended' to be working-class were viewed as unworthy of the term. These differentiations, judgements and resentments within intimate relationships highlight the emotive aspects of class meanings and identifications. Empathetic understandings were desired, but only from the proper, entitled source.

Although closeness and indeed distance was not always problematic, often the very presence of another problematised class definitions, leading to discomfort on both sides. In contrast to a process of imparting important information, reinforcing intimacy rather than distance, women often problematised and questioned their partner's working-class position, disputing their entitlement to identify: 'But she thinks she's working-class ... but I think she's just kidding on' (Amy). These judgements and differentiations, based on often painful and conflicting comparisons, produced resentments and generated distance rather than proximity, sameness or closeness. This is again indicative of the emotional meanings and embeddedness of class, which generate claims of il/legitimacy. Those with only 'surface', 'temporary' or 'little' emotional investments and/or experiences of class inequalities are disregarded as flawed 'fakes'. The process of comparison and contrast verges on competitiveness as several women in my study sought to find out if their partners *really* were working-class, if they had earned the right to be defined as such. The felt resentment when partners unjustifiably claimed the term 'working-class', appropriating something that was not theirs to touch, is a huge contrast with the positioning of working-classness as something to be escaped from, a slur and a one-way judgement (Johnson and Lawler, 2005; Skeggs, 1997):

> My ex used to say she was working-class and she was so not, do you know what I mean. Em, 'cause she said she was working-class when I first met her and I thought, you so aren't ... looking at the house that your mum and dad live in ... But, em, it caused her a problem 'cause she couldn't believe that I was challenging the fact that I didn't think she was, you know. (Grace)

Challenging a person's class generates hurt and disbelief, but these same feelings were responsible for causing Grace's doubt. While Grace dismissed her girlfriend's claims by pointing to the material markers of 'privilege', these markers remain intact. Amy also challenges her current partner's class position bringing in the embodied aspects of class: Steph is placed as middle-class, or at least not working-class, because of her investments in presentational standards and her deportment, 'the way she carries herself'.

Often the lack of working-class 'culture' is used to disprove girlfriends' working-class claims. Emphasising the importance of cultural factors over economic ones, Jeannette uses the lack of working-class cultural experience to define her girlfriend's class position. Although her girlfriend's family was 'flat broke' they had 'aspirations' and 'values' and 'pretensions', which, for Jeannette, made them middle-class. Similarly, Kelly and Lisa attempt to define the class position of Lisa's current partner, Beth, and conclude that 'she might be middle-class but poor', which again suggests that she is lacking the cultural signs and associations of being working-class. Estimations revolve around such judgements, defences and invalidations and class sometimes appears to be like a battle line, constantly re-drawn and negotiated.

In order to contextualise these tensions it should be noted that many women also spoke of the positive elements associated with relationships with other ('proper') working-class women. It was not all accusations and denials, sometimes common ground could be stable ground. For example, Sukhjit speaks of being able to share experiences and coming to a better understanding of her own life events, realising that 'her' problems were in fact social problems:

> She had quite a strong working-class identity, she grew up around the miners' strike, so it's a very *different* kind of working-class experience, but when I used to say things she'd say 'Yeah!' It kinda astounded me, it

was the first time I thought 'This isn't just to do with being Asian', and being brought up in this Asian environment when my parents didn't work, it's also about something bigger than that ... Yeah and it was fantastic just being able to talk to someone about different experiences and she knew not what you meant but where you were coming from and it didn't sound so strange to her and she had a take on it that wasn't individualistic, you know 'You find it hard because you're the one with the problem' kind of thing but something that was a bit more complex than that about, you know, wider society ... I'd say that most of the women that I relate to are working-class women, most of my friends. (Sukhjit)

Differences within this relationship were displaced through shared understandings and ability to empathise across different experiences. Personal disclosures were respected, rather than patronised, and re-interpreted rather than devalued. Similarly, Jo claims that she is not only able to share a similar culture with her working-class partner but also a sense of humour, informed by class position. Such jokes, told by an 'outsider' would take on a different set of meanings, they would not have the right to find them funny:

So we automatically connected on that and just like kind of stories about like, you know, stories about how it can be difficult if you're kind of growing up working-class but you can laugh about that as well, you know. Like our kind of drunken Irish grandfathers or whatever. But yeah, I think it's humour. (Jo)

Sharing 'common ground' may also be un/comfortable for a variety of (classed) reasons, thus shared gender, even sexuality, is often not enough in itself to produce affinities, equalities or so called lifestyle choices (Dunne, 1997; Weeks et al., 2001). The intersections between class and sexuality recreate expectations and assumptions about 'worth', 'decency' and 'excess', often materialised on the bodies of working-class lesbians, yet also expressly refused and simultaneously re-invoked by them.

Common ground (but not too common)

Many women spoke of being able to relate to other working-class people, generating a sense of empathy, understanding and affirmation of life experiences and identities, whereas middle-class individuals and lifestyles were viewed as remote and distanced from their lives. There is something very attractive about not having to explain. Class was felt to be important in the physical aspects of attraction, as an embodied characteristic, revealed through accent and appearance, something to be 'read' and understood:

> I'm more attracted to other women who then turn out to be from a working-class background. It's like I feel I can talk about things and there's a shared comprehension of what that means, you know … Like, it's quite difficult to explain … It almost feels like that kinda manifests itself on a kind of physical level in people … I feel like it's more possible to be more fully myself … Em, yeah I think it's security, it's that, it's something to do with like how people have to make their way in the world and if somebody just had to be more kind of, they've had to hold it together themselves a bit more and they've had to struggle a bit more, that's written into someone's face and that attracted me. (Fiona)

Appearance operates as the mechanism for authorisation, legitimation and delegitimation across various social sites (Skeggs, 2001), including within intimate relationships (Johnson and Lawler, 2005), and in this example working-class appearance is positively valued, as a way of recognising shared experiences and struggles. The ability to 'read' a physically embodied working-class narrative is seen as reassuring and reaffirming, a case of knowing what you are going to get from the picture on the label.

Jo asserts the importance of shared experience and values. Lacking shared understandings, Jo feels 'patronised' by middle-class women who then 'bring up insecurities' in her because of the perceived or real contrast with her own life. Kelly talks about 'inter-class' relationships as possibly being problematic, a factor, which she feels, is rarely acknowledged:

> I've got a dyke friend who I used to live with and she's Jewish and she's middle-class … She sees class, if she wants to have a relationship with someone she wants them to have an awareness of anti-Semitism and being Jewish, it's important to who she is, em, but she has a big awareness about class. She knows it's an important factor in going out with someone. 'Cause if people are Hindu or Jewish or Christian people go 'Oh, how difficult is it having an inter-faith relationship?' People are more aware of it. But *class*, if you said an 'inter-class' relationship' people would think you were being totally off your head and being over the top but it isn't any different. If you're having an inter-faith

relationship, whatever religion, it's just part of somebody's identity which is important. It's like, people often talk about non-Jewish people going out with Jewish people but she's middle-class, she has a different culture. (Kelly)

Kelly's comments suggest that 'inter-class' interconnections may not be all that 'interesting'; the 'difference' class makes is often not intriguing but is both irrelevant and 'extreme' – in highlighting it you may risk being seen as 'totally off your head'.

Working-class women are not always valued as a source of knowledge, embodying valued working-class existence. There may be no desire to share understandings, identifications and experiences. Instead, relationships with working-class women may constitute 'negative investments'; a case where one partner feels they are putting in but not getting anything out. May talks about the attitudes expressed by a middle-class woman who refuses to go out with those who have not been to university and challenges this devaluation of working-class individuals as 'stupid'.

In a class divided society, class position is equated with personal status and worth. Who you are seen to be with invariably says something about who you are. Differentiations between the 'deserving' and 'undeserving' poor are widely circulated and to this extent working-class people may feel the need to prove their 'decency' (Skeggs, 1997). Despite the commonalities, there were many difficult encounters even with other working-class women. Kelly and Lisa, who had previously emphasised the importance of shared working-class experience, also expressed negative views about other working-class women, that is, the ones who might drag them down. Here, the distinctions between the decent or educated working-class and the uneducated masses are drawn, with working-class women being positioned as unable to hold a 'proper' conversation. I am sure Lisa and Kelly would reject this assertion – but in their own personal relationships they too are making judgements on the basis of class:

K: It does affect the way I think about relationships as well. I really don't mean to sound awful but the relationships I've had before in the past, em, with women who are very ...

L: Oh, very working-class, you couldn't have a conversation with her, could you?

K: But it sounds awful when you say it. I've been out with two women before who've basically got a school education and nothing at all above that and even though you might fancy them physically and get on great in *that sense*, in other things, I'm going to blush now, on a different level, you can't have a conversation with them. In terms of what you want to go and do, like I go out to the cinema and stuff and they're like 'Why? Don't you want to go and get drunk?' you can't talk to them, they're just not interested in the same things. I just can't do it, I've tried a couple of times and it hasn't worked. It just doesn't work. I don't want to sound elitist or anything like that (laughs). I get told off for using big words when I'm around people like Sue and Sandra, who I've had relationships with before, very, very working-class. How do you end a relationship by saying 'I'm sorry I can't talk to you'? (laughs), I can't do it.

L: You need to have your mind stimulated and not just your clit! (laughs). (Kelly and Lisa)

The physical and emotional aspects of attraction are seen as opposing and incompatible and working-classness can serve to generate distance rather than compatibility as distinctions are drawn between un/worthy and in/decent 'others'. The working-class does not exist as a happy and cohesive group any more than all lesbians are best friends.

Such evaluations and devaluations also occurred through embodied class displays, which indicate the ways that class was being recognised and signified (Skeggs, 2000). The positive value of having relationships with working-class women were emphasised on the basis of empathetic understandings, but as Kelly and Lisa highlight, these were always subject to challenge and revision and never easily 'achieved'. Working-class women's attitudes were often claimed as more 'real', and this sense of 'reality' was believed to produce greater commonalities. Yet there was also a sense that working-class relationships could be 'too real'. Boundaries between in/decent, in/appropriate and 'unworthy' partners were drawn, as some working-class partners became representatives of general social problems (Skeggs, 1997, 2004).

For many women in my study, negotiating the positive and negative meanings of working-class positions produced complex tensions, evident in Ali's account as she talks of feeling 'ashamed' and 'embarrassed' by her 'rough' girlfriend, yet also feeling 'proud' of 'genuine' and 'real' traits. Ali speaks of an ex-partner as a member of the 'decent' working-class, with a class consciousness and political opinion and she contrasts her ex-partner with her current partner, who is subsequently devalued. Her current partner is described as 'common as muck' because of her 'choice' language use, her conversations, her behaviour and her (in) ability to socialise in the 'correct' manner – all embodied aspects of class position. Class in this case is fine so long as it is classy, selling the *Socialist Worker* is good, eating chips wrapped in it is not. Ali is ashamed about her partner's 'obviousness' and 'roughness' and attempts to silence her while in 'polite' society. Here her descriptions convey an image of excess and vulgarity, replicating typically classed judgements:

> Well actually, it's not just things she says, it's her behaviour and again, and I might be wrong thinking it's to do with class it might just be her ... With Helen, it was very much a case of 'Well, look, you like me, I like you, why don't we just go,' you know ... she was in the bath, now to me you don't get in the bath with somebody but it was 'Get in this water after me, it's alright, don't waste water, get in here after me' or 'Come in here with me' and I thought God, and it's just things like that. And the way she speaks as well. She's from St Helens, which is very, very much a working-class area, very deprived area, or is it depraved? (laughs) and she's got this what I call dead broad working-class accent. And you do, you attach certain things to different accents, don't you, you know? She talks as common as muck – which is a terrible thing to say, isn't it? That is awful. I'm trying to think of some of the things. As I said, she swears a lot ... There's no sort of, there's no edges ... it's awful, you know, I feel awful saying all this now. (Ali)

Ali's narrative is laced with qualifiers and tensions, also apparent in her contradictory emotions regarding the positive/negative aspects of working-classness. Contradictory emotions are experienced as a result of feeling proud of being working-class but not wanting to be 'too much', too embarrassing, or too 'common'. It would seem that to negotiate class is to walk a tightrope with a potential fall either into vulgarity or into pretentiousness, both of which can be painful, and, like all falls, embarrassing. Paradoxically, as well as being 'embarrassing', Ali also perceives Helen as 'genuine' and 'real':

> It's as if I'm embarrassed by her, what I would call class, yet I'm not because it's something I admire in people and it's something I look for in people is that a good genuineness of working, I always consider working-class people to be genuine. (Ali)

This is an account that is very difficult to unravel, as Ali appears to be taking the words back before they have even been fully formed. She is aware of the way in which her comments can be read and attempts to justify them by appealing to her audience, appealing to the classed assumptions that she believes are universally understood by 'us' about 'the others'. Is it 'our' guilty secret that cannot be repressed, but which 'we' all understand? In making investments in relationships everyone also makes investments in themselves and working-class lesbians had to manage devaluations of working-class identity, which produced dis/ identifications in intimate encounters. Sharing experiences or 'structural positions' is all well and good but, as Ali demonstrates, sharing bath water may not be. Devaluations also occurred through the inability to compete financially with partners, which generated discomforts across social sites where relationships occurred.

Keeping up with Ms Jones

Supposedly 'shared' positionings (Dunne, 1997, Giddens, 1992) are in fact experienced differently, mediated by class position. Inequalities within relationships extended to the varying cultural and emotional resources differentially available and capitalised upon within the relationship. Economic and cultural resources could work together to generate 'emotional capital' and a sense of security, which several working-class women perceived their middle-class partners as having, in comparison to their own 'insecure' positions (Illouz, 1997; Reay, 2002). The inability to match the spending power of middle-class partners, and to gain the comforts this entailed, extended beyond the economic and informed notions of self-worth.[5]

Some women felt dependent on middle-class partners, unable to negotiate middle-class leisure environments and 'ways of being'. This again reinforces boundaries and limits emotional 'investments' as middle-class women and associated 'lifestyles' are seen as incompatible with their own experiences and identifications. Several women also commented on the 'taken for granted' and 'spoiled brat' attitude of (predominantly) ex-partners. Refusals and challenges occurred as women described middle-class cultural and social practices as 'pretentious', even if the shame and embarrassment felt within these same social settings was not displaced. After all, not wanting to fit in is similar but not the same as being forced out.

Economic disparities produced more inequities within relationships, leading to feelings of superiority and inferiority. Becky challenges the equation between money and knowledge but notes the ways in which she was being re-produced as an ignorant, apolitical working-class woman in a previous relationship:

> Em, that had a *huge* effect on our relationship I think because she kinda, on reflection, she kinda looked at me as a silly little working-class girl who couldn't *possibly* have an idea or couldn't possibly have thoughts or feelings on anything, you know, political. She was very shocked that I knew anything about politics. Em, as far as I suppose money went it was very much 'Well you're working-class what do you expect?', which had a huge effect. She also had a rolling bank account that her mum and dad continued to put money into and I worked in a chip shop so as far as our kinda lifestyle together was that I was constantly having to match that and I couldn't you know, I couldn't match that. (Becky)

Economic dependence has rarely been theorised outwith heterosexual relationships (Dunne, 1997; Jamieson, 1998; Weeks et al., 2001). It is her ex-girlfriend's economic capital which generates a certainty and security about where she belongs, while Becky's 'lack' of capital is expected and her lack of value reinforced. Becky also speaks of being economically dependent in her current relationship, as did several other women, noting that they were, or had been, 'kept women'. Doris also notes the different relationship towards money that she and a previous partner had. She rejects her materialism and defends herself against any possible accusation of freeloading:

> I ended the relationship, so if I was on a gravy train so to speak I'd have got on that one and stayed. But I didn't want that, that didn't make me happy, don't go out with someone for money, it doesn't impress me, things like that don't impress me. It's nice, yeah, you know, you think 'that's nice' but if it affects the way you are then there's no point. (Doris)

Doris displays a degree of cynicism regarding the worth of economic power; she does not appear attracted by it, or resentful of it. However, there were numerous ways in which the daily reminders of difference caused irritation, generating incompatibilities and tensions. In a society so governed by economic power, financial disparity can signal more than just separate bank accounts.

Grace speaks of the 'inadequacy' felt when unable to 'match' her partner economically, which adversely affected her sense of comfort within social environments that her girlfriend viewed as extremely comfortable and entertaining. Grace also mentions the various displays required in such environments, including an ability to manage and present a certain classed image (Bourdieu, 1984; Skeggs, 1997). She describes feeling self-conscious and uncomfortable, but refuses to change her classed self, rejecting attempts to make her 'fit in':

> Things like that make me feel really uncomfortable about somebody having sort of different expectations ... I mean, where's the balance of power? ... 'cause if you're trying to impress somebody all the time, how do you actually deal with the relationship and how do you actually get to know that person if you're trying to, I don't know, learn. Or be something different. I don't know. Change into, I don't know, being manipulated into what they want you to be. (Grace)

Grace is extremely aware of the class meanings and consequences within the setting, not only for herself but also for those around her, speaking of restaurant staff she states: ' 'Cause at the end of the day, who are these people? They're people who are probably getting paid shite pence, who are probably really embarrassed about eating out themselves.'

Often women in relationships with middle-class women would get very irritated by the 'frivolous' spending of partners and their lack of concern about money, causing resentments which led Kelly to view an ex-partner as a 'spoiled brat'. Her challenge to economic privilege is made within her own framework that she, personally, has a problem or an 'unhealthy' relationship with money. Money, or lack of, has perhaps more 'meaning' for her than her ex-partner, hence her fear of it and inability to spend it even though she now has a higher income. Again this reveals the ways in which 'past' experiences impact upon 'present' selves and produce envy, annoyance and resentment in relationships:

> K: But I had Cat, she's been poor all her life as a result of risky behaviour, where she's put herself in situations where's she's been irresponsible ... Cat hasn't really grown up with the cultural stuff but she's grown up wealthy, so she doesn't have the same way of life. She doesn't look after anything. She will have money and blow it like that, but see I can't do that.
>
> L: I can't.
>
> K: And see that *annoys* me. It really annoys me.
>
> L: It annoys me.
>
> K: It annoys me in a relationship because when you're wanting to do things together like go out for a meal or something like that

and she'd blow it on a bottle of perfume which cost £60 quid and 'I've got no money', 'That's 'cause you blew it on a bottle of perfume if you don't have that much money why did you go and spend it on a bottle of perfume, why didn't you think about. ... ?' You know, it does affect your relationships because somebody's relationship with money, I mean, I started looking at my own relationship with money 'cause I think I've got issues (laughs). Just, I won't spend it! (laughs) (Kelly and Lisa)

Within this relationship both Kelly and Cat (Kelly's ex-girlfriend) may both have 'issues' with money but they do not experience this equally; for one this evokes memories of going without when it was not there, for the other it involves a cycle of risking and spending, apparently unacceptable behaviour of one who should know better, know what she has and not forfeit it. The 'common' issue does not generate commonality.

'Cultural' differences were seen to stand for, embody and signify wider class issues. Jeannette notes the cultural differences in her relationship as symbolised through tastes and interests; these 'differences' stand for broader (class) issues:

I think I find that my fondness for football is probably connected, it is connected with my upbringing and it's connected with class and I get really pissed off if she doesn't want me to watch it, you know, she wants me to do something else. Like yesterday was a case in point and we have these really ridiculous arguments where – I don't think it can be about football 'cause they couldn't get that heated if they were really just about football. (Jeannette)

Mavis had rejected the possibility of relationships with middle-class women – the differences caused by class, and not just football, were too vast. Mavis notes the requirement on the part of working-class women to 'understand' middle-class women, while middle-class 'certainty' is seen to protect middle-class women from such a requirement:

I think for working-class people having a relationship with middle-class people, em, there's a whole history that you don't share and there are understandings that, I mean I think that ... working-class people understand middle-class people in a way that middle-class people don't understand us, because they've never made an attempt, they've never *had* to understand us, whereas we've had to understand *them* and why they despise us so much and why they treat us the way they've treated us and why they think we're unintelligent and we can't be educated ... There's a whole background that middle-class don't share, there are privileges that they've had that they take for granted em, and as I say they've *never* made an attempt to understand because they have their place in the world, they can step out into the world with absolute certainty that they're accepted, that they're acceptable. I think we're always struggling with our respectability, you know. (Mavis)

Struggles based on respectability ensure that security cannot be achieved, or capital secured (Skeggs, 1997). The invalidation of respectability becomes the invalidation of struggle and the invalidation of history.

Many of the women's difficulties in relationships with middle-class women occurred through different and varied classed expectations, assumptions and behaviours. Often these aspects were the cause of increased tension and greater distance, rather than mutual appreciation of different life experiences, values and 'lifestyles'. In other words, the contrasting lifestyles were difficult to bridge, especially when these were judged as lacking value or indicative of an inferior/superior self. Possible disclosures between intimates, as well as mutual acceptance or appreciation, were fractured by misunderstandings, which were experienced as attempted erasures and denials of classed experiences.

Sometimes 'common' ground could be stable, certain, and equal ground, across respective friendship and family groups, but in the absence of working-class 'proof', or in the presence of middle-class indicators, many women resented the 'false' empathy offered. This produced misunderstandings and annoyance: a denial of difference and an erasure of meaning. There is still a fear of exposing classed and sexual selves, heightening non-disclosure and silence rather than disclosure and accountability.

The painful experience of inequalities within personal relationships contests the pervasiveness of 'democratic' and 'egalitarian' ideals. I am not arguing that the women's relationships were inevitably doomed to failure, but rather I would agree with Jamieson's assertion that '[it is not] the case that "disclosing intimacy" or the more varied types of "good relationships" that people have with each other are breaking down the pervasive divisions between socio-economic classes' (1998: 175). Unhappiness in intimacy is not the by-product of being working-class, but class is a significant factor in relational intimacies, and it continues to inform, enhance and disrupt personal relationships. In considering the interconnections between class and sexuality in the sphere of intimacy, a challenge can be made to the positioning of lesbian relationships as exemplarily sites of equality, paving the way for 'transformations' in intimacy (Giddens, 1992; Weeks et al., 2001). The intersection between class and sexuality prove pleasurable and painful in constructions of worth and value, applicable to friends and family, curtailing and allowing what can be said to whom and the ways in which classed and sexualised 'coming outs' can be heard, validated or negated. The material, cultural and subjective components of both class and sexuality bear upon a range of relationships, indeed they may well be the ties that bind, detach and dis/connect.

In thinking through intimate citizenship (Bell and Binnie, 2000; Bell and Binnie, 2002; Weeks et al., 2001) attention has to be given to who is excluded from formalised, legalised claims and how this impacts upon sexual, gendered and classed lives. With the Civil Partnerships Act in many European countries there now exists a formalised 'respectability' around certain lesbian and gay families, with 'responsible parenthood' arguably existing as another classed and sexualised signifier. There is an apparent contradiction between the alternative 'families of choice' identified by Weeks et al. (2001) and the bureaucratic and legalised processes of the Civil Partnership Act, which encourages traditional familial formations and responsibilities of a conventional nuclear family. Entering a civil partnership may not constitute a performative subversion, a queer erosion of the traditional version of coupledom, and the only 'queer tendencies' (Roseneil, 2000) allowable may be those which can be effectively capitalised upon (Chasin, 2000; Hennessy, 2000).

Knocking-Off: Conclusion

Throughout this book I have pointed to the continued salience of class in terms of identification, opportunity and constraint, and the ways that class and sexuality connect in the lives of working-class lesbians. In exploring their views and experiences, many relevant theories have been drawn upon, encapsulating the complexity of the intersections between class and sexual identity. Whilst some theorists see 'ambivalence' as a key site of renewed class analysis and as an adequate descriptor of current class identifications, whereby people are increasingly felt to make partial, hesitant, 'complex' and contradictory class identifications (Bradley and Hebson, 1999; Savage et al., 2001; Walkerdine et al., 2001) I have argued against the applicability of this to my data, given that 'working-class' remains a salient identification. Given that powerful, if varied and complex, certainties were made – and that working-class lesbians could point to, name and 'identify' class in their lives, I feel there is no need to 're-fashion' or rework the label. Similarly, my data suggests that the idea of 'dis-identification', whereby working-class people are seen to actively avoid being named through class (Skeggs, 1997) does not always hold true in all contexts.

Identity is constituted through material and cultural processes and I argued for the continued relevance of class as a way of explaining enduring inequalities. In this respect I concur with theorists who concede the continued relevance of class as a factor informing life experiences and life chances and against those who proclaim the 'death' of class. Many other debates have been drawn upon given the controversy aroused and the fact that identity questions, social divisions and social understandings cannot easily be polarised into 'for' and 'against', into definitive outcomes and solutions. I charted the changing nature of global society and shifting patterns of productions and consumptions which have been conceptualised as 'flows', 'mobilities' and 'choices' (Urry, 1995, 2000a, 2000b, 2002) or, more negatively, as exploitative and divisive, creating a global rich and a local poor (Hennessy, 2000). Within and between these arguments I put forward the case for establishing empirically grounded evidence to ascertain what these changes, if they were in fact experienced as that, meant for classed individuals. Hennessy's work usefully combines capitalist drives and changes with the commodification of sexual identity, as sexuality becomes a resource and a potential profit maker. She critiques the 'aestheticisation' of sexuality and the ways that material processes and constraints are often separated from sexual identity, which is increasingly thought of as a 'lifestyle' choice. In so doing, she situates her work against those more concerned with the performative aspects of identity construction and the queering of identity and sexuality (Butler, 1990; Fuss, 1991).

My own work potentially highlights the gaps in between materialist and queer perspectives on sexuality, although it has usefully combined elements of both. For example, the performativity of identity was demonstrated when discussing the appearance and embodiment of sexuality, utilising the work of Adkins (2000) and Holliday (1999): it was extended by utilising the concept of misrecognition and engaging with the work of Skeggs (1999, 2001), giving attention to the ways that bodies and identities are rendered un/entitled to occupy public space though in/adequate 'performances', echoing Fraser's (1999) call to 'class' queer visibility. To be recognised as something, as worthy, is to be in receipt of public legitimation and entitlement; systems of evaluation are deployed and these have real effects on movements through space – and for individual movers. There are powerful and resilient material components to spatial entitlements and im/mobilities. Bourdieu's (1984) conceptualisation of classed habitus and capitals, illustrates the ways that movements through space are still structured, via class: I found this to be a useful theoretical and analytical device, allowing for a sense of the entrenchment of class, materially and emotionally, which interviewees conveyed. The criticisms levelled against Bourdieu's work were given attention (Lovell, 2000) but I rejected the suggestion that, in his account, individuals simply become bearers of social positions.

Instead, I deployed his work alongside studies looking specifically at sexuality in space, from accounts of city space and scene spaces and the classing of each (Binnie, 1995, 2000), to those which looked at lesbians' perceptions and experiences of everyday space (Valentine, 1993a, 1993b, 1995). In this way, it was possible to extend Bourdieu's insights with a more appreciative awareness of gender and sexuality, as demonstrated by

Skeggs (1999, 2001). I considered the material, embodied and subjective consequences of occupying both working-class and lesbian identities, drawing upon studies that consider the negative consequences and discriminations faced by lesbians living in poverty (John and Patrick, 1999). My own data strongly contrasts with the findings of Dunne (1997) who, in exploring the materiality of lesbian lives across employment and private spheres, found a positive correlation between being a lesbian and 'achieving' economically. This, I suggested, isolates the respective influences of class and sexuality, a feature which is also apparent in recent studies of lesbian 'lifestyles' and relationships: all too often choice, as reflexivity, is prioritised and isolated from the materiality of different and unequal choices (Dunne, 1997; Giddens, 1992; Weeks et al., 2001; Weston, 1997) and, as such, I suggested that those theories which proclaim the widespread 'transformation' of intimacy are somewhat limited in applicability (Jamieson, 1998).

In analysing many aspects of working-class lesbians' lives and in seeking to situate my research in the broader literatures and debates on sexuality and class, I have constantly tried to avoid a deficit model where working-class or lesbian identity is inevitably seen as problematic, while at the same time striving to represent potential problems in all their variety and complexity. I contested the idea of an underclass (Murray, 1990,1994), the dual romanticisation/pathologisation of working-class life (Bulmer, 1986; Kefalas, 2003; Rubin, 1976) and the attribution of homophobia to the working-class (Moran, 2000). I showed that the women I interviewed had agency, opinions and choices – they resisted prevailing opinions of them as 'failures' while in school, the labelling of which is widely recognised as a classed operation (Mac an Ghaill, 1994; Skeggs, 1997) but which also has relevance to the consideration of lesbian identities (Epstein, 1994). Both class and sexuality were negotiated in – and out of – work, where structural and interpersonal positionings were daily experienced, performed (Adkins, 2000; Hoschild, 1983), recognised and misrecognised (Skeggs, 1999, 2001): there was an awareness amongst interviewees that what they did for a living positioned them in class terms while there was a simultaneous rejection of being told that what they did, where they lived and who they were, had no value. This was reflected in discussions about intimacy, for while many experienced devaluations and contentions, they were not without affirmation, emotional worth, value or capitals (Illouz, 1997; Reay, 2002).

The significance of sexuality and class position has been explored in relation to family background, schooling, work experiences, working-class areas and communities, leisure activities, scene spaces and intimate relationships. In looking at the operation of inequalities, experiences and identifications in these places, I have considered the economic, cultural, emotional and spatial aspects of class and sexuality, teasing out the tensions and pointing to commonalities. As has been seen, working-class lesbians' own identifications, thoughts and powerful descriptions highlight the continued significance of class and sexuality as factors shaping life experiences. Interviewees have pointed out obvious, as well as contradictory identifications and the pleasure and pain, rejection and affirmation, erasure and confirmation of these. This book has not sought to resolve these 'tensions', or to suggest that the women I interviewed should do so. Rather my purpose has been to highlight the interaction and relevance of both these positions and identifications. Class continues to exist – and these women know it.

In Chapter 2, 'Class And How To Get It', the continued importance of class identity was established, given the multiple, emotional, explicit and 'obvious' ways that many women spoke about their class identities and classed experiences. I began to outline the structuring of expectations, via class and sexuality, as well as the material components of these. Many interviewees recognised, challenged and were still positioned by such expectations and judgements. The variety and obviousness of class sometimes makes it difficult to pin down: even if we all know what is meant by it there are problems in relating something that is so personal and yet so social, something which occupies the past but which remains very much in the present.

Working-class lesbians' entrenched identifications, formed in childhood encounters and through an awareness of parental un/employment, communal vulnerability and difference, continued to impact upon who they were and who the 'others' were. Many of the women's classed perceptions involved an assessment of the 'real' aspects and attitudes of working-classness as opposed to the 'pretentious', 'conforming' associations of middle-classness. In (re)claiming their classed lives, rejecting notions of 'classlessness' and other individualistic discourses, many women resisted being positioned (through class) as members of an 'underclass'. But to resist the negative associations of class often re-invokes these; there is class and there is being classed.

'Close Encounters of the Classed Kind' (Chapter 3) examined experiences of growing up in working-class families and communities and attending (classed) schools. In-between these settings, comparatives between the 'norm' and the 'other' were constantly enforced. As children, many women first realised and encountered the subtle signifiers of class but they were already familiar with the economic consequences of being working-class and often did not need a reminder. Just as 'difference' was negotiated in inter-personal encounters within school settings so too was it negotiated in working-class communities. Gender, ethnic and sexual divisions exist within working-class communities, as they do in broader society and many women spoke with unease, implicatedness and disappointment about this.

In Chapter 4, 'What Now?' working-class lesbians' employment choices and ambitions, via school 'failures', were charted. For the vast majority of women, this transition was characterised by low-paid work, unemployment and sometimes, voluntary work. It may be that so much of what we can or cannot do is related to how much money we make, yet in Chapter 4, and in the thesis as a whole, I linked the ways in which the economic combined with social expectations, with subjective exclusions and inclusions, with interpersonal and spatial mis-recognitions and discriminations. Where we are going is a result of all these things and the ways that these combine, as each person moves through space. For the women I interviewed both class and sexuality constrained and affected employment choices and all sought to manage these, 'choosing' the best or coping with the worst. I have highlighted the structuring of these choices, rather than individualising them as the 'wrong' choices. For women who did work, they were often recognised as working-class: doing was equated with being and with this the complexity and emotionality of self-identification was denied. Similarly, to be 'out' at work was not a simple matter of self-identification – or indeed identification by other means. Many women experienced blatant discriminations, including losing their jobs, but what seemed more prevalent was an undercurrent of tolerance, a drive to assimilation, a refusal of existence rather than overt challenge. Their sexuality might be 'out' there, and so too might their class – but saying it once often isn't enough. Both these positions are negotiated in workplace settings, benefit agencies and in everyday settings.

The spatial aspects of identification were described in Chapter 5, 'Negotiation and Navigation: Emotional Maps', and Chapter 6, 'Scene Spaces – Inclusions and Exclusions', which combine class and sexuality in their respective focus upon working-class space as devalued territories in contrast to scene space as 'trendy', fashionable leisure space. Interviewees' powerful identifications with the areas they come/came from, as places of worth and emotional value, work to challenge the denigration of working-class areas as depressed sink estates. Movements through space were movements through differently classed territories, and shifting class boundaries of dis/identification. To belong somewhere is not easy to do when this space is vulnerable both in terms of the negative judgements incurred and the economic inequality experienced therein.

Yet a striking commonality amongst the women I interviewed was their, often emotional and positive, identification with specific classed areas – even when they recognised the 'problems'. Belonging is not sameness or cohesion; these spaces were neither conflict free nor abundant in resources. Many women experienced homophobic discrimination here, as in other settings: the classed aspects of homophobia were discussed and disputed by the women, not as inherently working-class or middle-class but rather as something that was always classed in its manifestations. Accessing scene space did not constitute an escape from discriminations.

Entry to scene spaces involved learning gay signs and dressing accordingly (Chapter 6, 'Scene Spaces – Inclusions and Exclusions'). Unfortunately, for many working-class lesbians, these 'designer' presentations were over-expensive and unachievable. Signifying sexuality becomes a pleasure and a danger – getting it right can be affirming, getting it wrong often means you can't, won't and don't fit in. The various restrictions, regulations, dominations and even emulations operating in scene space, and forming entitlements, work to exclude working-class lesbians, and this functions on an embodied level. Appearance becomes the mechanism for inclusion and exclusion as the central resource through which claims for legitimacy are made (Skeggs, 1999, 2001). The boundaries constructed around class, gender and age have been given particular attention in this book as those mentioned by interviewees, those affecting a sense amongst interviewees that it was not really *their* scene. Potential affirmations were fractured by classed discomforts and discriminations, also apparent in intimate relationships.

In Chapter 7, 'The Ties That Bind', I explored the operation of class in lesbian relationship setting this alongside idealised 'transformations' apparent in recent literature (Dunne, 1997; Giddens, 1992; Weston, 1997; Weeks et al., 2001). Because of the lack and inadequacy of infrastructure many women reported a degree of isolation and vulnerability in meeting women and in sustaining relationships, which necessitates a degree of 'outness' about sexuality and, as has been seen, about class. Class similarities as well as differences proved difficult, disruptive, emotive, enhancing and ultimately very relevant in most, if not all, of the women's relationships with partners and friends. This final chapter once again charted the multiple interactions of the subjective, emotional aspects of class experience and identification as well as the objective, financial limitations, negotiations and, often justified, resentments.

I have explored the relationship between class and sexuality across a range of social sites, pointing to the salience of class and sexuality as positions and identities which affect everything from growing up, going out, going to work; these areas are inseparable. The women I interviewed lived out both of these positions and identities, as 'working-class' and 'lesbian', and were very capable of making their own associations and linkages between these two categories – they knew who they were, where they were and how they wanted to be known, and that should not surprise us.

Appendix

1. **Ali**, 42 (Manchester – interviewed individually). Employed as a secretary earning £11,000–15,000, with '1 + A level/Highers'. Ali grew up with her mother, a housewife, and her father, a mechanical engineer. She is a single-parent with two children.
2. **Alice**, 25 (Edinburgh – interviewed individually). Unemployed. Alice grew up with mother and father who are both unemployed.
3. **Amy**, 29 (Edinburgh – interviewed individually). Employed in admin work, earning £16,000–20,000, with '5 + O levels/GCSEs/ Standard Grades'. Grew up with her mother, who works in a shop, and her father, who was a road foreman. She is currently in a relationship and has one child.
4. **Angela**, 42 (Glasgow – interviewed individually). Employed as a training and development officer earning £21,000–30,000, with '3 + A levels/Highers'. Grew up with mother and father, in a council estate. Mother was a 'homemaker' and father was a steel erector. Is currently in a relationship and has four children.
5. **Anna**, 21 (Edinburgh – Young Persons' Focus Group, Edinburgh). Unemployed for past two years, not a student, earning 'below £7000'. Missing data on qualification levels and parental employment details. Anna participated in an unrecorded discussion and drew a personal map.
6. **Becky**, 22 (Edinburgh – interviewed individually). Employed as a part-time development worker earning 'below £7000', has got '3 + A levels/ Highers'. Becky attended a college after school but later dropped out. Grew up with mother and step-father in a council estate but lived with a variety of relatives, mostly her gran, due to family circumstances. Becky described her relationship with her mother as 'violent';

she experienced physical violence from her mother when she was 'outed' by a girlfriend.

7. **Carol**, 50 (Glasgow – Older Lesbian Focus Group). Employed as a cleaner earning 'below £7000', with '5 + O levels/GCSEs/Standard Grades'. Data on parental occupation is missing. Commented that she grew up 'middle-class'.

8. **Cathy**, 37 (Manchester – Manchester Lesbian Group). Employed as an administrative assistant earning £16,000–20,000, with '1 + A level/higher'. Grew up with her mother and father, who came from Ireland. Her mother worked in a factory before marrying and her father worked as a boilermaker/welder.

9. **Charlotte**, 42 (Manchester – interviewed individually). Employed as a shop supervisor earning £16,000–20,000. Has '1 + O level/GCSE/Standard Grade'. Grew up with father and step-mother. Her father was a postman and her mother remains unemployed. Charlotte is a single-parent with two children.

10. **Chris**, 64 (Glasgow – Older Lesbian Group). Retired nurse. Current income between £21,000–30,000. Has an undergraduate degree. Data on parental occupation is missing but Chris grew up in a council estate.

11. **Dawn**, 22 (Yorkshire – interviewed individually), undergraduate student. Grew up in single-parent (mother) household. Her mother works as a cleaner.

12. **Diane**, 37 (Manchester – Manchester Lesbian Group). Employed as a care assistant earning 'below £7000', with '5 + O levels/GCSEs/Standard Grades'. Grew up with mother, who worked as a cashier, and her father, who worked in a factory.

13. **Doris**, 40 (Manchester – Manchester Lesbian Group). Employed as a support worker earning £11,000–15,000. Has 'no qualifications'. Grew up in a single-parent (mother) household. Her mum worked as a dinner lady in a local school. Doris lives on the same council estate where she grew up.

14. **Elaine**, 37 (Highlands – Rural Lesbian Group). Unemployed, not a student, income 'below £7000', with '1 + O level/GCSE/Standard Grades'. Grew up with mother and father in the Highlands. Her mother was a housewife and father was a clerk, who grew up in a black house.

15. **Emma**, 56 (Manchester – Manchester Lesbian Group). Retired teacher. Current income £21,000–30,000. Has an undergraduate degree. Data on parental occupation is missing and although Emma never identified as working-class, she also rejected being middle-class,

even while she described her childhood and current locality as 'middle-class'.

16. **Faye**, 45 (Manchester – interviewed individually). Faye is unemployed, not a student, income 'below £7000', with no qualifications. Grew up with her mother who worked as a cleaner, and her father worked as a bricklayer. Faye is a single-parent with two children.

17. **Fiona**, 29 (Edinburgh – interviewed individually). Employed as a cleaner earning 'below £7000', with '2 + A levels/Highers'. Fiona felt her schooling was adversely affected by periods of living with relatives, moving houses and living in poor conditions. She grew up in a single-parent (mother) household, mother 'never had a job – always on benefits'.

18. **Fliss**, 40 (Highlands – Rural Lesbian Group). Employed as a nurse earning £21,000–30,000, with 'other qualifications'. Grew up with her mother, who was a housewife but engaged in some secretarial work and her father who was a self-employed shop owner.

19. **Gemma**, 35 (Manchester – Manchester Lesbian Group). Employed as a support worker earning £7000–10,000, has 'other qualifications'. Data on parental employment is missing. Gemma lives on the same council estate where she grew up.

20. **Grace**, 30 (Edinburgh – interviewed individually). Employed in trade union work earning £16,000–20,000, with 'other qualifications'. Grace grew up with two parents; her mother is now working in a shop and her father is a janitor – both parents experienced unemployment while Grace was growing up which caused disruption and temporary separation of parents. Her mother now works as a school auxiliary and her step-father as a welder.

21. **Jane**, 25 (Yorkshire – interviewed in the presence of her partner May). Employed as a part-time youth worker earning 'below £7000', has '3 + A levels/Highers'. Jane grew up with her mother, a housewife, and her father, a HGV driver.

22. **Jean**, 54 (Manchester – Manchester Lesbian Group). Unemployed, income 'below £7000', with '1 + O level/GCSE/Standard Grade'. Data on parental employment is missing.

23. **Jeannette**, 39 (Glasgow – interviewed individually). Jeannette is now employed as a community worker earning £21,000–30,000 but has experienced both long-term (seven years) and short-term unemployment. She attended university via an access course and now has a degree. She grew up with mother and father but mostly with her mother. Her mother worked as a cleaner and her father as a labourer. Jeannette is currently in a relationship and has two children.

24. **Jenny**, 16 (Edinburgh – Young Persons' Focus Groups). Jenny is unemployed, having left school, earning 'below £7000'. Jenny participated in an unrecorded discussion and drew a personal map. Missing data on qualification levels and parental employment details.

25. **Jo**, 30 (Glasgow – interviewed individually). Employed as a gardener for a community project earning £11,000–15,000, with 'other qualifications'. Jo grew up with mother, who was predominantly a 'housewife' but engaged in part-time secretarial work, and her father, who worked as a delivery man.

26. **Jude**, 31 (Yorkshire – interviewed individually). She was an undergraduate student but had just left university because of financial and emotional pressure and was working in a restaurant. Jude grew up with her mother and father in an overcrowded council accommodation. She left school at 16, and moved to London with her cashed benefits cheque where she found a job in a restaurant. Her mother now works as an auxiliary and her father is unemployed.

27. **Karen**, 62 (Manchester – Manchester Lesbian Group). Unemployed, income 'below £7000'. Data on qualifications and parental employment is missing.

28. **Kate**, 16 (Edinburgh – Young Persons' Group). Kate is not currently working or studying, income 'below £7000'.Grew up in a single-parent (mother) household. Her mother works as a cleaner, described her father as a 'professional alcoholic and scrounger'. Kate participated in an unrecorded discussion and also drew a map, charting the places where she did and did not feel 'at home'.

29. **Kay**, 47 (Manchester – Manchester Lesbian Group). Unemployed, income 'below £7000 , with '5 + O levels/GCSEs/Standard Grades'. Kay grew up with her mother and father and described her background as 'middle-class'. Data on parental occupation is missing. Kay is a single-parent with two children.

30. **Kelly**, 23 (Yorkshire – paired interview with friend Lisa). Employed as a support worker earning £16,000–20,000. Has '3 + A levels/ Highers'. Kelly grew up first with mother and father, and then with mother and step-father. Her mother worked in a factory while she was growing up and is now employed as a community care worker. Her step-father is a factory worker.

31. **Kim**, 22 (Yorkshire – interviewed individually). Undergraduate student. Kim grew up with mother and father, who separated when she was a teenager. Her mother is now a teacher and father now works in sales. Kim was eager to point out that they had not always been

in these occupations – her mother, for example, had only recently qualified as a teacher having entered university via an access course, as a mature student.

32. **Kirsty**, 26 (Manchester – interviewed individually). Unemployed, not a student, income 'below £7000', with '1 + A level/Highers'. Kirsty initially lived with her mother, who worked as a bar maid, and her father, who worked as a bin man. Kirsty experienced much disruption and endured very stressful family circumstances while growing up, consequently living with a variety of relatives. Kirsty also lived in a woman's refuge at one point, having suffered from domestic violence at the hands of a (male)ex-partner. Kirsty is a single-parent with one child.

33. **Lauren**, 18 (Edinburgh – Young Persons' Focus Group). Lauren is not currently working or studying and has '1 + A level/Higher'. She grew up in a single-parent (mother) household, her mother is a nurse and father is a plumber. Lauren is living at home again, which she identified as very problematic, having left to live in a hostel due to mother's adverse reaction against Lauren's sexuality.

34. **Lisa**, 23 (Yorkshire – paired interview with friend Kelly). Employed as a teaching assistant earning £11,000–15,000, with '1 + A level/Higher'. Grew up mostly in a single-parent (mother) household until her mother married. Mother now works as an auxiliary, although they lived on benefits while Lisa was growing up. Her step-father is currently unemployed, although works as a factory worker when employed.

35. **Liz**, 23 (Manchester – interviewed individually). Employed as an information and administration worker for a lesbian project, earning £11,000–15,000, with '3 + A levels/Highers'. Liz grew up with her mother and father, both unemployed, on a council estate.

36. **Lynn**, 44 (Glasgow – interviewed individually although part of Older Lesbian Group). Employed as a social carer earning £16,000–20,000, has 'other qualifications'. She grew up with her mother and father, who both worked as cleaners. Lynn is a single parent with two children and is in a long-term relationship.

37. **Mandy**, 22 (Yorkshire – interviewed individually). Undergraduate student. Mandy grew up mostly in a single-parent (mother) household after her mum and dad split up. Her dad now works as a salesman while her mother is unemployed.

38. **Mavis**, 52 (Edinburgh – interviewed individually). Mavis is long-term unemployed due to a disability, income 'below £7000', has 'other

qualifications'. Grew up with mother and father. Her mum was unemployed and her dad worked in the shipyards. Mavis is a single-parent with three children.

39. **May**, 23 (Yorkshire – interviewed in the presence of her partner Jane). May is employed as a production worker earning 'below £7000', with '5 + O levels/GCSEs/Standard Grades'. At the time of the interview May was exploring local access courses which enable entry to university. She was very unhappy in her job and wanted to go to university. May grew up with her mother, a housewife, and her father, an electrician.

40. **Michelle**, 37 (Edinburgh – interviewed individually). Michelle is a care assistant earning 'below £7000', with '1 + A level/Highers'. Michelle engaged in a variety of Youth Opportunity Programmes and voluntary work after school and described her job as 'the first real job'. She grew up with mother and father; her mother worked as a lollipop lady and her dad worked as a road sweeper.

41. **Pam**, 24 (Yorkshire – interviewed individually). Undergraduate student and part-time shop assistant. Grew up with mother and father; both parents are unemployed.

42. **Rita**, 52 (Manchester – interviewed individually). Rita is employed as a part-time hairdresser earning £7000–10,000, has 'other qualifications' and is experiencing ill-health leading to concerns about her future employment status. She grew up with mother, who worked as a secretary, and father who worked as a mechanic; they came from Russia and Poland. Rita is a single-parent with two children.

43. **Sadie**, 28 (Edinburgh – interviewed individually). Employed as a project worker earning £16,000–20,000, with '1 + O level/GCSE/Standard Grade'. Grew up with her mother, a housewife, and her father, a chef who is currently unemployed due to illness.

44. **Sally**, 37 (Manchester – interviewed individually). Sally is a self-employed gardener earning £7000–10,000. Missing data on qualifications and parental employment. Sally is estranged from her family for a variety of reasons, including parental disapproval towards her sexuality. She is a single-parent with two children.

45. **Sam**, 22 (Yorkshire – interviewed individually). Undergraduate student. Grew up in a single-parent (mother) household, and her mother worked as a machinist.

46. **Sharon**, 47 (Glasgow – interviewed individually). Sharon is employed as a health promotion officer earning £21,000–30,000 and now has a degree, acquired as a mature student via an access course. Sharon previously felt this would be impossible to achieve given that she left school at 16 without being able to read or write.

Sharon grew up in a single-parent household (mother), her mother worked as a bus driver and Sharon also worked cleaning buses and then as a bus/taxi driver. She is currently in a relationship and has four children.

47. **Shona**, 39 (Edinburgh – interviewed individually). Employed as a youth support worker earning £11,000–15,000 stated that current job was the highest paid job she had ever had. Shona has '1 + O level/GCSE/Standard Grades'. She grew up with mother and father. Her mother worked as a care assistant, dad worked in a printing company in Glasgow before moving to the Western Isles. Shona is a single-parent with one child.

48. **Sonia**, 32 (Yorkshire – interviewed individually although partner, Joan, offered several comments as she passed through the kitchen where we were conducting the interview). Employed as a prison officer earning £21,000–30,000. Sonia did not like her current vocation but realised the financial benefits offered – she did not feel qualified for anything else; has '3 + A levels/Highers'. Sonia grew up in a single-parent (mother) household, her mother was a 'widowed housewife'. Sonia's partner is long-term unemployed due to a disability.

49. **Sukhjit**, 29 (Manchester – interviewed individually). Mature student with '3 + A levels/Highers'. Sukhjit grew up in an extended family household. Both parents came to Britain from Pakistan in the 1960s for 'a better life'. Unfortunately, Sukhjit believes this has not been realised, with resulting family trauma. Her mother was a housewife and her father was unemployed while she lived in the parental household. Sukhjit has no contact whatsoever with any member of her family for a variety of reasons. Leaving home at a young age, she has never discussed her sexuality with her family.

50. **Tina**, 41 (Glasgow – Older Lesbian Group). Employed as a nurse earning £16,000–20,000, with 'other qualifications'. Data on parental occupation is missing. Tina never spoke much during the focus group interview and later attempts at arranging a one-one interview fell through.

51. **Tracey**, 23 (Glasgow – interviewed individually). Employed as a carer earning £7000–10,000, with '1 + O level/GCSE/Standard Grades'. Tracey grew up in a single-parent (mother) household and her mother remains unemployed.

52. **Vanessa**, 16 (Edinburgh – Young Persons' Focus Group) Attends a local college on a part-time basis. Has '5 + O levels/GCSE's/Standard Grades'. Vanessa grew up with her mother and step-father who work

in banks. Vanessa lives in a hostel, she left the parental home after 'coming-out' and experiencing many conflicts.

53. **Vicky**, 46 (Glasgow – Older Lesbian Group). Unemployed, income 'below £7000', with '5 + O levels/GCSEs/Standard Grades'. Data on parental occupation is missing.

Focus groups

Manchester Focus Group

Cathy, Doris, Kay, Karen, Jean, Gemma, Emma, Diane.

Older Lesbian Group

Carol, Chris, Tina, Vicky.

Rural Lesbian Group

Fliss and Elaine were members of this group. Focus group conversations were unrecorded and, other than Elaine and Fliss, participants did not agree to take part in recorded discussions.

Young Persons' Group

Kate, Lauren, Vanessa, Anna, Jenny. This focus group was fairly informal because of the younger age of the participants. Lauren and Vanessa agreed to take part in a recorded discussion.

Notes

1 Reviewing the Literature: An Introduction

1. It is noteworthy that 'class' does not appear in the title, and is not a stated part of the research agenda. Perhaps the replacement of class with the terms 'lifestyle' and 'social capital' actually predetermines the authors' stance and their own 'ambivalence' towards class identities. In relation to Marshall et al. (1988) and Devine (1992), who speak of the continued relevance of class identities, it is claimed that 'because these writers emphasise the continued salience of class identity, this might be seen as the orthodox position' (Savage et al., 2001: 876).

2. 'Geordies' refers to people from the North East of England, traditionally synonymous with industrial labour, literally a term for pit workers (Nayak, 2003a, 2003b).

3. The National Statistics of Socio-Economic Classification (2001) replaced the RG's index and was also used to gather census data in 2001. Like the Goldthrope Scheme many occupations were outlined; interestingly the word 'class' does not appear within the table – nothing is named as 'middle-class' or 'working-class'.

4. Crompton et al. (2000) note that the debate has increasingly become focused on methodological questions, rather than on substantive issues of class inequality.

5. A number of attempts have been made to develop alternative scales for measuring the social class of women (Dale et al., 1985). Classifications construct understandings of what is un/skilled work, resting upon gendered assumptions (Crompton, 2000).

6. Symbolic capital is the form that different capitals take when they are recognised as legitimate; thus cultural capital has to be legitimated before it can have symbolic worth. Most representations of working-class people contribute to devaluing already limited capitals, denying conversion into symbolic capital (Skeggs, 1997).

7. Working-class families are often pathologised and blamed for the lack of their child's 'success'; another way of individualising structural inequalities. Depictions of working-class families and often entire working-class communities, seem to be caught between a binary of romanticisation/pathologisation, with a strong tendency towards homogenisation and stereotype (Bulmer, 1986; Jamieson, 1998; Rubin, 1976) – a habitus of deficiency, necessity (Charlesworth, 2000), or rose tinted tradition.

8. Dunne, Prendergast and Telford (2002) conduct research into homelessness among young lesbian, gay and bisexual people in England, looking at the impact of sexuality, rather than, for example, class. Their portrayal is perhaps overly optimistic: homelessness is seen to bring 'opportunities' to challenge assumed heterosexual identity.

9. In 2000, the EU agreed a directive banning discrimination in employment and vocational training on grounds of sexual orientation, religion and belief, disability and age. As a result, the United Kingdom had to introduce laws in 2003 to implement this ban. Various states in the United States of America have added sexual orientation to anti-discrimination laws. In Canada, all provinces (except Alberta) have included sexual orientation in their human rights laws.

10. See the section 'Written on the body' in this chapter for a fuller discussion of the concept of 'misrecognition'. This is a complex concept, which is deployed in different ways throughout this thesis. I will primarily be using it to show the ways that bodies in social spaces are read through appearance and judged as having no 'value'; they are 'misrecognised' and are unable to access certain forms of capital or to fully spatialise their claims and 'entitlements', upon space: I will be showing the ways that working-class lesbians are variously misrecognised as they are read and classified through appearance, according to both class and sexuality.

11. Adler and Brenner (1992) note that the gay men's 'community' is not homogeneous, warning against the stereotypical portrayal of gay men as uniformly affluent (Badgett, 2001). Similarly, it is claimed that the 'community' does include political activity that favours more radical politics, rather than dominant interest group strategies, which require consumer and political power.

12. Binnie and Valentine (1999) claim that geographical work on the production of sexualised space, and its linkage with processes of globalisation, function as a corrective towards the tendency in some writings on 'queer space', to separate considerations of sexual politics from wider political, economic debates.

13. Davidoff and Hall (1992) show the movement of the middle-classes out of city space to be a historical phenomenon. With increasing industrialisation, the urban landscape became ever more polluted. The middle-classes, facilitated by the development of transportation infrastructure, moved out to 'clean' space. This movement out of city space also produced clear gendered spatial division between work and home. There is a need to situate such movements in their historical context but despite differences in time and place, such movements show the abilities of the middle-class to move into more desirable space, to claim or reclaim space.

14. Skeggs suggests that 'respectability' is one of the central mechanisms through which present day class struggles revolve: 'Respectability is one of the most ubiquitous signifiers of class' (1997: 1). Heterosexuality is also aligned with respectability and those who threaten that respectability produce a disruption of the space. Furthermore, geographical areas and their inhabitants become un/respectable (fear of entering certain areas can also be figured through class defined respectability) (Moran and Skeggs, 2001).

15. Historically, appearance is the means by which knowledge about class, race, sexuality and gender is produced and values attached to bodies. As a mechanism of evaluative classification, appearance operates to class bodies.

16. Holliday notes that 'it is very unlikely that one would get beaten up for poor fashion sense' (1999: 482). Nevertheless, performances, which are subject to material constraints, are highly consequential for individual 'performers'. Such regulation can be perceived as an act of 'symbolic violence' (Bourdieu, 1984; Skeggs, 1997, 2001).

17. The term 'community' may be a troublesome concept but urban geography and sociology tend to use 'community' to indicate a geographically bounded area of people who share particular characteristics, such as ethnicity and class (Cohen, 1985; Phile, 1996).

18. Southerton (2002) suggests that mobility, like cosmopolitanism, is a feature of having high cultural resources, providing knowledge and experience of the 'other'. These 'others' are fixed, while the 'upwardly mobile' travel.

19. Castells (1983) explains the lack of visible lesbian communities, in comparison to gay spaces, by suggesting that there are gender differences in the ways that men and women relate to space. He argues that men try to achieve 'spatial supe-riority' while women have less 'territorial aspiration'. Bell and Valentine (1995) highlight this as an essentialist understanding, which ignores the economic factors constraining women's ability to use spaces. Middle-class women may have more ability to spatialise their interests than working-class women.

20. Anthias looks at the intersection of social divisions (class, race and gender) arguing that 'The concept of "social division" ... provides us with a useful conceptual tool for investigating the practices and outcomes of material inequalities ... . Such an approach treats persons as subjected to the effectivities of social location across dimensions of class, ethinicity/race and gender but in non-deterministic ways' (2001: 852). When theorising 'intersection' I resist, as Anthias does, an 'add on' approach, seeking instead to explore how these categories are lived in.

2   Class and How to Get It

1. Skeggs (1997) suggests that the UK Miners' Strikes, beginning in 1984 following an orchestrated attempt by the Thatcher government to destroy the Miners' Union as the strongest union in Britain, generated political 'resistances' amongst working-class women. I am suggesting that these moments provide enduring recognition and identification with working-class communities.

2. Other women (Fliss, Emma, Kay and Carol) from middle-class backgrounds spoke of how they distanced themselves from middle-class locations through their own attitudes. This reveals the link between displaying and 'investing' in certain 'attitudes' and class dis/identification. Carol argues that class is just a 'label' which she prefers not to have: 'If you asked me what class I was I wouldn't be able to tell you. First class, classless! I don't know, it's like a label I suppose that I don't want ... I just prefer not to have any label like that. If you asked me now I'd say "no class", I just wouldn't put myself in any class at all. But my childhood was middle-class' (Carol).

3   Close Encounters of the Classed Kind

1. See Appendix for a brief description of interviewees' employment and parental employment situations.

2. Jamieson (1998) argues that ideas about being a 'good' parent have changed in the course of history, and while some features of family household have a long history – like gender divisions, others do not. The changing conceptions of

mothering/fathering, apparent in the call for more 'sensitive' fathers, co-exist with the continuation of gender inequalities.
3. Lynn is describing Glasgow's Barrowland street market, known as 'The Barras'. The Briggate and the Saltmarket refer to the actual area, while the barras are the market stalls.
4. Twenty-four women said that they left school at 16yrs – there is some missing data on school leaving age/qualifications. Some respondents who left school at 16 went on to acquire qualifications through access courses.

4   What Now?

1. Their portrayal is perhaps overly optimistic: homelessness is seen to bring 'opportunities' to challenge assumed heterosexual identity, becoming somewhat separated from socio-economic contexts and constraints of such 'choices'.
2. Twenty women experienced unemployment immediately after school. For recent school leavers this was on-going (Kate, Lauren, Anna and Jenny). Elaine, Kirsty and Alice were unemployed on leaving school and were unemployed at the time of being interviewed although they had worked in secretarial (Elaine), shop (Kirsty) and care work (Alice) for short periods, while Diane, although initially unemployed, had worked as a care assistant for many years. Shona was initially unemployed after leaving school but had just found a job as a youth support worker, which she described as the most secure and highly paid work that she had ever done, as did Amy who now does secretarial/ administrative work. Having experienced long term unemployment (7 years) post-school, Jeannette currently worked as a community worker, earning a secure income (£21,000–30,000), while Jill now worked as a project worker after 7 years of unemployment. Having completed various Youth Training Programme's (YTS), after initial unemployment, both Grace and Michelle were now employed – Grace as a trade union organiser and Michelle as a care assistant. Jo and Tracey, who were also unemployed upon leaving school now worked as a gardener for a community project (Jo) and as a carer (Tracey). Sukhjit was unemployed on leaving school and had worked in a variety of shops and offices but now attended university as a mature student. Ten women were currently employed in secretarial/administrative or care work, although others, who gave their job titles as 'support work' may also be categorised as 'carers' although these women tended to earn slightly more (e.g., Doris earned £11,000–15,000 as a support worker while Kelly earned £16000–20000). Two women (Fiona and Carol) worked as cleaners. Rita worked as a hairdresser and May did production work.
3. The Youth Opportunities Programme (YOP) was introduced in 1978 with the intention of giving unemployed school leavers work experience and training. This was replaced in 1983 by the Youth Training Scheme (YTS) which was in turn replaced by 'Welfare to Work' schemes introduced as part of the New Deal in 1998. These schemes highlight the 'churning' of the poor around different de-standardised forms of work. Furthermore, MacDonald and Marsh (2000) suggest that policies aimed at combating youth unemployment are attempts to transform young people themselves rather than dealing with structural inequalities.

4. Mavis left her home in Glasgow in her early twenties, having worked in Glasgow's bars, and found secretarial work in London. She returned to Scotland in her mid-30s, relocating to Edinburgh. She has been long-term unemployed ever since due to a disability.
5. Jude left her home in Glasgow at the age of 16, heading for London with her cashed benefit money, where she found work in a restaurant. She attended university in York as a mature student in her late twenties but left in her second year and continued in her part-time restaurant work.
6. Twelve women spoke of previous heterosexual relationships and/or heterosexual marriage in the course of the interview. Many spoke of this being the expected, the only or even the best option available at the time.
7. Wilson's is a local food chain in Glasgow. Lynn had previously been married and has two children. She is now employed as a 'Social Carer' in Glasgow earning £16,000–20,000.
8. Kirsty has been unemployed, on and off, since leaving school at 18. She is a single-parent with a small child to look after.

5 Negotiation and Navigation: Emotional Maps

1. The women labelled the expected, and received negative evaluations of their communities as 'pretentious' and 'middle-class', which is suggestive of a superficial and false understanding of the area, in contrast to the 'real' understandings of working-class inhabitants (Howarth, 2002).
2. Hebden Bridge is a small town in West Yorkshire, UK, renowned for having a supposedly high lesbian concentration. It is also a relatively affluent area. Weeks et al. (2001) highlight the ways that lesbians and gay men seek to live in 'gay friendly' areas, with community support networks and/or commercialised scene spaces (Bell and Valentine, 1995; Weston, 1995).
3. Shona and Lauren came from rural areas, while Elaine, Fliss and Kay currently lived in rural areas.
4. Margaret Thatcher introduced the 'Right to Buy' scheme, covered in the 1985 Housing Act, through which council tenants could purchase their council houses.
5. Five women had experienced homelessness and two of the youngest respondents (Lauren, 18 and Vanessa, 16) lived in hostel accommodation at the time of the interview. John and Patrick (1999), Dunne et al. (2002), and O'Conner and Maloy (2001) all highlight the problem of homelessness amongst lesbians and gays. Rarely is poverty, or class inequality considered as a factor causing homelessness – rather the focus tends to be on hostile responses to sexuality as causal.
6. Hebden Bridge, West Yorkshire, UK.
7. 'The Broons' are a cartoon family who appear in a comic strip in the UK tabloid the 'Sunday Post'.
8. The areas also contain within them other classed markers, for example, specific schools, or 'failing' schools – through attending these schools, individuals are often immediately read as 'failures'(Furlong et al., 1996). This has been discussed in Chapter 3 'Close Encounters of The Classed Kind'.

7   Ties That Bind

1. In October 1989 two Danes became the first couple to enter a same-sex civil union. In the years since then, over twenty-two countries, including the United Kingdom, have taken steps towards providing legal recognition to same-sex relationships. Nearly half of countries in the European Union offer some legal recognition to same-sex couples, ranging from full civil marriage in Belgium, the Netherlands and Spain, to domestic partnerships in Portugal and Slovenia.

2. Several studies have highlighted the issue of violence in lesbian relationships as an under-researched area. Lobel (1986), Renzetti (1998) and Ohms (2002) all examine the prevalence, causes and effects of abusive lesbian relationships arguing that they are not so infrequent as to constitute an anomaly. All authors discuss aspects of heterosexism, internalised homophobia and lack of support and legal infrastructure. *Naming the Violence: Speaking Out About Lesbian Battering* (Lobel, 1986) includes accounts by women who have experienced abusive lesbian relationships and deals with community campaigning agendas. Renzetti (1998) specifically warns against explaining what happens in lesbian relationships through comparison with heterosexual relationships.

3. See Chapter 3 'Close Encounters of the Classed Kind' for an account of the ways in which the women, as children, initially recognised themselves as working-class, through the judgements of other young children.

4. See Chapter 6 'Scene Spaces – Inclusions and Exclusions'.

5. Just as Illouz (1997) is careful not to develop a classed binary of idealisation and deficit, I have to point out that working-class women are not without emotional 'worth' – rather they experience devaluation in intimate relationships. Illouz (1997) argues that middle-class women, with the emotional and verbal 'habitus' necessary to achieve dominant definitions of intimacy are far more likely to attain emotional well-being for themselves and their families than their working-class counterparts.

Bibliography

Abbott, P. and Sapsford, R. (1987) *Women and Social Class*. London: Tavistock.

Adkins, L. (1995) 'Gendered work', *Sexuality, Family and the Labour Market*. Buckingham: Open University Press.

——. (2000) 'Mobile desire: aesthetics, sexuality and the "lesbian" at work', *Sexualities* 3(2): 201–218.

——. (2001) 'Risk culture, self-reflexivity and the making of sexual hierarchies', *Body and Society* 7(1): 35–55.

——. (2002) 'Reflexivity and the politics of qualitative research', in May, T. (ed) *Qualitative Research in Action*. London: Sage.

Adkins, L. and Skeggs, B. (2004) (eds) *Feminism after Bourdieu*. Oxford: Blackwells.

Adler, S. and Brenner, J. (1992) 'Gender and space: lesbians and gay men in the city', *International Journal of Urban and Regional Research* 16(1): 24–34.

Adler, S. and Brenner, J. quoted in Valentine, G. (1995) 'Out and about: geographies of lesbian landscapes', *International Journal of Urban and Regional Research* 19 (1): 96–111.

Ainley, R. (1995) *What Is She Like? Lesbian Identities from the 1950's to the 1990's*. London: Cassell.

Allen, S., Dale, A., Gilbert, G.N. and Arber, S. (1985) 'Integrating women into class theory', *Sociology* 19(3): 384–409.

Allison, D. (1988) *Trash*. Ithaca: Fireband Books.

——. (1992) *Bastard out of Carolina*. Penguin: New York.

Altman, D. quoted in Binnie, J. (2000) 'Cosmopolitanism and the sexed city', in Bell, D. and Haddour, A.(eds) *City Visions*. Harlow: Prentice Hall.

Anthias, F. (1998) 'Rethinking social divisions: some notes towards a theoretical framework', *Sociological Review 46* (3): 505–535.

Anthias, F. (2001) 'The concept of "Social Division" and theorising social stratification: looking at ethnicity and class', *Sociology* 35(4): 835–854.

Armstead, C. (1995) 'Writing contradictions. Feminist research and feminist writing', *Women's Studies International Forum* 18 (5/6): 627–636.

Badgett, L.M.V. (2001) *Money, Myths and Challenges: The Economic Lives of Lesbians and Gay Men*. Chicago: Polity Press.

Barbour, R.S. and Kitzinger, J. (1999) *Developing Focus Group Research. Politics, Theory and Practice*. London: Sage.

Barrett, M. (1992) 'Words and things: materialism and method in contemporary feminist analysis', in Barrett, M. and Phillips, A. (eds) *Destabilizing Theory*. Cambridge: Polity.

Bauman, Z. (1990) *Thinking Sociologically*. Oxford: Blackwell.

——. (1998) *Work, Consumerism and the New Poor*. Buckingham: Open University Press.

Beck, U. (1992) *Risk Society*. London: Sage.

——. (2000a) *What is Globalization?* Oxford: Blackwell.

——. (2000b) 'Zombie categories', in Rutherford, J. (ed.) *The Art of Life: On Living, Love and Death*. London: Lawrence and Wishart.

Becker, D.P. (1997) 'Growing up in two closets: class and privilege in the lesbian and gay community', in Raffo, S. (ed.) *Queerly Classed. Gay Men and Lesbians Write about Class*. Boston, MA: South End Press.

Bell, D. (1990) 'Doing anthropology at home: a feminist initiative in the bicentennial year', in Sirman, N. and Ganesh, K. (eds) *Anthropological Perspectives on Research and Teaching Concerning Women*. New Dehli: Sage.

——. (1991) 'Insignificant others: lesbian and gay geographies', *Area* 23(4): 323–329.

——. (1995) 'Pleasure and danger: the paradoxical spaces of sexual citizenship', *Political Geography* 14(2): 139–153.

Bell, D. and Binnie, J. (2000) *The Sexual Citizen: Queer Politics and Beyond*. Cambridge: Polity Press.

——. (2002) 'Sexual citizenship: Marriage, the market and the military', in Richardson, D. and Seidman, S. (eds) *Handbook of Lesbian and Gay Studies*. London: Sage.

Bell, D. and Valentine, G. (eds) (1995) *Mapping Desire : Geographies of Sexualities*. London: Routledge.

Bell, D., Binnie, J., Holliday, R., Longhurst, R. and Peace, R. (2001) *Pleasure Zones: Bodies, Cities, Spaces*. New York: Syracuse University Press.

Benjamin, S., Nind, M., Hall, K., Collins, J. and Sheehy, K. (2003) 'Moments of inclusion and exclusion: pupils negotiating classroom contexts', *British Journal of Sociology of Education* 24(5): 547–558.

Bettie, J. (2003) *Women without Class: Girls, Race, and Identity*. London: University of California Press.

Binnie, J. (1995) 'Trading places. consumption, sexuality and the production of queer space', in Bell, D. and Valentine, G. (eds) *Mapping Desire*. London: Routledge.

——. (2000) 'Cosmopolitanism and the Sexed City', in Bell, D. and Haddour, A. (eds) *City Visions*. Harlow: Prentice Hall.

——. (2004) *The Globalization of Sexuality*. London: Sage.

Binnie, J. and Valentine, G. (1999) 'Geographies of sexuality – review of progress', *Progress in Human Geography* 23(2): 175–187.

Blumenfeld, W.J. and Raymond, D. (2001) *Looking at Gay and Lesbian Life*. Boston: Beacon Press.

Bondi, L. (1998) 'Gender, class and urban spaces: public and private space in contemporary urban landscapes', *Urban Geography* 19(2): 160–185.

Bourdieu, P. (1984) *Distinction. A Social Critique of the Judgment of Taste*. London: Routledge.

——. (2000) *Pascalian Meditations*. Cambridge: Polity.

——. et al. (1999) *The Weight of the World*. Cambridge: Polity.

Bowring, B. (2000) 'Social exclusion: limitations of the debate', *Critical Social Policy* 20(3) August Issue 64: 307–330.

Bradley, H. and Hebson, G. (1999) 'Breaking the silence. The need to re-articulate class', *International Journal of Sociology and Social Policy* 19(9): 178–203.

Bradshaw, J., Finch, N., Kemp, P., Mayhew, E. and Williams, J. (2003) *Gender and Poverty in Britain*. Working Paper Series (No 6). Social Policy Research and Development Unit: University of York.

Brekhaus, W.H. (2003) *Peacock, Chameleons and Centaurs. Gay Suburbia and the Grammar of Social Identity* Chicago: University of Chicago Press.

Brickell, C. (2001) 'Whose "Special Treatment"? Heterosexism and the problems with liberalism', *Sexualities* 4(2): 211–235.

Brown, L.M. (1997) 'Performing femininities: listening to White working-class girls in rural Maine', *Journal of Social Issues* 53(2): 683–701.

——. (2000) *Closet Space: Geographies of Metaphor from the Body to the Globe.* London: Routledge.

Browne, K. (2004) 'Genderism and the bathroom problem: (re)materialising sexed sites, (re)creating sexed bodies', *Gender, Place and Culture* 11(3): 331–346.

Brownworth, V.A. (1997) 'Life in the passing lane: exposing the class closet', in Raffo, S. (ed.) *Queerly Classed. Gay Men and Lesbians Write about Class.* Boston, MA: South End Press.

Bulmer, M. (1986) *Neighbours: The Work of Philip Abrams.* Cambridge: Cambridge University Press.

Burchardt, T., Le Grand, J. and Piachaud, D. (1999) 'Social exclusion in Britain 1991–1995', *Social Policy & Administration* 33(3): 227–244.

Burrows, R. and Ellison, N. (2004) 'Sorting places out? The social politics of neighbourhood informatization', *Information, Communication and Society* 7(3): 321–336.

Buston, K. and Hart, G. (2001) 'Heterosexism and homophobia in Scottish school sex education: exploring the nature of the problem', *Journal of Adolescence* 24: 95–109.

Butler, J. (1990) *Gender Trouble.* New York: Routledge.

——. (1997) 'Merely cultural', *Social Text* 52/53, Vol, 15(3 and 4): 265–277.

Byrne, D. (2005) *Social Exclusion.* Berkshire: Open University Press.

Campbell, B. (1993) *Goliath: Britain's Dangerous Places.* London: Lime Trees.

Carabine, J. (ed) (2004) *Sexualities. Personal Lives and Social Policy.* Milton Keynes: The Open University Press.

Casey, M. (2004) 'De-dyking queer space: female heterosexual access and visibility within lesbian and gay space', *Sexualities* 7(4): 446–461.

Castells, M. (1983) *The City and the Grassroots.* London: Edward Arnold.

——. (2000) *The Rise of Network Society.* Oxford: Blackwell.

Chambers, D., Tincknell, E. and Van Loon, J. (2004) 'Peer regulation of teenage sexual identities', *Gender and Education* 16(3): 397–415.

Charlesworth, S. (2000) *A Phenomenology of Working Class Experience.* Cambridge: Cambridge University Press.

Chasin, A. (2000) *Selling Out: The Lesbian and Gay Movement Goes to Market.* Basingstoke: Palgrave.

Code, L. (1995) *Rhetorical Spaces: Essays on Gendered Locations.* London: Routledge.

Cockburn, C.K. (1987) *Two-track Training: Sex Inequalities and the YTS.* London: Macmillan.

Cohen, A. (1995) *The Symbolic Construction of Community.* London: Routledge.

Collins, P.H. (1991) *Black Feminist Thought: Knowledge, Consciousness and the Politics of Empowerment.* New York: Routledge.

Cooper, D. (1998) 'Regard between strangers: diversity, equality and the reconstruction of public space', *Critical Social Policy* 18(4): 465–492.

Corteen, K. (2002) 'Lesbian safety talk: problematizing definitions and experiences of violence, sexuality and space', *Sexualities* 5(3): 259–280.

Crompton, R. (2000) 'The gendered structuring of the middle classes: employment and caring', in Crompton, R., Devine, F., Savage, M. and Scott, J. (eds) (2000) *Renewing Class Analysis.* Oxford: Blackwell.

Crompton, R. and Scott, J. (2000) 'Introduction: the state of class analysis', in Crompton, R., Devine, F., Savage, M. and Scott, J. (eds) (2000) *Renewing Class Analysis.* Oxford: Blackwell.

Crompton, R., Devine, F., Savage, M. and Scott, J. (eds) (2000) *Renewing Class Analysis*. Oxford: Blackwell.

Dale, A., Gilbert, G.N. and Arber, S. (1985) 'Integrating women into class theory', *Sociology* 19(3): 384–409.

Davidoff, L. and Hall, C. (1992) *Family Fortunes: Men and Women of the English middle class, 1780–1850*. London: Routledge.

Davis, M.D. and Kennedy, E.L. (1993) *Boots of Leather, Slippers of Gold*. London: Routledge.

Devine, F. (1992) 'Social identities, class identity and political perspectives', *Sociological Review* 40: 229–252.

——. (2004) *Class Practices. How Parents Help Their Children Get Good Jobs*. Cambridge: Cambridge University Press.

Devine, F. and Savage, M. (2000) 'Conclusion: renewing class analysis', in Crompton, R., Devine, F., Savage, M. and Scott, J. (eds) (2000) *Renewing Class Analysis*. Oxford: Blackwell.

Duncombe, J. and Marsden, D. (1993) 'Love and intimacy: the gender division of emotion and emotion work', *Sociology* 27: 221–241.

Dunne, G.A. (1997) *Lesbian Lifestyles. Women's Work and the Politics of Sexuality*. London: Macmillian Press.

——. (ed) (1998) *Living Difference. Lesbian Perspectives on Work and Family Life*. New York: Haworth Press.

Dunne, G., Prendergast, S. and Telford, D. (2002) 'A story of "difference," a different story: young homeless lesbian, gay and bisexual people', *International Journal of Sociology and Social Policy* 21(4/5/6): 64–91.

Dutton, K.R. (1995) *The Perfectible Body: The Western Idea of Physical Development*. London: Cassell.

Edwards, P. (2000) 'Late twentieth century workplace relations: class struggle without classes in analysis', in Crompton, R., Devine, F., Savage, M. and Scott, J. (eds) (2000) *Renewing Class Analysis*. Oxford: Blackwell.

Egerton, J. (1990) 'Out but not down: lesbians' experience of housing', *Feminist Review* 36: 75–88.

Ehrenreich, B. (2001) *Nickel and Dimed: On Not Getting By in America*. New York: Henry Holt.

Epstein, D. (1993) *Changing Classroom Cultures: Anti-racism, Politics, and Schools*. Stoke-on-Trent: Trentham.

——. (1994) *Challenging Lesbian and Gay Inequalities in Education*. Buckingham: Open University Press.

Evans, D. (1993) *Sexual Citizenship. The Material Construction of Sexualities*. London: Routledge.

Eves, A. (2004) 'Queer theory, butch/femme identities and lesbian space', *Sexualities* 7 (4): 480–496.

Faderman, L. (1991) *Odd Girls and Twilight Lovers: A History of Lesbian Life in Twentieth-Century America*. New York: Penguin Books.

Farquhar, C. (with Das, R.) (1999) 'Are focus groups suitable for "sensitive" topics?', in Barbour, R.S. and Kitzinger, J. *Developing Focus Group Research. Politics, Theory and Practice*. London: Sage.

Featherstone, M. (1991) *Consumer Culture and Postmodernism*. London: Sage.

Feinberg, L. (1993) *Stone Butch Blues*. Ithaca, NY: Firebrand Books.

Field, N. (1997) 'Identity and lifestyle market', in Hennessy, R. and Ingraham, C. (eds) *Materialist Feminism. A Reader in Class, Difference, and Women's Lives*. London: Routledge.

Finch, J. (1984) ' "It's great to have someone to talk to": the ethics and politics of interviewing women', in Bell, C. and Roberts, H. (eds) *Social Researching: Politics, Problems, Practice*. London: Routledge Kegan Paul.

Flaherty, J., Veit-Wilson, J. and Doran, P. (2004) *Poverty: The Facts* (5th edition). London: Child Poverty Action Group.

Fraser, N. (1997) 'Heterosexism, misrecognition, and capitalism. A response to Judith Butler', *Social Text* 52/53, Vol 15(3 and 4): 279–289.

——. (1999) 'Classing queer. Politics in competition', *Theory, Culture and Society* 16(2): 107–131.

——. quoted in Skeggs, B. (2001) 'The toilet paper: femininity, class and misrecognition', *Women's Studies International Forum* 24(3/4): 295–307.

Frazer, E. (1988) 'Teenage girls talking about class' *Sociology* 22(3): 343–358.

——. (1989) 'Feminist talk and talking about feminism: teenage girls' discourses of gender', *Oxford Review of Education* 15(3): 281–290.

Freund, P. (1990) 'The expressive body: a common ground for the sociology of emotions and health and illness', *Sociology of Health and Illness* 12(4): 454–477.

Furlong, A., Briggart, A. and Cartmel, F. (1996) 'Neighbourhoods, opportunity structures and occupational aspirations', *Sociology* 30(3): 551–565.

Fuss, D. (1989) *Essentially Speaking: Feminism, Nature and Difference*. London: Routledge.

——. (ed) (1991) *Inside/out: Lesbian Theories, Gay Theories*. New York: Routledge.

Gabb, J. (2001) 'Desirous subjects and parental identities: constructing a radical discourse on (lesbian) family sexuality', *Sexualities* 4(3): 333–352.

——. (2005) 'Locating lesbian parent families', *Gender, Place, Culture* 12(4): 419–432.

Gagnier, R. (2000). 'The functions of class at the present time: including taste, or sex and class as culture', *Women: A Cultural Review* 11(1/2): 37–44.

Gagnon, J.H. and Simon, W. (1973) *Sexual Conduct*. Chicago: Aldine.

Gardner, S. (1993) 'What's a nice working-class girl like you doing in a place like this?', in Tokarczyk, M. and Fay, E. (eds) *Working-Class Women in the Academy. Labourers in the Knowledge Factory*. Amherst: The University of Massachusetts Press.

Gershuny, J. (2000) 'Social position from narrative data', in Crompton, R., Devine, F., Savage, M. and Scott, J. (eds) *Renewing Class Analysis*. Oxford: Blackwell.

Giddens, A. (1992) *The Transformation of Intimacy: Sexuality, Love and Eroticism in Modern Societies*. Cambridge: Polity Press.

Glendinning, C. and Miller, J. (eds) (1992) *Women and Poverty in Britain in the 1990s*. London: Harvester Wheatsheaf.

Glennie, P.D. (1998) 'Consumption, consumerism and urban form: historical perspectives', *Urban Studies* 35, 927– 951.

Glucksmann, M. (1994) 'The work of knowledge and the knowledge of women's work', in Purvis, J. and Maynard, M. (eds) *Researching Women's Lives from a Feminist Perspective*. Brighton: Flamer Press.

Gluckman, M. and Reed, B. (eds) (1997) *Homoeconomics: Capitalism, Community and Lesbian and Gay Life*. New York: Routledge.

Goffman, E. (1968) *Stigma: Notes on the Management of a Spoiled Identity*. Harmondsworth: Penguin.

———. (1969) *The Presentation of Self in Everyday Life*. Harmondsworth: Penguin.

———. (1983) 'The interaction order', *American Sociological Review* 48(1): 1–17.

Griffin, C. (1985) *Typical Girls: Young Women from School to the Market*. London: Routledge and Kegan Paul.

Griffin, C. (1988) 'Youth research: young women and the "gang of lads" model', in Hazekamp, J., Mees, W. and Peol T, Y. (eds) *European Contributions to Youth Research*. Amsterdam: Free University Press.

———. (1996) quoted in Reay, D. (1997) 'Feminist theory, habitus and social class: disrupting notions of classlessness', *Women's Studies International Forum* 20(2): 225–233.

Griggers, C. quoted in Adkins, L. (2000) 'Mobile desire: aesthetics, sexuality and the "lesbian" at work', *Sexualities* 3(2): 201–218.

Hanafin, J. and Lynch, A. (2002) 'Peripheral voices: parental involvement, social class and educational disadvantage', *British Journal of Sociology of Education*, 23(1): 35–49.

Harding, S. (ed) (1987) *Feminism and Methodology*. Milton Keynes: Open University Press.

Hawkes, G. (1996) *A Sociology of Sex and Sexuality*. Buckingham: Open University Press.

Haylett, C. (2000) ' "This is about us, this is our film!" Personal and popular discourses of "underclass" ', in Munt, S.R.(ed) *Cultural Studies and the Working Class: Subject to Change*. London: Cassell.

———. (2001) 'Illegitimate subjects?: Abjects whites, neoliberal modernisation, and middle-class multiculturalism', *Environment and Planning D: Society and Space* 19: 361–370.

Heath, S. and Cleaver, E. (2003) *Young, Free and Single? Twenty-Somethings and Household Change*. Basingstoke: Palgrave.

Hennessy, R. (1995) 'Queer visibility in commodity culture', in L. Nicholson and S. Seidman (eds) *Social Postmodernism : Beyond Identity Politics*. Cambridge: Cambridge University Press.

———. (2000) *Profit and Pleasure. Sexual Identities in Late Capitalism*. London: Taylor and Francis Group.

———. and Ingraham, C. (eds) (1997) *Materialist Feminism. A Reader in Class, Difference, and Women's Lives*. London and New York: Routledge.

Hey, V. (2003) 'Joining the club? Academia and working-class femininities', *Gender and Education* 5(3): 319–335.

Holliday, R. (1999) 'The Comfort of Identity', *Sexualities* 2(4): 475–491.

———. (2001) 'Discomforting identities', in Bell, D., Binnie, J., Holliday, R., Longhurts, R. and Peace, R. (eds) *Pleasure Zones*. Syracuse, NY: Syracuse University Press.

Holliday, R. and Thompson, G. (2001) 'A body of work', in Holliday, R. and Hassard, J. (eds) *Contested Bodies*. London: Routledge.

hooks, b. (1989) *Talking Back: Thinking Feminist, Thinking Black*. London: Sheba.

———. (1994) *Teaching To Transgress. Education as the Practice of Freedom*. London: Routledge.

Hoschild, A.R. (1983) *The Managed Heart. Commercialization of Human Feeling*. London: University of California Press.

Howarth, C. (2002) ' "So you're from Brixton?" The struggle for recognition and esteem in a stigmatized community', *Ethnicities* 2(2): 237–260.

Illouz, E. (1997) 'Who will care for the caretaker's daughter?: towards a sociology of happiness in the era of reflexive modernity', *Theory, Culture and Society* 14(4): 31–66.

Ingraham, C. (1997) 'The heterosexual imaginary. Feminist sociology and theories of gender'. in Hennessy, R. and Ingraham, C. (eds) *Materialist Feminism. A Reader in Class, Difference, and Women's Lives*. London: Routledge.

Jackson, S. (1998a) 'Telling stories: memory, narrative and experience in feminist research and theory', in Henwood, K., Griffin, C. and Phoenix, A. (eds) *Standpoints and Differences. Essays on the Practice of Feminist Psychology*. London: Sage.

——. (1998b) 'In a class of their own. Women's studies and working-Class students', *The European Journal of Women's Studies* 5(2): 195–215.

Jackson, S. (1999) *Heterosexuality in Question*. London: Sage.

——. (2001) 'Why a materialist feminism is (still) possible – and necessary', *Women's Studies International Forum* 24(3/4): 283–293.

Jagger, A.M. (1989) 'Love and knowledge: emotion in feminist epistemology,' in Jagger, A.M. and Bordo, S.R. (eds) *Gender/Body/Knowledge: Feminist Reconstructions of Being and Knowing*. New Brunswick: Rutgers University Press.

Jamieson, L. (1998) *Intimacy. Personal Relationships in Modern Societies*. Cambridge: Polity Press.

Jeffreys, S. (1994) *The Lesbian Heresy*. London: The Women's Press.

——. (2003) *Unpacking Queer Politics: A Lesbian Feminist Perspective*. Oxford: Polity.

Jenkins, R. (1996) *Social Identity*. London: Routledge.

John, S. and Patrick, A. (1999) *Poverty and Social Exclusion of Lesbians and Gay Men in Glasgow*. Glasgow: Glasgow Women's Library.

Johnson, P. and Lawler, S. (2005) 'Coming home to love and class'. *Sociological Research Online* 10(3): 1–2 http://www.socresonline.org.uk/10/3/johnson.html.

Johnston, L. and Valentine, G. (1995) 'Wherever I lay my girlfriend, that's my home. The performance and surveillance of lesbian identities in domestic environments', in Bell, D. and Valentine, G. (eds) *Mapping Desire*. London: Routledge.

Kadi, J. (1997) 'Homophobic workers or elitist queers?', in Raffo, S. (ed) *Queerly Classed. Gay Men and Lesbians Write about Class*. Boston, MA: South End Press.

Kefalas, M. (2003) *Working-Class Heroes. Protecting Home, Community, and Nation in a Chicago Neighbourhood*. California: University of California Press.

Kelly, L. (1988) *Surviving Sexual Violence*. Minneapolis: University of Minnesota Press.

Kidger, J. (2005) 'Stories of redemption? Teenage mothers as the new Sex educators', *Sexualities* 8(4): 481–496.

Kitzinger, C. (1987) *The Social Construction of Lesbianism*. London: Sage.

Knopp, L. (1995) 'Sexuality and urban space. A framework for analysis', in Bell, D. and Valentine, G. (eds) *Mapping Desire*. London: Routledge.

Kuhn, A. (1995) *Family Secrets: Acts of Memory and Imagination*. London: Verso.

Lamont, M. (1991) *Money, Morals and Manners: The Culture of French and American Upper-Middle class*. London: University of Chicago Press.

——. (1992) *Cultivating Differences: Symbolic Boundaries and the Making of Inequality*. Chicago: University of Chicago Press.

Lareau, A. (2003) *Unequal Childhoods. Class, Race and Family Life*. London: University of California Press.

Lash, S. and Urry, J. (1987) *The End of Organized Capitalism*. Cambridge: Polity.
——. (1994) *Economies of Signs and Space*. London: Sage.
Lawler, S. (1999) 'Getting Out and Getting Away: Women's Narratives of Class Mobility' *Feminist Review* 63: 3–24.
Lawler, S. (2000) *Mothering the Self: Mothers, Daughters, Subjects*. London: Routledge.
——. (2002) 'Mobs and monsters. Independent man meets Paulsgrove woman', *Feminist Theory* 3(1): 103–113.
——. (2004) 'Rules of engagement: Habitus, class and resistance', in Adkins, L. and Skeggs, B. (eds) *Feminism After Bourdieu*. Oxford: Blackwell.
Lees, S. (1986) *Losing Out*. London: Hutchinson.
——. (1993) *Sugar and Spice: Sexuality and Adolescent Girls*. London: Penguin.
Leidner, R. (1993) *Fast Food, Fast Talk. Service work and the Routinization of Everyday Life*. London: University of California Press.
Leslie, D. and Reimer, S. (2003) 'Fashioning furniture: restructuring the furniture commodity chain', *Area* 35(4): 427–437.
Levitas, L. (1998) *The Inclusive Society? Social Exclusion and New Labour*. Basingstoke: Macmillan.
Levitas, R. (2001) 'Against work: a utopian incursion into social policy', *Critical Social Policy* 21(4): 449–465.
Lewis, J. (ed) (1986) *Labour and Love. Women's Experience of Home and Family 1850–1940*. Oxford: Blackwell.
Lewis, R. and Rolly, K. quoted in Holliday, R. (1999) 'The comfort of identity', *Sexualities* 2(4): 475–491.
Lobel, K. (ed) (1986) *Naming The Violence: Speaking Out About Lesbian Battering*. Seattle: The Seal Press.
Lovell, T. (2000) 'Thinking feminism with and against Bourdieu', *Feminist Theory* 2000 1(1): 11–32.
Luke, C. (1994) 'Women in the Academy: the politics of speech and silence', *British Journal of Sociology of Education* 15(2): 211–230.
Lynch, K. and O'Neil, C. (1994) 'The colonisation of social class in education', *British Journal of Sociology of Education* 15(2): 307–342.
Mac an Ghaill, M. (1994) *The Making of Men: Masculinities, Sexualities and Schooling*. Buckingham: Open University Press.
MacDonald, R. and Marsh, J. (2000) 'Employment, unemployment and social polarization: young people and cyclical transitions', in Crompton, R., Devine, F., Savage, M. and Scott, J. (eds) (2000) *Renewing Class Analysis*. Oxford: Blackwell.
Mahony, P. and Zmroczek, C. (eds) (1997) *Class Matters, 'Working-Class' women's perspectives on Social Class*. London: Taylor and Francis.
Mansfield, P. and Collard, J. (1989) *The Beginning of the Rest of Your Life?* London: Macmillan.
Marshall, G., Newby, H., Rose, D. and Vogler, C. (1988) *Social Class in Modern Britain*. London: Hutchinson.
Mason, G. (2002) *The Spectacle of Violence. Homophobia, Gender and Knowledge*. London: Routledge.
Mason, G. quoted in Corteen, K. (2002) 'Lesbian safety talk: problematizing definitions and experiences of violence, sexuality and space', *Sexualities* 5(3): 259–280.
Mason, J. (2002) 'Qualitative interviewing: asking, listening and interpreting', in May, T. (ed.) *Qualitative Research in Action*. London: Sage.

Mayer, M. (1993) 'The onward sweep of social capital: causes and consequences for understanding cities, communities and urban movements', *International Journal of Urban and Regional Research* 27(1): 110–132.

McDowell, L. (1997) *Capital Culture: Gender at Work in the City*. Oxford: Blackwell.

McDowell, L. (2001) *Young Men Leaving School. White, Working-class Masculinity*. Leicester: Youth Work Press.

McRobbie, A. (1982) 'The politics of feminist research: between talk, text and action', *Feminist Review* 12: 46–57.

——. (2000) *Feminism and Youth Culture*. London: MacMillan.

——. (2004) 'Notes on Bourdieu and post feminist symbolic violence', in Adkins, L. and Skeggs, B. (eds) *Feminism after Bourdieu*. Oxford: Blackwell.

Mead, G.H. (1927) *Mind, Self and Society, from the Standpoint of Social Behaviourism*. Chicago: Chicago University Press.

Medhurst, A. (2000) 'If anywhere: class identifications and cultural studies academics', in Munt, S.R.(ed.) *Cultural Studies and the Working Class: Subject to Change*. London: Cassell.

Mitchell, L. (1999) 'Combining focus groups and interviews: telling how it is; telling how it feels', in Barbour, R.S. and Kitzinger, J. *Developing Focus Group Research. Politics, Theory and Practice*. London: Sage.

Moran, L. (2000) 'Homophobic violence: the hidden injuries of class', in Munt, S.R.(ed.) *Cultural Studies and the Working Class: Subject to Change*. London: Cassell.

Moran, L. and Skeggs, B. (2001) 'Property, boundary, exclusion: making sense of hetero-violence in safer spaces', *Social and Cultural Geography* 2(4): 407–420.

Moran, L., Skeggs, B. with Tyler, P. and Corteen, K. (2004) *Sexuality and the Politics of Violence*. London: Routledge.

Morley, L. (1992) 'Women's studies, difference and internalised oppression', *Women's Studies International Forum* 29 (1): 23–41.

Morris, L. (1994) *Dangerous Classes: The Underclass and Social Citizenship*. London: Routledge.

Munt, S.R. (1998) *Butch and Femme*. London: Cassell.

—— (ed.) (2000) *Cultural Studies and the Working Class: Subject to Change*. London: Cassell.

Murray, C. (1990) *The Emerging British Underclass*. London: Institute of Economic Affairs, Health and Welfare Unit.

——. (1994) *Underclass: The Crisis Deepens*. London: Institute of Economic Affairs, Health and Welfare Unit.

Namaste, K. (1996) 'Genderbashing: perceived transgressions of normative sex-gender relations in public spaces', *Environment and Planning D – Society and Space* 14(2): 221–240.

Nayak, A. (2003a) *Race, Place and Globalization. Youth Cultures in a Changing World*. Oxford: Berg.

——. (2003b) 'Last of the 'Real Geordies'? White masculinities and the subcultural responses to deindustrialisation', *Environment and Planning D: Society and Space* 21: 7–25.

Nayak, A. and Kehily, M.J. (1996) 'Playing it straight: masculinities, homophobias and schooling', *Journal of Gender Studies* 5: 211–230.

Nestle, J. (1987) *A Restricted Country*. Ithaca, NY: Firebrand.

Nettleton, S. and Burrows, R. (2000) 'When a capital investment becomes an emotional loss: the health consequences of the experience of mortgage possession in England', *Housing Studies* 15(3): 463–479.

O'Conner, W. and Maloy, D. (2001) *'Hidden in Plain Sight': Homelessness amongst Lesbian and Gay Youth.* London: National Centre for Social Research.

O'Dair, S. (1993) 'Vestments and vested interests: academia, the working class, and affirmative action', in Tokarczyk, M. and Fay, E. (eds) *Working-Class Women in the Academy. Labourers in the Knowledge Factory.* Amherst: The University of Massachusetts Press.

Ohms, C. (ed) (2002) *Against Violence. Guidelines for Counselling Services on Dealing with Violence in Lesbian Partnerships.* Anti-Violence Project of the Lesbian Information and Counselling Service Frankfurt.

Okely, J. (1992) 'Anthropology and autobiography. Participatory experience and embodied knowledge', in Okley, J. and Callaway, H. (eds) *Anthropology and Autobiography.* London: Routledge.

Oppenheim, C. and Harker, L. (1996) *Poverty: The Facts.* London: Child Poverty Action Group.

Paechter, C. (2006) 'Reconceptualizing the gendered body: learning and constructing masculinities and femininities in school', *Gender and Education*, 18 (2): 121–135.

Pahl, J. (2000) 'Social polarization in the electronic economy', in Crompton, R., Devine, F., Savage, M. and Scott, J. (eds) (2000) *Renewing Class Analysis.* Oxford: Blackwell.

Pakulski, J. and Waters, M. (1996) *The Death of Class.* London: Sage.

Penelope, J. (ed.) (1994) *Out of the Class Closet: Lesbians Speak.* Freedom, CA: The Crossing Press.

Phile, S. (1996) *The Body in the City: Psychoanalysis, Space and Subjectivity.* London: Routledge.

Phoenix, A. and Tizzard, B. (1996) 'Thinking through class: the place of social class in the lives of young Londoners', *Feminism and Psychology* 6(3): 427–442.

Plummer, G. (2000) *Failing Working-Class Girls.* Staffordshire: Trentham Books.

Plummer, K. (1995) *Telling Sexual Stories. Power, Change and Social Worlds.* London: Routledge.

——. (1996) 'Intimate citizenship, and the culture of sexual story telling', in Weeks, J. and Holland, J. (eds) *Sexual Cultures. Communities, Values and Intimacy.* London: Macmillan Press Ltd.

Probyn, E. (1990) quoted in Skeggs, B. (1997) *Formations of Class and Gender.* London: Sage.

Putnam, R.D. (1993) 'The prosperous community. Social capital and public life', *The American Prospect* 13: 35–42.

Quilley, S. (1997) 'Constructing Manchester's "new urban village": gay space in the entrepreneurial city', in Ingram, G.B., Bouthilette, A. and Retter, Y. (eds) *Queers in Space: Communities, Public Places, Sites of Resistance.* Seattle: Bay Press.

Qvortrup, J. (1994) 'Childhood matters: an introduction', in Qvortrup, J., Bardy, M., Sgritta, G. and Wintersberger, H. (eds) *Childhood Matters: Social Theory, Practice and Politics.* Aldershot: Avebury.

Raffo, S. (ed) (1997) *Queerly Classed. Gay Men and Lesbians Write about Class.* Boston, MA: South End Press.

Rahman, M. (2000) *Sexuality and Democracy. Identities and Strategies in Lesbian and Gay Politics.* Edinburgh: Edinburgh University Press.

——. (2004) 'The shape of equality: discursive deployments during the section 28 repeal in Scotland', *Sexualities* 7(2): 150–166.

Reay, D. (1996) 'Insider perspectives or stealing the words out of women's mouths', *Feminism and Psychology* 6(3): 57–73.

——. (1997) 'Feminist theory, habitus and social class: disrupting notions of classlessness', *Women's Studies International Forum* 20(2): 225–233.

——. (1998) ' "Always Knowing" and "never being sure": familial and institutional habituses and higher educational choice', *Journal of Educational Policy* 13(4): 519–529.

——. (2000) 'Children's urban landscapes: configurations of class and place', in Munt, S.R.(ed.) *Cultural Studies and the Working Class: Subject to Change*. London: Cassell.

——. (2002) 'Gendering Bourdieu's concept of capitals?: Emotional capital, women and social class', Paper presented at the *Feminists Evaluate Bourdieu Conference*, Manchester University, UK, 11 October 2002.

——. (2004) 'Gendering Bourdieu's concept of capitals?: Emotional capital, women and social class', in Adkins, L. and Skeggs, B. (eds) *Feminism after Bourdieu*. Oxford: Blackwell.

Reay, D. and Ball, S. (1997) ' "Spoilt for Choice": the working classes and educational markets', *Oxford Review of Education* 23(1): 89–101.

Reay, D. and Lucey, H. (2000) ' "I don't really like it here but I don't want to be anywhere else": Children and inner city council estates', *Antipode* 32(4): 410–428.

Reese, E. (2005) *Backlash against Welfare Mothers: Past and Present*. Berkeley: University of California Press.

Renold, E. (2000) ' "Coming out": gender, (hetero)sexuality and the primary school', *Gender and Education*, 12(3): 309–326.

Renzetti, C.M. (1998) 'Violence and abuse in lesbian relationships: theoretical and empirical issues', in Bergen, R.K. (ed.) *Issues in Intimate Violence*. London: Sage.

Rich, A. (1980) 'Compulsory heterosexuality and lesbian existence', *Signs* 5(4): 631–660.

Richardson, D. (2004) 'Locating sexualities: from here to normality', *Sexualities* 7(4): 391–411.

Roberts, K. (2001) *Class in Modern Britain*. New York: Palgrave.

Robinson, V., Hockey, J. and Meah, A. (2004) ' "What I used to do … on my mother's settee": spatial and emotional aspects of heterosexuality in England', *Gender, Place and Culture* 11(3): 417–435.

Robson, R. (1997) 'To market, to market: considering class in the context of lesbian legal theories and reforms', in Raffo, S. (ed) *Queerly Classed. Gay Men and Lesbians Write about Class*. Boston, MA: South End Press.

Rose, G. (1993) *Feminism and Geography. The Limits of Geographical Knowledge*. Minneapolis: University of Minnesota Press.

Roseneil, S. (2000) 'Queer frameworks and queer tendencies: towards an understanding of postmodern transformations of sexuality', *Sociological Research Online* 5(3) http://www.socresonline.org.uk/5/3/roseneil.htm.

Rubin, L. (1976) *Worlds of Pain: Life in the Working-class*. New York: Basic Books.

Sacks, K. quoted in Armstead, C. (1995) 'Writing contradictions. Feminist research and feminist writing', *Women's Studies International Forum* 18 (5/6): 627–636.

Sandell, J. (1997) 'Telling stories of "Queer White Trash": race, class and sexuality in the work of Dorothy Allison', in Wray, M. and Newitz, A. (1997) *White Trash. Race and Class in America*. New York: Routledge.

Sapsford, R. and Jupp, V. (eds) (1996) *Data Collection and Analysis*. London: Sage.

Savage, M., Bagnall, G. and Longhurst, B. (2001) 'Ordinary, ambivalent and defensive: class identities in the Northwest of England', *Sociology* 35(4): 875–892.

Sayer, A. (2002) 'What are you worth?: Why class is an embarrassing subject', *Sociological Research Online* 7(3) http://www.socresonline.org.uk/7/3/sayer.html.

Segal, L. (1987) *Is the Future Female? Troubled Thoughts on Contemporary Feminism*. London: Virago Press.

Sennett, R. and Cobb, J. (1977) *The Hidden Injuries of Class*. Cambridge: Cambridge University Press.

Shilling, C. (1997) 'The body and difference', in Woodward, K.(ed.) *Identity and Difference*. Milton Keynes: Open University Press.

——. (1999) 'Towards an embodied understanding of the structure/agency relationship', *British Journal of Sociology* 50(4): 543–562.

Sibley, D. (1995) *Geographies of Exclusion*. London: Routlege.

Skeggs, B. (1994) 'Situating the production of feminist ethnography', in Maynard, M. and Purvis, J. (eds) *Researching Women's Lives From a Feminist Perspective*. London: Taylor and Francis.

——. (1995) ' "Women's Studies in the 1990s". Entitlement cultures and institutional constraints', *Women's Studies International Forum* 18(4): 475–485.

——. (1997) *Formations of Class and Gender*. London: Sage.

——. (1999) 'Matter out of place: visibility and sexualities in leisure spaces', *Leisure Studies* 18(3): 213–232.

——. (2001) 'The toilet paper: femininity, class and mis-recognition', *Women's Studies International Forum* 24(3/4): 295–307.

——. (2002) 'Techniques for telling the reflexive self', in May, T. (ed.) *Qualitative Research in Action*. London: Sage.

——. (2004) *Class, Self and Culture*. London: Routledge.

Skolnick, A. (1992) *The Intimate Environment: Exploring Marriage and the Family*. New York: Hapercollins.

Smith, D. (1987) *The Everyday World as Problematic: A Feminist Sociology*. Milton Keynes: Open University Press.

Southerton, D. (2002) ' "Boundaries of us" and "them": class, mobility and identification in a new town', *Sociology* 36(1): 171–193.

Sperling, L. and Owen, M. (eds) (2000) *Women and Work. The age of post-feminism?* Aldershot: Ashgate.

Squirrell, G. (1989) 'Teachers and issues of sexual orientation', *Gender and Education* 1(1): 17–35.

Stable, C.A. (1997) 'Feminism and the ends of postmodernism', in Hennessy, R. and Ingraham, C. (eds) *Materialist Feminism. A Reader In Class, Difference, and Women's Lives*. London: Routledge.

Stanley, J. (1995) 'Pain(t) for healing. The academic conference and the classed/embodied self', in Morley, L. and Walsh, V. (eds) *Feminist Academics. Creative Agents for Change*. London: Taylor and Francis.

Stanley, L. and Wise, S. (1993) *Breaking Out Again: Feminist Ontology and Epistemology*. London: Routledge.

Steedman, C. (1986) *Landscape for a Good Woman: A Story of Two Lives*. London: Virago.

Taylor, Y. (2004a) 'Hidden in the small ads: researching working-class lesbians', *Graduate Journal of Social Science*, 1(2): 253–277.

———. (2004b) 'Negotiation and navigation: an exploration of the spaces/places of working-class lesbians', *Sociological Research Online*, 9 (1): 1–24. Available at http://www.socresonline.org.uk/9/1/taylor.html.

———. (2005a) 'The gap and how to mind it: intersections of class and sexuality', *Sociological Research Online*, 10(3): 1–20. Available at http://www.socresonline. org.uk/10/3/taylor.html.

———. (2005b) 'Inclusion, exclusion, exclusive? Sexual citizenship and the repeal of Section 28/2a', *Sexualities* 8(3): 375–380.

———. (2005c) ' "Real politik or real politics? Working-class lesbians" political "awareness" and activism', *Women's Studies International Forum* 28(6): 484–494.

———. (2005d) ' "What now? Working-class lesbians" post-school transitions', *Youth and Policy* 87: 29–43.

———. (2005e) 'Classed in a classless climate', *Feminism and Psychology* 15(4): 491–500.

Thomas, M.E. (2004) 'Pleasure and propriety: teen girls and the practice of straight space', *Environment and Planning D: Society and Space* 22: 773–789.

Thomson, R. and Scott, S. (1991) *Learning about Sex: Young Women and the Social Construction of Sexual Identity*. London: Tufnell Press.

Thrift, N. (1997) ' "Us" and "Them": re-imagining places, re-imagining identities', in H. Mackay (ed.) *Consumption and Everyday Life*. London: Sage.

Thrift, N. and Johnson, R. (1993) 'Ringing the changes: the intellectual history of Environment and Planning A', *Environment and Planning A* Anniversary Issue: 14–21.

Tokarczyk, M. and Sowinska, S. (1997) 'Lesbians, class and academia. Some thoughts about class-based identity and difference', in Mintz, B. and Rothblum, E.D (eds) *Lesbians in Academia*. London: Routledge.

Twigg, J. (2000) *Bathing – The Body and Community Care*. London: Routledge.

Urry, J. (1995) *Consuming Places*. London: Routledge.

———. (2000a) 'Mobile sociology', *British Journal of Sociology* 51(1): 185–203.

———. (2000b) *Sociology beyond Societies: Mobilities for the Twenty-First Century*. London: Routledge.

———. (2002) 'Mobility and proximity', *Sociology* 36(2): 255–274.

Valentine, G. (1993a) 'Hetero-sexing space: lesbian perceptions and experiences of everyday spaces', *Environment and Planning D- Society and Space* 9(3): 395–413.

———. (1993b) 'Negotiating and managing multiple sexual identities: lesbian time-space strategies', *Transactions of the Institute of British Geographers* 18: 237–248.

———. (1995) 'Out and about: geographies of lesbian landscapes', *International Journal of Urban and Regional Research* 19 (1): 96–111.

Valentine, G. and Johnson, L. (1995) 'Wherever I lay my girlfriend: that's my home', in Bell, D. and Valentine, G. (eds) (1995) *Mapping Desire*. London: Routledge.

Valentine, G., Skelton, T. and Butler, R. (2003) 'Coming out and outcomes: negotiating lesbian and gay identities with, and in, the family', *Environment and Planning D: Society and Space* 21:479–499.

Walby, S. (1997) *Gender transformations*. London: Routledge.

Walkerdine, V. (2003) 'Reclassifying upward mobility: femininity and the neo-liberal subject', *Gender and Education* 15(3): 238–249.

Walkerdine, V. and Lucey, H. (1989) *Democracy in the Kitchen: Regulating Mothers and Socialising Daughters*. London: Virago.

Walkerdine, V., Lucey, H. and Melody, J. (2001) *Growing up Girl. Psychosocial Explorations of Gender and Class*. Basingstoke: Palgrave.

Warde, A., Martens, L. and Olsen, W. (1999) 'Consumption and the problem of variety: cultural omnivorousness, social distinction and dining out', *Sociology* 33(1): 105–127.

Warner, M. (ed.) (1993) *Fear of a Queer Planet. Queer Politics and Social Theory*. London and Mineapolis: University of Minnesota Press.

Webster, C., Simpson, D., MacDonald, R., Abbas, A., Cieslik, M., Shildrick, T. and Simpson, M. (2004) *Poor Transitions: Young Adults and Social Exclusion*. Bristol: Policy Press.

Weeks, J., Heaphy, B. and Donovan, C. (2001) *Same Sex Intimacies: Families of Choice and Other Life Experiments*. London: Routledge.

Weston, K. (1995) 'Get thee to a big city: sexual imaginary and the great gay migration', *GLQ* 2: 253–277.

——. (1997) *Families We Choose: Lesbians, Gays, Kinship*. New York: Columbia University Press.

Wilkinson, R. (1996) *Unhealthy societies: the afflictions of inequality*. London: Routledge.

Williams, S. (2001) *Emotion and Social Theory. Corporeal Reflections on the (Ir)rational*. London: Sage.

Willis, P. (1977) *Learning To Labour: How Working Class Kids Get Working Class Jobs*. Farnborough: Saxon House.

Willow, M.G. (1997) 'Class struggles', in Raffo, S. (ed.) *Queerly Classed. Gay Men and Lesbians Write about Class*. Boston, MA: South End Press.

Witherow, J.K. (1997) 'Not just merely queer', in Raffo, S. (ed.) *Queerly Classed. Gay Men and Lesbians Write about Class*. Boston, MA: South End Press.

Wray, M. and Newitz, A. (1997) *White Trash. Race and Class in America*. London: Routledge.

Wright, D. (1996) 'Beyond the predatory male: the diversity of young Glaswegian men's discourses to describe heterosexual relationships', in Adkins, L. and Merchant, V. (eds) *Sexualising the Social: Power and the Organizing of Sexuality*. London: Macmillan.

Wright, E.O. (1985) *Classes*. London: Verso.

Youdell, D. (2005) 'Sex-gender-sexuality: how sex, gender and sexuality constellations are constituted in secondary schools', *Gender and Education* 17(3): 249–270.

Zmroczek, C. and Mahony, P. (eds) (1999) *Women and Social Class – International Perspectives*. London: UCL Press.

Zweig, M. (2000) *The Working-Class Majority: America's Best Kept Secret*. Ithaca: ILR Press.

Index

217